ACKNOWLEDGEMENTS

Part One of this book was made possible only through the research undertaken by my daughter, Toni Strasburg. She had never known my father, and had only known my mother when she, Toni, was very young. She became interested in her grandparents and transcribed and put in order my father's letters, and, some years ago, interviewed friends of my father who have since died. She wrote up this material, and because it had never been printed she has let me make ample use of it.

Professor C. Friedmann and Professor L. Cardozo both made generous donations that enabled me to visit Moscow and contact some of my sister's former pupils. I am very grateful to them for their interest and assistance.

My thanks to I.L. Shcherbakova, the Russian historian who interviewed former inmates of the camps, among them Ray, some of whose experiences are incorporated in this book.

Since beginning to write this book I have come to know as close friends Irina and Vladimir Volosov. Irina, who was befriended by my sister when she was young and later became her pupil, translated Ms. Shchebakova's interview from Russian into English for me. She also told me of her own family's experiences, some of which are incorporated in this book. Vladimir read the manuscript and helped with the spelling of names and places. I am grateful to them for their interest and assistance.

Professor Apollon Davidson of Moscow University read an early draft of the book, discussed it with me, and made useful corrections.

I was fortunate to have the cooperation of my husband Rusty, who worked with me on this book before he died. His contributions were invaluable. He acted as my live-in editor, advisor and critic and suggested many changes. He was always interested in what I was writing and ready with his sharp, critical intelligence and wonderful understanding to discuss my problems and difficulties.

As there are often many different ways of spelling Russian names, I have used the version of original English documents, or as advised by Russian speakers.

HILDA BERNSTEIN
SEPARATION

Moscow, 20-xi-26

My dear Vera,

Many Happy Returns.
Sorry can-not be with
you on your birthday,
but hope to be with you
on Christmas.

Love Papa

SEPARATION

ALSO BY HILDA BERNSTEIN

The Rift – The Exile Experience of South Africans
Death is Part of the Process
No. 46 – Steve Biko
For Their Triumphs and Their Tears
The World That Was Ours

SEPARATION

HILDA BERNSTEIN

CORVO

First published in Great Britain in 2003 by
Corvo Books Ltd
34A Highbury Hill
London N5 1AL
www.corvobooks.co.uk

A catalogue record for this book is available from the British Library.

Jacket design by Richard Roberts.

Typeset by SJM Design.

Printed and bound in Great Britain by
Biddles Limited, Surrey.

ISBN: 0-9543255-2-4

For my family – all of them.
Including the ins the grands and the greats.

PROLOGUE

THERE are two sets of documents in my possession. The first is a collection of letters written by my father during years in which he was living apart from his family, unable to return. The second is a set of short descriptive pieces of a time a decade later when my sister too was away from her home in England, trapped in the same country where my father had been.

They are subjective, personal; both reveal aspects of the life of that foreign land – Russia – that they were unable to leave. They share one thing: both wanted to leave Russia and return to their family in London, and each lived in expectation that they would, soon, return. But every time they made arrangements to go events beyond their control intervened and made it impossible (for my father) and difficult (for my sister) to return. There is a ten-year gap between the times of their writing, and they wrote from opposing standpoints – my father from a close involvement in and sympathy with the problems of life around him, my sister from detachment and hostility.

One day my father's work took him out of our lives. He went away, believing that he would soon return to his wife and children. For months, then for years we waited for him, always with the expectation – his, as well as ours – that he would soon be with us again. In the first weeks after his departure we expected him back. Then, as weeks grew into months and months to a year, to two years, it still seemed that he was always about to return to us. As time went by, as our lives adjusted and changed to living without him, we still believed he would, one day, come back to our home, his home, to us who belonged to him as he belonged to us. Although he kept contact through his frequent letters, the years went by; we grew up without him.

A decade later my sister Olga left home to follow his trail, to find out what had happened. It was to have been a short trip, two weeks. Yet as a result of a chance meeting, she later went there again, and she, too, did not come back, and it was nearly twelve years before she was able to return to England.

Both had become victim to extraordinary times, and experienced distant, little-known places. They could not change the circumstances in which they found themselves, but within those constraints they each had to make their own moral choices. It is these choices that make the humble and obscure lives of ordinary people testaments to unrecorded sacrifices and personal heroism.

Their experiences were the products of two world wars; by the world-remaking that arose from the First and the Russian Revolution that it set in motion in 1917. And by the Second, particularly from 1941, when Hitler invaded the Soviet Union.

The written fragments that I have of those certain periods in the lives of my father and my sister only become comprehensible when set against the background of those extraordinary times, a world-shaking period of history. My father's letters are mainly self-explanatory; my sister's essays need to be set in the context of the history of that time. My contribution is to fill in the necessary background.

This, then, is their story.

BOOK ONE

THE FATHER

CHAPTER I

An English Family

WE were, I always believed, an ordinary English family, like all our neighbours. My two sisters and I were born and grew up in London. We were educated at local schools in the areas where we lived, our friends were English, our only home language was English. Our lives were limited to the suburbs and to annual holidays in the country or at the seaside, always in Britain. The furthest we travelled was to Wales and the Isle of Wight. We never went abroad; ordinary people in those pre-war days did not travel far.

But both my parents were immigrants. Papa had been born in Odessa. As a nineteen-year-old he had emigrated to England in 1900, in all probability to escape conscription into the Tsar's army. Thousands were emigrating at that time from Russia and the countries of eastern Europe – young men like my father, and very many Jewish families escaping from the persecution they suffered in ghettos. Some settled in Britain, some went to America and further afield – to South Africa. Any country where they believed they would find work and build a new and better life.

How would my father be classified today – as an asylum seeker? An economic migrant? Would he have been permitted to stay or be turned back? Those were different times; there were no problems to his entry.

He settled in London and established a small business as a house painter and decorator.

I assume he had been well educated, for he was fluent in Russian, German and Yiddish, and spoke English with no trace of an accent. He was a burly man, of average height, with red hair and a red moustache.

In his twenties he married Dora who had been born in one of those border regions which history and politics shuffled between Polish, German and Russian rule. When she was only seven she had been sent to live with her older brother Louis in London. Louis was married with children and Dora had become an unpaid maid in her brother's house. One of her tasks was to fetch her brother's children from school. She herself did not go to school, but every day when she went to deliver or collect her cousins she would stand outside the school gates hoping a teacher would see her and ask her why she too was not in school. She was never asked.

She grew up to be a very pretty young woman, with thick curly black hair and a beautiful complexion. She remembered her childhood as an intensely unhappy time. When she was old enough – still without any schooling – she went to work in a basement shirt factory, sewing buttonholes. She only learned to read and write as an adult. She enjoyed reading, admired Ruskin, and loved music. Because of her own lack of formal education she keenly desired that we, her children, should be well-educated.

It was a time when religion tended to play a more important part in defining who people were than it does today. In our house there was no religion; what we knew of it came from our schools where religious instruction – fundamentally Christian – was part of the curriculum. Our father – Papa – was an atheist but did not try to influence us; he left us to decide for ourselves to accept or reject whatever religious faith we chose. As a child, by my own choice, I went to Sunday School.

'Am I Jewish?' my sister Vera asked him once.

'Why do you ask?'

'A girl at school asked me.'

'Tell her you are a human being.'

Because our parents practiced neither the religious customs of their own parents, nor the cultural customs of their countries of origin, the only religious festival my sisters and I knew of was Christmas. We were taught the religious significance of Christmas at school, and there was always a nativity play; but to us – as to most British children – its religious significance tended to be of less importance than the holiday festivities; and the excitement of making and receiving gifts, of constructing decorations that we looped across the rooms, with a tree we loved to decorate.

Our mother did not fully share Papa's atheism. She was ambivalent about the existence of a God and she retained some lingering memories of the customs of her early childhood. She would later express regret that her daughters had never learned anything about the culture from which she had come. Her politics were vaguely social-democratic; she favoured the Fabian society and admired the Labour MP, George Lansbury. Communism was a closed book to her.

Papa believed that émigrés should assimilate in their new country. He did not categorise people by race or religion. He accepted that his home was England, and he anglicised his first name from Simeon to Samuel; everyone called him Sam. During the First World War, because of anti-German hostility he found it necessary to change his German-sounding surname from 'Schwartz' to the eminently English 'Watts'. But he did not legalise the change.

Our family evolved in an unexceptional British way. We were a product of the social life and schools of the suburbia of a big city. In times that were more class-ridden than today we were what would be termed 'upper working-class'.

To our neighbours in the suburbs where we lived we were socially undifferentiated, ordinary in the sense that we lived as they did. We never felt ourselves to be different in any way from them or from our school friends.

But we were different. Despite his belief in assimilation, Russia was always a presence in Papa's life, and so, in a shadowy way, in ours. As children we often went to the houses of other émigrés where friends of our parents, with their more open, expansive hospitality, their foreign accents and interesting food, seemed to bring a slightly exotic element into our conventional English lives.

Because of our father's love of music all three of us had music lessons. We had a piano in our house – a good one, an upright Bechstein – which would later become an element in dividing our family. Papa wanted us to be a trio: Vera the eldest, learned to play the piano, Olga the violin, and I, it was hoped, would play the cello. Until I was old enough and a cello could be bought, I had piano lessons.

By the time he married, our father already had an active social life in émigré circles where he played chess and indulged his interests in music, particularly opera – he had a good singing voice. He loved the theatre and took part in amateur theatricals. One of the clubs where Russian émigrés gathered was in Charlotte Street, a cultural and political centre that organised lectures, meetings and theatricals. There his interest in politics was stimulated.

The First World War awakened a new awareness of national feelings and patriotism. Papa decided that the time had come for him to acquire British nationality. He applied for citizenship but was turned down, for what reason I do not know – perhaps because of his association with radicals and revolutionaries in the émigré circles, perhaps because the patriotic passions of war created a distrust of all foreigners. He thought of joining the British army; but without British nationality he was afraid that if he was wounded or killed he might not have any claim to compensation or a pension.

He lived two different lives – the ordinary English life of work, home and family; and a Russian émigré life as a member of the cultural and political centre with regular meetings in Charlotte Street. In our neighbourhood surroundings the war raging in Western Europe was at the centre of peoples' lives. In his Russian circle composed almost entirely of refugees from Tsarism, intense and passionate interest centred on the war raging on the Eastern Front. As the war dragged into its third year the numbers of dead and wounded on both fronts rose to thousands and then hundreds of thousands. The misery, hunger and suffering of civilians all across Europe and Russia seemed to be – like the war – without end in sight.

Rumours of revolt and incipient uprisings on the Russian front inspired political hope in the émigré circle which included radicals and revolutionaries of all political groups seeking the overthrow of the Tsar's feudal despotism. Amongst them were communists like Maxim Litvinov, who had come to London as a political exile in 1908 (he was later to become Minister of Foreign Affairs in the Soviet Union); Peter Kropotkin who led the anarchist faction, and others. In this circle Simeon's political commitment grew. He joined the Russian Social Democratic Labour Party group before it split into two groups, the more moderate Mensheviks and the Bolsheviks – who would become the Russian Communist Party.

But Dora never became involved in that second life. Like many communists, my father's belief in equality for women was not carried into the life of his own home. For all his progressive views he was a man of his times, subject to the conventions of the society in which he lived, a time when women did not have the right to vote and were excluded from any positions of power. He went to meetings, Dora stayed at home and looked after the children. From the time that Vera was born Dora was housebound and thus excluded from participation in that second life. When she complained about the fact that she was only able to do ordinary 'little' things, he assured her that his work was little in comparison to hers. The most important job in the world was the nurturing of a new generation. 'You cannot compare yourself to the Master Builder's wife,' he wrote to her once when she had complained. 'You have got your realm; the very biggest of all works.'

Simeon never took time off from his many activities to persuade her of his beliefs, of what communism meant to him, nor how deeply it influenced his life. Because of this a fatal fault line developed in their relationship which would later become too deep to bridge, with tragic consequences.

With so many interests in addition to his work, we often saw little of our father during the week. But we adored him. He was a man who enjoyed his children. He had a happy nature, made friends wherever he went and was popular with everyone who knew him. In summer when we spent some weeks at the seaside, he stayed in London working and visited us at weekends. Whenever we were separated he sent us postcards. He played games with us, did tricks, made pennies disappear from his fingers and come out behind our ears, told us stories, brought us little treats when he had been away. He gave attention to each of his daughters, made each of us feel special. He was a lovely father to have.

When I was ten years old he went away, and I never saw him again.

CHAPTER 2

Revolution

In every way, the idea of communism embodied the hope of human transformation. It transcended the blind nationalism behind the appalling slaughter of World War One. It offered an alternative to the despair and unemployment of the Great Depression. It promised a sense of comradeship that would gradually spread to all countries of the earth.

Adam Hochschild, *The Unquiet Ghost* (Viking, 1994)

I WAS born in 1915, during the First World War. I was three when the war ended, and even when I went to school I knew almost nothing about it, nor of the Russian Revolution in 1917. To those in authority it must have seemed too near, too raw and perhaps too controversial to include in our school curriculum. Our history lessons ended before the First World War. So, as a child, I learned nothing of the upheavals which destroyed the old order in Europe, where empires disappeared and new frontiers were drawn, new countries born.

It has taken many decades for a true history of those times to become generally known. Today, nearly ninety years later, contemporary writers and film makers have brought to life the massive destruction

9

and senseless loss of life of that war; the futility and, enormous suffering and sacrifices of 'the lions led by donkeys'.

By 1917 people were becoming weary of war, of the huge losses inflicted on a generation of the young and most able men. In Britain many of the men called up for military service proved to be physically unfit to go into the army; a reflection of their poor living conditions, the malnutrition and illnesses of urban poverty. The huge advance of industrialisation had been uncontrolled by legislation and unrelieved by government welfare. It condemned millions to lives crammed in disease-ridden slums, where poverty and over-crowding produced high infant mortality and physically under-nourished and feeble adults. The war had added to the discontent and desire for change.

It was not only in Britain that people were war-weary. All Europe was in turmoil as in many countries the population turned against the autocratic rule of those who held power – a decadent coterie of Lords, Kings, Tsars. Everywhere people longed for peace; and more than that they wanted society to change, they wanted an end to poverty and unemployment, to the ignorance and disease of the cities. They wanted governments that would represent their interests, not those of closed hierarchies run by self-appointed upper classes, by hereditary kings and tsars. The countries of Europe were seething with pressure for change.

Nobody could have predicted that this desire for revolutionary change would burst into flames in the most backward country of Europe – the vast Russian empire. No country needed it more.

The Russian Revolution came with devastating effect. It has been described by the historian E.H. Carr as a turning point in history that may well be assessed by future historians as the greatest event of the twentieth century.[1] Not only socialists and idealists greeted it with optimism; it was celebrated by enlightened, progressive people all over the world. Bolshevism seemed to promise a radiant future in which socialism would transform society and at the same time transform human nature.

My father, too, nursed this great utopian dream. While still in his teens, he had turned his back on the horrors and brutality of the Russian empire, the cruelty, backwardness and feudalism of Tsarism. He had decided to assimilate in the country to which he had emigrated. He had discarded the religion, the rituals, the social customs of his childhood. Yet despite this he remained a Russian at heart. The years of childhood and young adulthood had shaped his attitudes, his personality; he could not discard them.

Now, despite his efforts to integrate himself and his family into English, life the events in the land of his birth exercised a powerful pull on him. The Russian Revolution seemed to promise an end to the poverty and exploitation of capitalism. The Russian Revolutionaries were pioneers setting out to build a better world.

For him – as for other émigrés in his circle – all social strivings came to focus on the life and death of the revolution which was being fought out in his far away homeland. They believed, like the Bolsheviks themselves, that the revolution would be the signal for uprisings in Central and Western Europe, where antagonism to the war was leading to disaffection in the armies and among civilians. They saw their revolution as the fuse that would ignite socialism in all Europe. It seemed miraculous that this great leap forward should come from within such a backward country. If Russian workers could set out to change the nature of their society surely the workers of the more advanced nations of Europe would follow suit. The revolutionary anthem, *The Internationale*, called upon 'the wretched of the earth' to inherit the new order, dispelling forever poverty and unemployment.

Simeon was one of those for whom the revolution and the survival and success of its radical government became the driving force in his life. He decided that his place was now as a full-time member of the Bolshevik Party. As soon as conditions made it possible we would emigrate to Russia as a family, where he would serve in whatever capacity

11

he could, and we – his daughters – would be able to grow up in the new and better world of socialism.

The Bolsheviks' most urgent task was peace with Germany. On October 26,1917, immediately after seizing power, Lenin announced a Decree on Peace. Another first step was the Decree on Land announcing the expropriation of all the big estates and their equipment, and converting them into the property of the entire people. These decrees were swiftly followed by others instituting an eight-hour day and giving workers control of factories and mines.

While the communist objective of a socialist society was rooted in the dream of a more just society, for the Russian ruling classes whose estates were being confiscated it spelt disaster. Russian generals opposed to the Bolsheviks formed a counter-revolutionary army. Other groups opposed to the Bolsheviks joined what was to become known as the White Army. The Bolsheviks' Red Guards rallied to defend the revolution and by 1918 Russia and the countries that had comprised the Tsarist empire were at civil war.

The Soviet dream was also a nightmare to some in the governments of Western Europe, many of whose aristocrats had dynastic relations with the Tsar and aristocracy of Russia, and who saw in Russian communism the threat of revolution closer to home. 'The revolution was the first challenge to the capitalist system in Europe,' wrote E.H. Carr. 'It could be thought of as both a consequence and a cause of the decline of capitalism.'[2] As the world war came to an end with the defeat of Germany, the Allies began to pay more attention to Russia's civil war.

By the beginning of 1919 the disparate and undisciplined Red Guards had developed into the Red Army, and the Soviet government was fighting for its life on four fronts. Counter-revolutionary armies were advancing under Admiral Kolchak in the east, General Deniken in the south, and General Yudenich in the north. The British landed an expeditionary force in Archangel and Murmansk; the French landed a naval garrison in Odessa; the Japanese occupied territory in the Far East.

But the Allied armies were war-weary and opinions about Russia were divided. Their aid to the Whites was half-hearted. Meanwhile, the Generals and the White Army had no real political goal to offer people except the defeat of communism and a return to the old regime; while the Red Army had the crusading fervour of those fighting for a new world order. The civil war ended with the defeat of the Whites, and the withdrawal of foreign troops.

The war had torn communities and societies apart. Large-scale atrocities had been committed by both sides, and the prolonged period of war from 1914 followed by civil war left the country impoverished and brutalized. On top of the toll of war dead, in the years 1918 to 1920 millions died from disease and malnutrition.

On this disaster-stricken society the new Union of Socialist Soviet Republics was erected – a vast area stretching across one sixth of the world, an empire of many countries, ethnically diverse, divided by language, religion, culture and traditions. It was predominantly agrarian, and lacking in modern facilities, administration and communications. Socialists believed that socialism – even more so communism – could only be achieved on the basis of a highly industrialised, technologically advanced society with an educated working class and professionals of every kind – engineers, scientists, researchers, administrators; and with the co-operation of the intelligentsia. The new order lacked them all. They would have to create them as they built their socialist order.

While the British expeditionary force was fighting the Bolsheviks the British government had been reluctant to encourage British residents to travel; they favoured the opposition parties within Russia, mainly the Mensheviks under Kerensky, and tended to withhold visas from known Bolsheviks. The émigrés set up their own committee of four to decide who amongst them should return to Russia. They listed first Ivan

Maisky (later to be Soviet Ambassador in Britain), Maxim Litvinov, Georgi Chicherin and Zundelevich. This committee felt that for the time being my father, Simeon, with his familiarity with British life would play a more useful role in London.

In due course the new Soviet government appointed Litvinov as its representative in London; he opened the first Soviet Embassy and formed a Russian Delegates Committee to co-opt the services of émigré comrades. Simeon became honorary secretary of the Executive Committee of this organisation, in effect Litvinov's secretary and right-hand man. But in 1918 in reprisal for the Soviet government's expulsion from Moscow of a British engineer, Bruce Lockhart, who was accused of espionage, Litvinov was expelled from Britain. Simeon was now left acting Consul until such time as the British government would recognise a new official representative.

He wound up his interest in the house-painting business. We moved from a small house in Hampstead Garden Suburb to a larger house in Wessex Gardens in Golders Green. The house was newly-built in a street of houses that eventually would cover the fields which surrounded the house when we moved in. My sisters remembered the changes in our family's life that took place at that time. They remembered attending functions in a chauffeur-driven car and that there were many visitors to our house.

In 1921 an Anglo-Russian trade agreement was signed and George Krassin arrived in Britain to open trade relations between the two countries. Simeon then went to work for the new Russian trading organisation, Arcos.

For six years he waited for his chance to return to his homeland. Late in 1924 he was recalled to the USSR on official business. The journey to Moscow was complicated and slow. After the channel crossing to France, he took a train to Paris, and then on to Berlin, Warsaw, Leningrad and finally Moscow. He stayed in Moscow with Communist

Party officials for a few days, writing his first impressions to his family, and then went to visit his childhood home and his brother in Odessa.

As the train continued its long journey across the steppes he watched the landscapes with increasing excitement.

Oh, what glory! Only in my childhood do I remember such a beautiful sky. The vast fields and trees all sprinkled with snow, and the glorious sun, so big and round; what beauty, what glory. How could I live all those years in such gloomy, rainy, foggy London!

He went to visit his brother's home in Odessa and wrote that the weather was *glorious, dry, frosty after sunshine. What a beautiful town this is still, in spite of the terrible demolition and ruins in many streets. The sea is so near the centre, and the streets are lined with trees.*

He sent us postcards from Odessa, Kiev and Moscow and wrote regularly to Dora. He returned to England. In the summer of 1925 he was again recalled to the USSR. He thought that he would be there for about six months.

CHAPTER 3

Another Life

IT was nearly twenty-five years since he had left Russia. He had been born and grown up in the southern Ukraine, in Odessa on the Black Sea, one of the world's most beautiful towns, situated on terraced hills overlooking the harbour. It has a warm, benign climate, in many ways like a Mediterranean city, with architecture influenced by French and Italian styles. A British journalist described Odessa as 'a port where the breezes of Europe blew, a town of gamblers, good weather and Italian opera'. My father must have grown up listening to opera, for it was his abiding passion. He had never lived in the cold north, in Moscow.

It was a time long before reports and pictures of events in distant parts of the world could be transmitted as speedily as they are today. Embassies reported to their own governments, but there were few foreign reporters, no on-the-spot journalists with cameras, no means of transmitting pictures and stories within hours of their occurrence, no television to bring the reality of starving children into peoples' homes. Those who lived in the safety of the British Isles, where not since ancient times had wars been fought on their territory, had no comprehension of the extent of the devastation that war, revolution and civil war had brought to Russia.

My father had left his homeland before the years of war and revolution, when society, although oppressive, had been relatively stable. If he had known of the real situation or had any understanding of the chaos and destruction, the poverty and horrific living conditions that war and revolution had created he would not have contemplated emigrating with his family.

He was sent to Moscow. Although it was the capital of the Soviet Union, much of the city was in the nature of a provincial town, a huge sprawl with unpaved dirt roads, some cobbled streets and houses built of wood. Only in the central area were there many fine buildings – the Kremlin at the heart of the city, with the Bolshoi Theatre, the Metropol Hotel and public buildings nearby; and around the centre and along the banks of the Moskva river the houses of the nobility and merchants.

He had left his country in pre-war peace; he was not prepared for the immensity of the post-war poverty and suffering of ordinary people in the streets around him. He had been away too long, living in the largest capital city of the industrialised West, to have anticipated the backwardness and primitive living conditions of even a large town like Moscow.

A decade of war and civil war had brought industrial and agricultural collapse and its aftermath – a famine which claimed millions of lives. The countryside had emptied its starving people into the city. But the city had no heating or lighting and no space for the newcomers. Once-spacious apartments had been divided up with families often restricted to only one room, and with facilities for cooking and washing shared with several other families. In some apartments rooms had been sub-divided by a curtain to accommodate two families. Many single people without even a room slept in corridors or on the floors of friends' rooms.

And it was not only the starvation, the squalor and the extreme poverty that so shocked him, but the apparent acceptance – or even indifference – shown by his friends and comrades to conditions he found intolerable.

On his previous visit he had not really experienced what it was like to live in post-revolutionary Russia. He had been accommodated in a hotel, had been able to take in visits to the theatre and ballet, had travelled around in a car with little real contact with the life of the city. Now, no longer a short-term visitor but a working citizen, he was experiencing the reality of it every day. He wrote of his feelings about what he saw. He was finding it very difficult to adapt to the harsh living conditions which his comrades seemed to accept as normal: the dirt, the vermin and rats in the apartments, the homeless children, barefoot and in rags, and the hordes of beggars in the streets.

He wrote to Dora every two or three days. Some of these letters were sent through the regular post; others, describing his reactions to the conditions, he gave to friends to post for him in England when they arrived there.

At present I feel very strange and lonely, and believe me, if it were not for the sake of the children's future I would ask you to come over and leave everything behind. But the thought of the change for the children holds me back.

He believed – in fact had been assured – that, by virtue of his nearly a quarter of a century of life in England, his fluency in English and his familiarity with life in the West, he would soon be given a post in Britain or America. But for the meantime how could he bring his daughters, born in England, British subjects who spoke only English, from the ordered and protected life they had known in their suburbia, from their house with separate rooms for every function, the garden with its apple trees, their pet Airedale dog – to this deep poverty, chaos and turmoil. Realising how difficult it was for himself to adjust even though he was Russian born, fluent in the language and familiar with the customs, he understood that for us it would be traumatic. We would be deprived and alienated.

It is terribly difficult to take it all in. People who come here for a few weeks are conscious all the time that they themselves will not remain, but will return to their own more cultured life; they brag about the wonderful progress made; all very well for others. How much misery!! – the beggars in the streets, cripples, men, women and little children crawling about, begging, simply barring the way and you cannot pass...

He quotes a friend who advises him to '*take it all philosophically. Those beggars are mostly professionals exposing themselves like business people expose their wares; every cent you give them only encourages them to greater effort in the art of their profession. Such scenes are seen in all the Eastern countries, they are relics of medieval times – Moscow is now and always was a semi-Eastern town; such things are inevitable and will re-main for years until the government is rich enough to clear all the beggars and cripples off the streets into decent houses. But now we have more im-portant work on hand.*'

He breaks off with disconnected pictures of life in Moscow:

Evening. Young folks walking, laughing, joking as though life is quite normal. A little mite with practically no clothes on stands under a lamp post singing and begging for a kopek for food; no one seems to take any notice.

He gives an amusing sketch of an altercation between a drunk and a policeman. Then simply adds:

<u>*Finis*</u>

But continues:

<u>*12.30 midnight*</u>

Rats!!! Giving no rest, impossible to get to sleep. Oh, that's nothing, they tell me. Nichevo. You're too fussy, you ought to have lived here in 1920 –

you have no idea what life was like then. You are spoilt. You will get used to it. You've been living as a bourgeois too long. The wretchedness and misery is appalling. What people must have lived through!

Streets are better lit, but oh! the street beggars – they give you no respite. At every inch there is an old woman or cripple stretching hands for only one kopek… how many years before we really begin to live as we dreamed. It seems so slow.

Sometimes he writes sketchily of his own circumstances, of his exceptional good fortune in obtaining accommodation where there is a bathroom with a geyser and a bath – inevitably shared with all the other tenants in the building – a rare luxury. *Not very clean because everybody washes there and spits in it but still I can have a bath… the only thing to do is to imagine it is very, very clean.*

This philosophy does not always work. He is living in a very large apartment previously belonging to a nobleman. He describes the grandeur of the rooms, very large and lofty, with floors of parquet and furniture that is very heavy and antique.

But it has been neglected, and is infested with rats. *As soon as you retire to bed the commotion begins. For nights I could not sleep, and when I told some of the people who live here they said, Oh yes, it is very unpleasant, but we take no notice of it.*

If you can shut your eyes and only think of what will be in ten, fifteen years, or twenty, then you are very lucky.

Sept 12, 1925:

It seems that to understand all that is taking place one has to live through the misery in order to appreciate the improvements. I am unable to take it all in yet.

A gigantic stagnant pool, the bottom of which was full of filth and dirt. To clear the stinking filth out it was impossible not to stir the whole pool, and consequently the whole pool looks filthy. The objects were there all the time, unseen and unobserved, and now everything is seen in its naked truth. It cannot be cleaned without stirring the bottom. The process is a long one, not for one year, but for many, many years, but a beginning is made.

The crowds scurry like ants whose nest has been destroyed; they are running everywhere, looking, seeking for new nests which do not as yet exist… everything is done in slow and primitive ways that seem part of the poverty and backwardness.

Queues! Everywhere… whatever you want you have to queue and wait your turn, queue and queue again. These are small things admitted, but life itself is made up of small things and why not make it pleasant? But no one cares. People have got accustomed to discomforts and do not care. Nichevo.

He thinks the problem is that he is seeing Moscow through 'London eyes' and he worries that he is thinking like a White Guard.

Possibly I am spoilt by the middle class petty-bourgeois life in London, but at present life seems very sordid.

Yet in spite of all said, many, many things are interesting. The great thirst for knowledge, young and old, literature shops are always full, young and old buying books, tracts, etc.

But *people don't know how to do things, everything is done in a primitive way, slow and somehow without interest. Something will have to be done to develop initiative otherwise we shall stand still for years to come.*

But is there any other way? I doubt it, there seems nothing else. Twenty, thirty years! What changes – they must come. But when you try to do things you find difficulties in your way. We do not lack in ideals, but we lack the material necessary to carry these ideals into practice.

And then like a cry of despair:

Only seven weeks here and it seems like seven <u>months</u>! Somehow I have grown out of all this. Everything is so backward and strange as though no changes have taken place – and yet – <u>twenty-five years</u> have gone since I left – and a revolution!

The Letters

I have many of the letters that Papa sent to Dora, spanning seven years from 1925 to 1932. Although some are missing, particularly from the later years, I believe she had tried to keep all the letters written in his clear and elegant script, even those sent by hand which he asked her to destroy. But there are gaps in time where I assume either that letters did not arrive, or that they have not survived the disruption and our many moves over the years. There are none of the letters that Dora sent to him, but from what he wrote in response to her letters it is not difficult to deduce what was in them Apart from news of the children – school reports, illnesses, holidays – she wrote constantly about what she seemed to regard as his refusal to return; and more persistently about one thing – her chronic shortage of money.

He had arranged for the main part of his Moscow salary to be paid to her. This had not been easy. His superiors could not understand why anyone would need to send money from the poverty-stricken Soviet Union to prosperous England; and the limitations that the Soviet government imposed on obtaining foreign exchange were compounded by bureaucracy. Its arrival was erratic, leaving Dora endlessly struggling to make ends meet, to pay the bills. He used his influence to get her a job at Arcos; but she had no training in office work, nor did she appreciate the necessity for diplomacy in a Soviet-run office where her political attitudes were under constant observation; and after some time she lost this job, probably more through lack of caution in voicing her political opinions than through inefficiency.

From the first the difficulties of managing the flow of money for his family to retain their standard of living was a constant problem for Simeon.

I am sorry you are having all the trouble, I knew you would have your hands full, what with the care of the house, children, dog, and going out to work. I can quite understand how you feel. I am sorry to say I can help you very little as yet and most probably for some time to come until my own position becomes quite clear. You will have to arm yourself with plenty of patience and courage.

His letters are filled with concern, even with guilt. But clearly Dora did not share either his sense of dedication, nor an understanding of the realities of Soviet life. Unwittingly, by voicing her resentment of and hostility to the communists whom she held responsible for keeping him away from her, she was weakening his own opportunities for return to England. She was voicing these feelings both to people in the Arcos office, and also to those she considered friends in the wider émigré circle.

In his letters, (these are the hand-delivered ones) over and over he pleads with her to be more cautious in what she says and to whom she speaks of her problems. He suggests she should take in lodgers to help financially, but specifically asks that she should *not* let rooms to communists. He was aware of the consequences of reports being made to the Party both of her hostility to communism and of what they considered the bourgeois life style of his family. But she never understood. Despite his warning, she rented a room to a Russian couple who duly reported her increasing hostility to communism and her regular criticisms of the Soviet leaders, and also our 'bourgeois' standard of living; apart from the house and garden, *we had a piano*!

She began to see herself and her family as victims of the new Soviet society, while those friends who had been part of the former émigré circle but who had chosen not to return continued to live their comfortable lives. Only *her* husband had chosen to sacrifice his family for an ideal; it was beyond her comprehension. As time went by her sense of grievance grew with the constant worry about money and involuntary privations she now suffered.

She was trusting, gentle and unassertive. She had no skills other than those of a housewife and mother. She had been left with the responsibilities of a house, a mortgage, bills, three children and an erratic income. After she lost her job at Arcos she took up ventures for which she was unsuited. She tried selling underwear door to door, dealt with difficult lodgers, dreamt endlessly of schemes that could never materialise, and wrote her sad letters of complaint and distress to Simeon. Communism, she had read, believes in free love and destroys family life. Hadn't it ruined hers? And he in turn wrote sympathetic but unsatisfactory replies in an attempt – too late – to make her understand what his beliefs meant to him and how fundamental they were to the course of his life.

He tries to explain:

I am a communist, but very far from the conception of a communist in Russia. No one here would understand or believe it is possible for a communist to have a house of his own – they cannot understand it, after all they have lived through these years. And a piano! How dare I have a piano!

In September of that year he has, however, been offered a choice of two important jobs, one as chairman of a state company, or the other as chairman of a government shipping concern. But he has refused them both, deciding instead to work for Sovkino, a state organisation connected with film-making. He explains that he has turned down the more prestigious positions: *because that would mean that I have to settle here for a few years, whereas in the cinema business I may have an opportunity within a few months to be appointed representative in England or America. I will get enough money to enable me to support you and the children until they are on their own feet; that is my only thought.*

You think you would like to come here? As far as you yourself is concerned I should like it very much. Mind you, you must not think that you can come here and, if you don't like it, you will go back. Oh no! But that *is not all, that would not matter. It is only when I begin to think about the children that the whole question takes a different turn. <u>I feel that I have no right to bring them here at this age</u>. Later on they can do as they please, but as they were not born here, and have been educated in English schools as far as secondary school under conditions as yet unknown here, it would cripple them for many years; they would be neither one thing nor another and they would suffer from a lack of knowledge and education. I cannot write you this in an open letter by post. You will understand that.*

But what is to be done? Believe me, if I had another way I would have taken it. Suppose I give it all up and by some means come back? Even supposing I am allowed in again – which is not certain – what would I do there – or anywhere? I have no business to rely on, no rich friends to fall back upon, no prospects.

He explains that with what he is sending together with her earnings from her job, and if needs be, the letting of a room or two, she should be able to manage for a year although he hopes it would be less than that. By then he believes that if things go well he will be sent to England and America regarding the import and export of Russian films as well as to arrange the joint production of films. This is his only reason for working in Sovkino.

I am practically certain that in time – it may be a year, maybe less – I will get some sort of work abroad and will go back to London.

He says he will not have time to write such long letters when he begins to be involved in this new work.

As well as party activity which for me is the most important question of all – to get into my party work and find myself on a level with those who on the whole know much more than myself – in particular on questions concerning the party machinery and Soviet institutions of which unfortunately I know very little as yet. And only when I have worked here for a time the question of my going abroad can be raised.

Have you any other way out? I am prepared to listen, but do not send it by post. You can always find out from R who is going to Moscow, and send it by hand.

There are several more pages of this letter, going into details about how she might make better use of what money she has, and how he manages on thirty shillings a week, which is what he has allotted to himself. He details all his difficulties, and speculates about the future. He concludes:

It is not the fault of the government when the Russian peasant is <u>one hundred years behind</u>; they are trying their very best under terrible odds, but the progress is so slow! So slow! For those who imagined things better… this time will soon pass, and I dare say you will be glad you stuck it out and the children will have the benefit for their lives. I am sorry you may feel different, I can see no other way.

There is no further news of the Sovkino job, but by September of the following year, 1926, he reports that he is being sent on a fortnight's tour of the Ukraine, and on his return believes he is going to be able to go to London for a holiday. He has also been offered a post in New York.

When this comes off I will tell you; it is only possible when all the formalities have been gone through. It is a question if the Party will give me permission to work abroad after only one year's work in Russia. They may say I am not sufficiently Russianised – or Bolshevised (and they would be right, believe me!!!). The question is now being considered by the Central Bureau of the Party; they must give their consent… However, as soon as I am told all clear for America I am going, and of course will come to London. So be prepared to go…

The year is winding down. Dora has lost her job at Arcos, and Simeon is trying to use his influence to get her reinstated, or to obtain another position.

I have, as you already know, been appointed to go to New York. The matter is now in the hands of the Central Committee dealing with appointments for abroad. I have every confidence that they will agree to my appointment, as there are no people here with a fair knowledge of English …

My great worry is how you will keep on until I come. The money I am sending, small as it is, is <u>beyond</u> my earnings. I am doing all I can to save every coin and send it over… I am hoping that in January or the latest in February some one must go to New York and by then the matter will be quite clear.

He is still wearing his London clothes – light shoes and overcoat, his only protection against Moscow's sub-zero winters; but he is sending all his money to his family.

At the end of December, he is able to send her a letter by hand.

It is quite evident from your last letter that you do not realise the situation when you say that we have to decide in one month what to do. I have many times attempted to explain to you that we are in an exceptional position with regard to the question of all of you coming here. But should you after all decide that you will under any circumstance prefer to be here, I warn you that I cannot be responsible for all the sufferings you may have to endure. I want to be quite frank with you, and will say at once without hesitation that I myself would not mind staying on if I cannot be appointed anywhere abroad. But my own personal case is quite different from yours.

I am up at eight in the morning and away all day, busy all the time and most of the evenings. I have nothing whatever to do with the obtaining of food, or preparing it in a kitchen where five, six or seven other families are doing the same.

I know the language, and feel at home. The time passes quickly, I have no time to bother about anything or anybody. You on the other hand would have to bear the load of all the shortcomings. You cannot do any social work here, you do not know the language. You would have to put up with being alone; and as far as the children are concerned – well, I really do not know how they would fare, all of us living in one or two rooms. It is quite different for people who were born and brought up here, and who went through the horrors of war, revolution, famine, etc. They have got hardened to everything.

So it is with a full conscience that I have told and advised you in the past as well as I am doing now, to remain where you are under any circumstances.

You think I do not understand how you were feeling at Arcos all the time? Oh! I do know quite well that you did not have a very nice time. And though you did not feel nice there, it will be heaven in comparison with the position you would undoubtedly find here.

I am trying very hard to get a position abroad, anywhere, Germany, America, wherever they need some one. But it does not rest with me. If I am definitely told that permission to go abroad is refused I will ask to be given a chance to bring my family over. I do hope, however, that it will not be refused.

He asks her not to pay attention to a friend who has told her he will never come back.

Of course it was very foolish of you to tell him that they have taken me away from you (I do not understand how you could do it) and of course he was quite right in telling you that I need not have gone. Of course not! But I would have been thrown out of the Party. It may not mean anything to you, but it would have meant <u>everything</u> to me, and consequently to all of you. I went of my own free will, but if I did not I would have lost all standing, and would have to look for a job. I have told you this many times before.

In short, my advice to you is as before: try and get a second mortgage on the house, or take my life policy to the bank and get a loan. I keep sending you my very last penny leaving me with practically nothing for myself. I will not leave a stone unturned to get abroad, even for a year or two, so that the children can continue their education. That is my last word to you. I hope Arcos will take you back. I will not keep quiet here about it.

By January he has been away two years. He writes that he has asked a friend to lend Dora some money, and is trying to get her another job. In March he is still waiting to hear about his own future, but retains his expectation of being sent abroad, as he has had provisional permission to enter America; and he has hopes of being able to make a short visit to London.

In June he knows that his posting abroad is not going to materialise – at least, not in the foreseeable future. And a 'new situation' has arisen.

I hope it will not worry you, but it seems my hopes of a short visit to London have been shattered. My mission to America has also been postponed; on the other hand I have had an offer to go to another place, far away from Moscow, on a better salary which will enable me to provide you with the necessary means to keep yourself and the children in comparative comfort. I have dried my brain to find a solution, and I think under the present circumstances it will be the best way out of the situation. I will at least know that you are not in want, and that will give my mind a rest.

He says he is preparing a full power of attorney for her during his mission. Then, bitterly, he attributes his problems to Dora's indiscretions.

Speak less your mind to other people, he writes in a last desperate letter before he finally decides to take on what will be a difficult and hazardous job. *Had you not done so all along, things would have been different. I used to tell you this often.*

The Journey East

On July 28, 1927, he began a very long letter:

It seems at last I will get a chance to relate to you fully what I could not do before, to give you an idea of the position I found myself in from the very beginning, almost two years ago; and the reason I accepted new work at the very end of the world.

He added to the letter as he was travelling, but it was nearly four months before he had an opportunity to post the letter, on November 20.

We shall be travelling through Japanese territory from where I can post this letter without running any risk of being called a White Guard.

When, two years ago, I set out for Moscow, I myself and many others believed that it would not be long before I would be back in London. It seemed obvious to everybody. I possessed all the qualifications necessary to be entrusted with any work in connection with trade, or any other position requiring a knowledge of English. I was quite confident that in six months, at the most, I would be sent back to London.

This belief, he wrote, had been strengthened by what had happened to others, including a man who had been expelled from the party and, reinstated, was permitted to return to London.

However, this did not happen to me, and as soon as I arrived in Moscow it became clear to me that I shall have to stick it out for at least a year before I will get a chance to return to you. For three months I nearly went out of my mind. It was maddening. I could not get used to all the ways here not only in life personally, but everything seemed so strange and primitive after twenty-four years' life in the centre of cultural Europe that I was afraid I would not be able to bear it.

Nevertheless, after a few months I began to look at life philosophically and to find excuses for many things. For six months I worked hard on myself personally in order to get acquainted with the framework and vocabulary of Soviet 'political literacy' as it is called. I was allotted to conduct a school of young communists and I accepted a position as chairman of a company, a post quite envied by others, and I was confident that with this rehabilitation I would gain the confidence of those necessary to give me permission to go abroad.

After nine months he had approached his superiors, who said they were willing to send him to London as a representative of the state maritime agency Sovtorgflot, but doubted that the party committee controlling foreign appointments would agree. He then made an informal approach to the official who controlled appointments abroad.

I gave him my reasons: that you were there, the children go to English schools and do not speak a word of Russian. He told me that was all the more reason that you should come here; it was my duty to bring you all over so that you as well as the children should get the necessary grounding for the future Communist commonwealth. My children should be brought up in proletarian schools, and not in bourgeois schools. I gathered that nothing would help induce anyone to give me the opportunity to return to you.

People told him that he was lucky to be in Moscow, as many others who had been called back from abroad had been sent to a provincial town or village where there was hardly any life. The purpose was to bring to reality those who had lived abroad in comfortable surroundings, to remind them that such life, for the proletariat, is unobtainable.

I know that it is very difficult for you to understand all this. One has to understand the psychology prevailing here – not without reasons, of course. Many people who went through the horrors during war and revolution, having been denied the most elementary requirements of life, when they go abroad at once lose their heads, take advantage of their positions, live like lords, and spoil the very life of others. For such reasons stringent rules have been made for people working a few years abroad. And, as is always the case, the guilty invariably escape punishment and those who are straight suffer for the guilty ones.

Believe me, no one is to blame. Once you are disappointed in people you are always suspicious of everybody. After all, why should I be the exception to the rule? How is anyone to believe that I have never taken advantage of my position and will remain so? Besides there are always *'friends' to give you a lift in life. Reports are being sent of every slip you make. Only think of it: I, a communist, own property – even a piano!; my family are not far from ordinary <u>White Guards</u>. Of course, you have never made any secret of your hostility to many things existing in Russia today. I cannot blame you for it, except tactlessness. (<u>Walls have ears, you know</u>.) All you said was transmitted and put down in a notebook against me. So that when the question of going abroad was raised, apart from everything else, it was found that I was not to be trusted, as my family lives very well and my children are not being brought up in a communist way. And so you will understand it was terribly hard for me to overcome such prejudice against me.*

And then in January 1927 I was finally appointed representative for Sovtorgflot in New York and began the ordeal one has to go through before receiving the blessings of all the committees. At the beginning all went well, I got through nearly all the stages – I was almost sure the matter was settled. But alas! At the last minute I received the terrible blow – No! For a day or two I did not know what to do. I knew exactly your position: Rent, rates, taxes, school fees, and means to live on. I had drained all cash resources. I could not think of anyone to ask for a loan again. There was nothing left for me to do but finish it all… But what good would that have done? I kept on receiving letters from you reproaching me for saying I was coming and then that my visit had been postponed, as though it depended on my will or wish. I could not write you plainly by post, though I gave you plenty of hints to understand it.

There seemed to be no other way for me than to ask for a little assistance in order to bring you all over to Moscow. I did not want to do that. Heaven only knows how I struggled against that. If I were to tell you all the reasons I did not want to take this last step, you probably would not understand it. You may have been told all sorts of things – and no doubt you have been told many things; but I only know one reason, and that is, that all of us – apart from anything else, apart from the fact that it would

*have been terribly difficult for you and especially for the children to put up
with all the inconveniences, we, all of us, would remain <u>poverty stricken</u>
for the rest of our days. If our children were at least boys, not girls, perhaps
it would have been best under the circumstances to come over and be together. But you do not know the psychology of the young generation here,
and the results that this would have on young girls having been brought
up in quite a different atmosphere. I have seen some results myself, and do
not wish my children to have such experience… it may be foolish on my
part, but there!!*

He then asked a friend to intervene with an under Minister to obtain
accommodation for his family. His request for a permit to visit London
for just two days was refused; but the official was prepared to provide
two rooms in Moscow and some material assistance to bring his family
over.

He was on the point of agreeing, when a friend, Natzarenus, who was
staying with him for a few days, was appointed chairman of a new company formed by the government for the purpose of organising and exploiting the material resources of the most remote and little known region of the Soviet Union, Kamchatka. Would he be prepared,
Natzarenus asked him, to head a project to research the place?

*It has never been properly investigated. Many stories are related about
the hidden treasures that can be found there. But the climate is so terrible
that up to now very few Europeans have penetrated there. All the best furs
come from animals found on this great territory. In other parts the
seashores and lakes are full of the richest fish, such as salmon and stur-
geon. There is also supposed to be gold as well as platinum. Americans and
Japanese are anxious to penetrate and exploit these mines and fisheries.
The Government has decided to organise the industries without the help
of foreign capital, and formed a company with Natzarenus at the head
of it.*

Far beyond Siberia, Kamchatka is a peninsular jutting out between the Bering Sea and the Sea of Okhotsk. It is separated from Alaska (once also Russian territory) by only a narrow passage of icy ocean. A chain of small islands directs its tip towards Japan. It is now known to be rich in many natural resources, and rich reserves of minerals such as coal and gold; but at that time it was unexplored. Life was primitive, the people had no connection with the world that lay beyond their separate and scattered communities and tribal regions. There were no roads, no transport. They were isolated not only from the distant centres of power and authority but from each other. He would be exchanging the poverty and deprivation of life in the city for an even deeper poverty, deprivation, and unknown dangers of life in a harsher and unforgiving countryside.

Because of the climate, very few people are anxious to go and work there. There are no railways leading to this territory. One can only get there by sea, and as the shore freezes in winter – for about eight or nine months – one is cut off from the rest of the world until spring, about May or June. The winter is very severe. Snow falls about September, and frost reaches fifty degrees below zero.

To induce people to go there to work, the Government pays double salaries to those paid in Moscow. That means that if my salary in Moscow is £25 a month, I will get about £50 per month. In addition, I get two months salary as an inducement. Being confronted with the ever-lasting question of bills growing daily in London and no prospect of settling them; also the fear that I may remain in such a state of stagnation for a year or two with no prospect of finding a way out; having all the time the question of the children's education in front of me I have decided to accept a position to work there knowing full well that, for maybe a year or maybe longer I will have no chance of seeing you. For peace of mind, that at least part of my salary will be more or less sufficient to keep the children at school – I was prepared to do anything. Then I got £100 right away which settles the big question of rent, rates, taxes, clothes for them. Have I done right? I know not myself! Temporarily I am satisfied. My head does not ache and I can sleep at night .What the future will bring I do not know and do not even think.

There is one other thing. When I consented to go to this place Natzarenus told me that in all probability we shall need machinery for the mines and fisheries; this machinery can only be got from Japan or America, and as I am the only one amongst them who can speak English, he promised that at the first opportunity he will send me abroad; and then I will get as far as London. All this put together seemed irresistible.

He was a man of the cities. He loved the cultural life. He did not relish leaving Moscow for the hardships that would be an inevitable part of the adventure of exploring such a country.

I can assure you I was not a bit anxious to go, and now half way already I am still in doubt whether I did the right thing… I was like a drowning man clutching at a straw. I am not worrying now because I know that you and the children are not in want. I know you are in want of <u>me.</u> I myself feel it but it cannot be helped. Heaven knows, I tried my very best, but I could not knock through the steel heads of the bureaucrats who think they are saving humanity by such methods…

He had even, he wrote, considered abandoning his allegiances in an attempt to get back to England. But even then, to take such a step, first he would need permission to enter England, which as a Russian subject and known communist he might possibly find difficult to obtain. But he would also need permission to leave the Soviet Union.

<u>The last I would never have got</u>. Secondly, it means cutting myself off from the world in which I lived the whole of my natural life… The fact of my treatment, and a thousand other such acts on the part of some silly asses does not blind me to seeing many great things being achieved in spite of all.

He wrote of the slow and tiresome process towards changing society, the need always to be able to visualise the future, and his belief that the results of this tremendous experiment would be seen by generations to come.

Have I done right? I know not myself. But temporarily I am satisfied.

And then he wrote:

The desire to live personally, and to live well takes very often the upper hand. It requires the world of strength to withstand all the temptations.

I know that the best days are meanwhile running, the most interesting years of our lives. The children need my advice and presence. At times I feel this very deeply indeed, but am trying to comfort myself with thoughts of the future, hoping for the best.

He began writing while he was still on his way to Kamchatka. Now he had arrived in Vladivostock on the trans-Siberian railway and continued the letter:

We are staying here for a few more days waiting for some instructions and regulating some formalities, without which not a step can be made here. The routine of getting anything through is so slow that it is a wonder that anything gets done at all. However, I hope that in a week or so we shall be passing through Japanese territory where I intend posting this letter. I have done my best to explain to you the situation and hope you will understand it. There is no use whining. It cannot be helped for the present. Heaven knows I have only one thought and only one: that is to lighten your burden and give my children an opportunity to achieve something in life.

Not until four months later, after a long period of waiting at Vladivostock for a steamer going to Kamchatka, was he was able at last to post the letter from Hakodate in Japan. Before posting it he added a final note:

I think I have said all I could in this letter. You will have some sort of idea of the way I lived for the last two years. What awaits me in the future I do not know yet. I hope you will all keep well and do your best as I am trying to do myself.

I am finishing this letter. I think you had better destroy it. Love to you and the children.

As ever, yours Sam.

I will write from wherever I'll be.

CHAPTER 4

Years of Turmoil

My father had not appreciated the enormity of the problems facing the Bolsheviks in establishing and in maintaining power, in instituting structures of government; and in transforming the huge Russian empire into a multi-national Soviet state.

His personal experiences, the problems that he encountered during those years were revelatory of the obstacles and problems of the new regime, foreshadowing the direction it would take in the future. They were also indications of deeper social flaws which would come to characterise the Soviet Union, distort the attempts to build a socialist society; and in the end lead to Stalin's gulags.

Although he realised that the problems were enormous and believed that change would come, he had been appalled by the easy acceptance of unacceptable social conditions by those in authority. He suffered under the weight of a strangling bureaucracy, the red tape that delayed the smallest procedure, the enforcement by an unreachable leadership of unbending policies, the infuriating, time-wasting slowness, the inability to move things forward; and the rigidity that could not recognise personal, human problems, nor make exceptions.

But these were not just the teething problems of the new social order, not minor irritations. They were deeply embedded in a society that had never known the structures and functioning of a democratic system; a society where absolute power had always come from above; where only individuals who held power could take decisions; where those in lower ranks of the civil service would never take a decision on their own; and where time was of no importance.

None of the Russian people nor of the many nationalities that comprised the new USSR had ever experienced any form of democratic government. They had been ruled by an autocratic Tsar and other tsars before him. It was not so many years since serfdom had been abolished; life for the peasants – and the majority of the population were peasants – was primitive and except in the southern regions exacerbated by a difficult cold climate. The tempo of life was a peasant tempo where seasons and weather determined the course of life; time did not count; waiting was constant.

The upper classes – those around the Tsar and his court – noblemen and leading military men – led corrupt and dissolute lives. Chekhov's plays convey a true picture of the decadence and purposelessness of life among the aristocracy, the nobles and owners of huge estates. The problems were not simply the consequences of the revolution of 1917, nor of the subsequent devastation of invasion and wars. 'The heritage of a more distant past also bore down on them. Russia's size, climate and ethnic diversity greatly complicated the tasks of government. She also lagged behind her major competitors in industrial and technological capacity; she was threatened by states of the West and the East; and her frontiers were the longest in the world. Arbitrary state power was a dominant feature in public life.'[3]

The Bolsheviks carried the burden of this past – their past – with them into the new society.

Through Simeon's letters one can already discern the obsessional mistrust by those in power towards even the most loyal and dedicated Party members – a distrust that as the years went by would mushroom into a great explosion of reprisals against innocents. Not just against individual dissenters and critics, but their families, children, working associates; and ultimately become the murderous madness of the Stalin era, that would strangle so much of the brilliance and initiative of those early years of socialism.

Those of his friends who seemed indifferent to my father's complaints in 1925 had truly lived through more terrible times. The long years of war, revolution and civil war and famine had devastated and impoverished a land that was now stricken by an enemy none could repel. In 1921, civil war requisitions and crop failure were followed by prolonged drought, particularly to the area which was known as the 'bread basket', the Ukraine. With drought came famine. Everything that lived could be – was – consumed. Writers describe how fields were stripped of every last blade of grass, every stalk of straw; even trees of their bark. And with famine came typhus.

The survivors who could manage the journey came to the cities with their rags and lice to seek food, to beg and to die on the streets. Hunger, suffering and disease invaded the cities. Life for the city-dwellers themselves was a bitter struggle. The apartment blocks had been heated by central furnaces that were no longer functioning. Home-made stoves called *bourzborki* were used for heating, the iron pipes protruded from windows of every apartment. The *New York Times* correspondent, Walter Duranty, described Moscow as a city incredibly broken and dilapidated. 'The streets were full of holes where water mains had burst, and there had been digging in an attempt to clear choked drains…There was also a breakdown in running water and sanitation.'[4]

Urgent action was required to try to deal with such conditions in town and countryside. A radical measure, introduced by Lenin in 1921, in response to massive popular revolts, was the New Economic Policy – NEP – a concession which replaced the requisitioning of grain by a tax in kind; and permitted private small-scale manufacturing and the private ownership of retail shops in order to stimulate positive growth both in the countryside and the towns.

There were deep disagreements among the leaders of the Bolshevik Party about this and other policies; it was the force of Lenin's personality and prestige which held together the Politburo (the central policy-making and governing body of the Soviet Union, made up of the top members of the Central Committee). But in May 1922 Lenin suffered a major stroke, and although he made a partial recovery his influence diminished. After a second stroke in December, he prepared what was to become known as 'Lenin's testament', with pen portraits commenting on the personalities of six leading members of the Politburo: Stalin, Kamenev, Zinoviev, Pyatakov, Bukharin and Trotsky. Lenin hoped that a collective leadership would remain in place regardless of what happened to him. In 1923 he dictated an addendum to his testament: to the effect that Stalin was too crude to be retained as General Secretary of the Party. But in March Lenin suffered a third stroke, and a few months later he died.

Differences of policy among the members of the Central Committee led to struggles for power. It was these internal political struggles within the highest echelons of the Party together with the physical and economic crisis that prevailed after 1917 that enabled Stalin to build up his power base. From his place of influence as General Secretary, he consolidated his grip. In January 1925 Trotsky was removed from his post as Commissar for War and Zinoviev sacked from his position as Chairman of the Leningrad Soviet. A year later Trotsky was ousted from the Politburo, and in November Trotsky, Kamenev and Zinoviev were expelled from the Party. By January 1928, when Trotsky was sent into internal exile, Stalin was on his way to becoming the supreme dictator.

Kamchatka

Simeon was no longer young. Perhaps twenty years before he might have relished this new experience. But the past two years had been a time of stress, both physical and mental. Now he was suffering from those strains: from the difficulty of adjusting to the sordid and hard living conditions, the food shortages and poor diet and the constant anxieties and problems about his family.

Still, there was the innate buoyancy of his nature, and as the journey proceeded he became keenly interested in this unexplored world, and wrote about it whenever he could.

Even today Kamchatka is sparsely populated – 400,000 people in a territory the size of California and Oregon put together; and more than half that population lives in the largest city, Petropavlosk-Kamchatsky. These days there are tourist agencies arranging adventure holidays in what they advertise as the last of the earth's really wild places – a country with vast white-capped mountain ranges and 160 volcanoes, many of them active; with uncharted forests and rivers teeming with many varieties of fish. The tourists fly in – there is still no overland route – at the right season for river and fishing jaunts, or mountain climbing. And fly home again at the end of their holiday. It was no holiday for my father.

On December 10, 1927 he sent a letter from Petropavlovsk.

As you will see by this, I have at last reached my destination for a time. The journey from Vladivostok to this place was the worst journey I have ever yet experienced. We travelled a fortnight on a steamer that was not the sort you expect to find for a long sea journey. It was too small and light in weight to withstand stormy waves on the open ocean. Two days it took us to reach Hakodate, a Japanese port town, from where I sent you and the children some postcards and I sent you a long letter telling you everything.

I hope you have got it and you will be in a position to judge the real circumstances in which I found myself.

From Hakodate we travelled eleven days and nights without a stop. The sea was all the time stormy. Our ship was at times tossed about on the waves like a small piece of wood. Most of the passengers were sick. It was frightful at night, and the feeling of horror at times seemed to creep and eat at your very heart. All around pitch dark. The noise of the great rolling waves beating against the ship walls again and again, lifting our ship, tossing it up high… and then letting it down into a valley of gathering waves. The feeling that one is quite helpless in case of emergency is enough to make you sick at heart.

However, there were very nice travelling companions. I kept quite well and fit all the time. We played chess. I had a good appetite. And so the time passed, though at the finish all of us were tired of the journey. So on the 29 November we reached Petropavlovsk at last.

As they approached the port he saw the ring of high mountains, crowned with eternal snow. Through the pure and lucid air, everything was: *so clear and bright that you see for thirty and more miles as clearly as just across the road.*

Petropavlosk is a small town in a valley, sheltered by mountains on all sides. The houses are primitive – no water taps or lavatories; no electricity or gas. No trams, trains or taxis. There are a little over 1,000 inhabitants. There is practically nothing growing here, so no factories or workshops of any kind. Practically everything – food, clothes and other necessities are shipped in over the ocean.

The climate here and for a few miles around is quite mild – not quite so cold as it is sometimes in Moscow. I have a big shuba – a winter hat of fur – and also fur high boots up to the very stomach, so I am quite prepared for a much colder climate.

Later on I will be leaving to visit other villages on a dog sleigh, the only means of transport as the snow is so deep that horses are of no use. Sometimes one travels on deer. The distance between one village and another is as far as from London to Manchester, and further, so you will get some idea of how long it takes when travelling by dog sleigh.

People here however are not very perturbed by such distances. They sometimes travel a week or a fortnight to have tea with friends… and so life goes on, untouched by civilisation as we know it.

I am anxious to send this before the ship leaves for Vladivostock. You will, of course, only get this letter about the middle of January, as it takes two weeks to get there, and about three weeks from there. I may yet send you one more letter as we are expecting another steamer about the end of this month, and then goodbye until May.

Two more letters arrived for Mamie – as he called Dora – and his children.

December 18, 1927.

Today is Sunday. The other day we had the first serious fall of snow, when waking in the morning the doors and windows of all the houses were blocked with snow. It was necessary to clear a hole first to climb through and then begin clearing some of the snow away. To walk to the shop is not an easy matter. The snow in some parts is six to seven feet deep, the ground below is slippery, so each step must be taken carefully.

Soon after Christmas I am to set out for a journey on dog sleigh, for about two months. It all depends on the weather. At times, I am told, when a purga (a violent snow storm) overtakes one on the road there is very little chance of moving anywhere. If one is caught by such a snow storm away from any living place, as the villages are so few and far between you have to stop for a day, or two or three in the snow covered never ending space until the purga ends. All the time you feed yourself and the dogs on the provisions taken beforehand.

It sounds interesting, does it not? But give me a nice soft bed, a fairly warm room, and blankets or a quilt and I will gladly give up all this adventure. When I tell people here that I lived over twenty years in London they look at me doubtfully. They cannot understand what silly motive brought me out here. Surely I must be touched.

He reports that he is reading books about the various tribes that inhabit the territory, how they live, what they eat, and would soon be seeing for himself. Because the weather has been fine and the snow fell late, he is able to send one more letter before he leaving Petropavlosk.

For three days and nights it has been snowing continuously and where the paths have not been cleared – and most of them have not – the depth is more than the height of a tall man. The snow is soft like feathers... you grope as best you can fighting your way through the depths. Younger people walk on broad boards. But curiously enough, it is not at all cold... There is one thing which is quite unique in its way, for me, after so many years in cities like London and Moscow: the quietness of the night is marvellous. You hear no sound anywhere, except the noise of the sleigh dogs who make such a pitiful crying noise you would like to close your ears.

I read a great deal, play chess and drink tea in the evenings. Often there are meetings. As everywhere else in the USSR people are active, seeking, learning.

As I write this letter I am watching the snow gradually rising to the level of my window at the office. The men have cleared the front door several times, but it is of little use. In half an hour it gets as high as six or seven feet.

December 23. When I got home, after dinner, I went round the next street to some friends who came over here the same time as me. Normally it is a three minute walk. Well, I walked for over an hour, up to my belly in snow, and worst still I could not get back and had to sleep there. If it keeps on a bit longer like this, we shall climb through the chimneys and walk on the roofs of the houses – as often the snow is higher than some of the roofs.

Finally he writes:

I hope to get your first letter with the first ship arriving here about the beginning of April. You can begin writing about the beginning of March. I hope you are getting the £36 per month.

Mosquitoes

Whatever letters Simeon wrote over the next seven months have been lost. We know that he did write, not only because he obviously enjoyed describing his experiences, but also because he refers to them.

How much I have seen and lived through is all written down, and it will make a very interesting tale.

It is clear he had continued writing, but there is no way of knowing what adventures he experienced during his expeditions on the dog sleigh to outlying villages. It is not until summer, July 1928, that there is any record of his new adventures.

For eight days he has travelled into the interior on the river Kamchatka, which runs right down the centre of the peninsular; two days by steamer, and then another six days on a small launch. His mission is to find out about the possibilities of exploiting the forests of Kamchatka.

Again I am in a small village far away from civilisation. The climate here is quite good. It is indeed warm. The sun shines as brightly as anywhere in central Europe – but Oh! A plague of mosquitoes makes you curse the very day you set out for this place. My face, neck and hands are one mass of blisters, smarting all over, and yet this is only the beginning; our party is to stay here for at least two months. How can one stand this? I have a veil for my face, gloves and suitable clothes, but the miserable ghastly creatures penetrate through anything and poison your very flesh. The misery one experiences when compelled to expose part of the naked body to administer natural functions – it is hell!! It is indeed a nightmare!

And yet people live here, true not very many, but human life exists. In winter the temperature reaches fifty degrees below zero, and summer brings this plague of mosquitoes that poison the air.

I wonder how you are now. I am held here for a couple of days, as the rivers run fast, and we cannot get across to the place where we begin our work, and must hire horses and go on horseback for a few days through the marshes.

How I would love to see you all! How peaceful it must be where you are. The garden must be looking beautiful with flowers and fruit. How nice it would be to sit on a chair on the green lawn and read a newspaper. These things won't give one rest even at night time. They work twenty-four hours a day.

That couple of days became eight, with nights that are eight hours of hell. Exploring the forests of Kamchatka had been an interesting adventure in the beginning, and even pleasant on the motor launch. But now, no more. In the woods, he would give anything in the world for one hour of rest in a place where there were no mosquitoes; and he faces another six to eight weeks of this life, and does not know how he will endure it. But endure it he must; his salary is double what he earned in Moscow, which enables his children to continue at school in London. In the forefront of all his letters is his desire for us to get a good education; and his distress when our music lessons had to be discontinued for lack of money. At that time in England compulsory schooling ended at age fourteen, but he wanted to ensure we continued on to high school.

It is impossible to lie abed. Abed? No such dreams of luxury. One room where a man and his wife sleep in one corner, I and my learned friend on forest questions in another corner, and our assistant in the middle of the room. All on a wooden floor. The room is full of mosquitoes. Their music sounds like a Zulu war dance. They attack you everywhere – face, neck, arms, legs, and laugh at you. You exterminate a few hundred and it makes no difference at all. How nice it would be to get up and have a nice warm bath, breakfast, go into the garden and sit down on the green lawn and read a newspaper. What dreams!

For six more days they wait for the horses to arrive, unable to leave the room because of the mosquitoes. *I would not dream of touching them if only they would leave me alone. But they won't do that. Expecting the horses to come today. Fancy for six days not being able to leave the room for fear of mosquitoes.*

At last the horses arrive and his expedition of six people sets out. The horses are small and clumsy, he writes, laden with all sorts of things, and he rides his horse with a rifle on his shoulder in case he meets a bear in the forest.

The day is a wet one. It rains slowly, and riding through thick woods one has enough to do to look in front so as not to lose part of the face, or an arm. On we go, slowly over hills, dales and lakes. I am getting tired, we stop for a breath, light a camp fire, make tea, have a rest, proceed further...Oh! The mosquitoes! Terrible, impossible to stand it!!! I cannot hold a pencil in my hand.

The night comes as a great blessing. They put up their tents, drive out the mosquitoes and can sleep. When they wake they see through the white linen of the tent hordes of mosquitoes: *defying you to come out. But out we must come.*

As they ride on he writes that he has not had a proper wash for weeks although they have passed many rivers; he cannot uncover any part of his body. *My face and hands are already more or less used to it, but other parts of my body cannot stand it. Perhaps in a few days we will reach a village, possibly have a bath.*

They come to a place where there is one miserable old house and a man living there with stores of goods for the neighbouring villages a few miles around. *He keeps on fighting bravely but soon another man will take his place.*

The filth in this place is an example of how a human being can exist in unbearable conditions. He has a cow and gets milk, but the milk becomes a white soup as mosquitoes turn it into a meaty porridge... he himself does not mind. I make coffee and drink, but was sick afterwards. They stay for two days and then ride on. He describes the various bushes in the woods, and the berries from which people make jam.

July 19. Now after two days in the woods on horseback one feels great relief to come to a village and be let into a house where one can have a hot meal in peace without being attacked all the time. Here I am going to stay a few days. I do feel so tired and need a real rest. I can only stay two or three days here. A clean little house of only two small rooms, but a 'vapour bath' attached. The family consists of two people, a man and wife, Russians, they came from the Ukraine. They are already old. They have lived here for about twenty years. They have a garden, chickens, a cow, a horse, a small boat near the river which is at the back of the house, so live quite in peace here.

But they complain that at times they feel a real loneliness and would wish to return to the Ukraine; but they are afraid they will not get on so well there, as they receive letters from relatives that life is very hard in the Ukraine. So they prefer to stay where they have practically everything they need. They catch fish when they want; especially for about four months in the summer, one only needs to go out into the back yard and there is the river full of salmon – have your pick and cook your dinner. Always fish, as meat is rather dear here. However, if not for the mosquitoes for most of the summer, life would not be bad here.

The view all around is amazingly lovely. Only but a few miles away (it seems only yards away) these high mountains covered with snow glittering in the sun, and yet here below them it is as hot as an August day in London. Glorious sun, mountains, sky...Oh! Mosquitoes!

July 27. After a weeks stay in this little village we are starting out again on the river in a small boat. In a few days from now we shall reach the point from where we board a steamer bound for Petropavlosk. Then I think I am going to Vladivostock, and if true, I hope, I am being sent abroad…

I wonder how you all fare? I have had a very hard time here. Nearly a fortnight on horseback and the life of a vagabond. All my body is aching. I can hardly sit on my behind, and bitten all over by beastly mosquitoes. It was interesting in a way, but oh! how hard! Age is beginning to tell. Shall we meet this year? I hope so!! However, I am quite fit and well.

You must be wondering why I haven't written for such a long time. Of course I said I would be away for two or three months where there was no chance of writing.

I am getting tired of waiting for the steamer which is due here in three or four days time.

On August 20 he writes that at last he is back in Petropavlosk.

Everything is the same. The high mountains are cleared of their winter dress of snow, except for one – afraid to undress altogether as it stands so high – nearly reaches the sky; and so keeps a layer of snow on its back.

Then on August 26, he is plunged into agitation by a telegram from Natzarenus asking him to travel on a steamer bound for London – but then to return immediately to Vladivostock via Odessa.

'What can I do? What will a few days in London give me? It will probably make things worse – how can I go and come back?? What shall I say? It is however best to go if only for one day and see you all – and then – oh hang – let come what will. I will go!'

Valediction

There are only two more letters in my possession, one from Vladivostock in 1930, and the last from Moscow in October 1932.

There is nothing in either of them to indicate why he did not reach London, nor what had happened to the promised overseas posting at the end of his Kamchatka expedition. A torn fragment of a letter written to my sister Olga was posted from Okhotsk in September 1929 – Okhotsk is a port on the Sea of Okhotsk, to the west of Kamchatka. That, and the 1930 letter, posted from Vladivostock seems to indicate that at that time he was still working on the same project.

He addresses the letter to all of us, not, as in the past, only to Dora. He writes, almost formally.

My dear family, I am pained to inform you that so far I have not suc-ceeded in obtaining permission to transmit any more money. The question is still unsettled, and I am trying hard to get it settled.

I was asked to go back for one year to Okhotsk, but in view of the fact that I could not get the transmission of money settled while here, I thought it best to take my holiday and go to Moscow, where perhaps I could get matters put straight more quickly.

I am glad to say I keep well in health. I am worrying how you manage without means. It must be a hell of a job, and yet I am unable to do a thing.

I only hope you will keep well and get out of this muddle somehow. Maybe later on I will try while in Moscow to get another appointment which will make it easier for you. It would be useless to build any plans at the present stage because I know very little of the sort of appointment I will get when I go back to Moscow. I hope for the best. But whatever will come I will let you know.

In the last five years undoubtedly a great change has taken place. The children have grown up and I dare say become quite independent. It is only natural.

Fondest love to all of you. I will not write much at present.

Your loving Papa.

I read that letter as a valediction. Seven years have passed since he went back to Moscow on what he thought was to be a six-month as-signment. He has been forced at last to acknowledge the real situation: that he will never receive the foreign posting; that his separation from his dearly loved family is a permanent one. (He could not even get permission for a two-day visit after five years.) The dream of sitting on the lawn in that English garden is a dream of the past. Although he has never ceased thinking of us, writing loving letters, sending postcards from every place he went to and small gifts whenever he could, he recognises that he has lost the years of his children growing up; he has accepted now that he must make his own life entirely in his work in the country where he was born, and to which he returned in fulfilment of his dream of helping to create a new kind of world.

He had never intended to sacrifice his family for his cause. He plunged into his political life believing that it would not involve relinquishing his family life or his family, only relocating them to that new dream world. As soon as he saw the realities of Moscow life, of the conditions under which we would have to live, he knew he could not bring us there; so the only way we could be reunited was through the expected, the promised, the logical foreign posting.

The stringencies of party demands, the view those above him held that he had been corrupted by his own bourgeois life in England, reinforced by reports of his family's lifestyle and his wife's hostility to communism, made it impossible for him to serve both his cause and his family adequately. He did not intend it that way, but in the end he sacrificed the joys of a family life so that those he loved best – his own children – would not have to adjust to a harsh and difficult life in a strange country during the vital years of their youth and their education.

But in doing so he also lost the opportunity to fulfil his own potential contribution to his dream of a better world, to exercise to the full whatever talents and experience he possessed. He believed he could make that contribution in a job that was not just predicated on his need to earn money; he wanted jobs that would enable him to make a worthwhile contribution to the building of a socialist society. So he refused the opportunities held out to him – only because of us, to enable us to continue our bourgeois life-style, to provide the money for our school fees, our music lessons, our seaside holidays, our comfortable home; and also because he believed that by forgoing those posts he would be available to take up that elusive posting abroad, and so he would be re-united with us. But for that he needed to climb the ladder in the Soviet hierarchy and to comply with all the tests set for him by his superiors, not to exile himself in Kamchatka but to stay in Moscow, to be in the heart of the political scene, to participate in all the endless meetings, exercise responsibility, prove his worth, be more than just an employee. To step up the party ladder he had to be present on the political scene, to be known and recognised. He knew that, but put our immediate needs first.

He had to give up the family he loved, the familiarity of home, garden, known streets, the companionship of friends to become the true revolutionary that was required of him. In a way his position was like that of the Soviet government itself, determined to make a new, different future – and finding itself still chained to the customs and habits of the past. So Simeon was still chained to his family, his London home, all those years of English life.

I cannot ever know how the way he was treated affected his faith or his loyalty. It was more than just a personal matter; it was part of the whole bureaucratic structure of the new society and of the theories that propelled it; the rigidity of party organisation, the submission of the individual to collective decisions that did not allow for any relaxation or considerations of common humanity. He was a victim of the exercise of that authority; he saw the exercise of power. But however he felt, he would have had no choice. His beliefs might have been shaken but there was no way to deviate from them; nor was there even any way to escape out of that vast country had he decided to relinquish his party, his beliefs.

My father's idealism revealed to us a world larger than the suburb where we lived. He had created a legacy for us. What he had succeeded in achieving in the early part of our lives and sustaining for some years after he went to the Soviet Union was to open windows for my sisters and myself that may otherwise have remained closed. We did not know it when we were young, but these were the most enduring parts of our education.

He was essentially an outgoing and social person, who derived great pleasure from the company of friends; wherever he went he made friends and all those who knew him spoke of him with affection. But over all there were two abiding passions in his life – his love for his family and his devotion to the idealism of his party.

The two had become incompatible. In the end, he lost out on both.

CHAPTER 5

Death

SINCE she left school my sister Olga had also been working at Arcos. Always careful about money, by the summer of 1932 she had saved up enough to go to Moscow to visit our father. He arranged to take his leave, then went to meet her in Leningrad when she arrived by boat.

He was overjoyed to see his pretty, dark-haired daughter and had arranged a programme of activities for her. He introduced her to all his friends, among whom were the talented and intellectual Bronstein family – cousins of Trotsky; and he took her to the theatre and ballet. She met many interesting people in Moscow. She met John Grierson the documentary film-maker, and a famous actor from the Arts Theatre. He took Olga on a trip down the Volga, and to the country to visit a friend's dacha.

I am glad to think that Olga had a nice time. It was certainly lucky that I had free time to be with her, and I did not care how things would be later as long as I gave her a jolly good time. I think she deserves everything. She is lovely, and very sensible. I dare say the others are like her too.

I did not write to tell you how life is, and what you may or may not expect, because I am sure Olga has had the opportunity of seeing everything, and will tell you how you may fare here.

I have said in the letter I gave to Olga how I am fixed at present. <u>No room yet</u>. Hope to get something soon.

To get a room in Moscow it was necessary to have a job there. This indicates that he must have finished with the Kamchatka project, and was considering what to do next. And it is confirmation that he had by then relinquished all hopes of a foreign posting. Then he asks: *how about Hilda?* He is obviously responding to a letter in which Dora must have told him that I had decided that I wanted to be an artist.

Of course it would be fine for her to keep at what she likes, but I doubt very much if art will give her anything in life except perhaps a nice hobby. You know, that to be an artist and earn a living at it, one must be an absolutely born genius. Well, if you think Hilda has got this in her, it may be a very good thing. Otherwise, she will be able to draw very nice things, but not for money. However, try, and if I can do anything to help, I certainly will.

Do I want anything? Well, you cannot fill a bottomless case. There are so many things one needs, but it is of no use sending anything. We get on without.

My love to Vera and Hilda – let them write to me.

Before Olga left Moscow, he received confirmation that he had been given a job with the state travel organisation, Intourist. The Soviet Union was gradually opening up to tourists, and his job would involve travelling around the country to find sites suitable for the building of tourist hotels. Although he would be travelling again, the job would entitle him to a room in Moscow.

*

Some time before 1932 he had met and formed a relationship with Tamara, a woman of about his own age, with whom he lived until he died. He had taken a room in a hotel for the period of Olga's visit. He must have had some alternative accommodation, but did not take her there. Olga gave no indication on her return that she knew anything about Tamara, and she may not have known. But she was always the secretive sister. Vera, like myself, was outgoing and expansive; Olga did not talk about her feelings and relationships. If she knew about Tamara (and I think that she did) it was certainly not she who imparted the news to Dora. But, as always, there were others who were ready and eager to tell Dora that her husband had taken another wife in Moscow.

My mother never spoke about it to me; I heard that part of the story from Olga only many years later, by which time I was old enough to understand that it was an inevitable outcome of their long separation. It must have been this, I believe, more than his letter, that finally persuaded my mother that he would never return. After all those years of waiting and expecting she felt bitter and abandoned, and she decided to join her older sister in South Africa, who had been trying for a long time to persuade her to come and live with her in Johannesburg.

The long struggle to keep us at school, to maintain the house and pay all the bills was over. We were no longer the children that Papa had said goodbye to all those years ago. My sisters were adults; Vera had qualified as a teacher; Olga had a well-paid office job; both were self-supporting, and neither of them had any wish to emigrate.

I was a teenager; I had left school the year before when I was sixteen without any qualifications; and the only direction in my life was the wish to be an artist. I had won a scholarship that would pay art school fees for full-time instruction for three years, but it did not cover the cost of art materials nor my upkeep. The authorities then agreed to pay my fees for evening classes, so that I could work during the day.

My first job had been in a small shop that sold sweets and cigarettes. A spell as assistant cashier at Selfridges in Oxford Street proved to be a failure – my maths was pathetic. I found a more permanent post at the telephone switchboard of a company that made carburettors. I had no interest in these jobs apart from earning money, and my mother thought I was too young to leave behind. I liked the idea of seeing another country, so I went with her to South Africa.

The house was sold, my sisters went to live in a flat on the Vale of Health. And my mother and I sailed off to South Africa on the Union-Castle Line.

Although none of the letters that Simeon wrote from that time on have survived, we know he did continue to write to Dora in Johannesburg and he sent postcards from places he visited. But after we had been there for some months, the letters ceased. Dora waited and worried, and asked her daughters in England to see if they could find out why.

Olga spoke about this with some of the staff at the Arcos office, and was even contemplating going to the USSR to see if she could find out for herself. Someone suggested she contact a man who had been in Moscow and allegedly had seen Simeon a few months before. She was invited to dinner at his home, and he, not realising that he was breaking the news to her for the first time, handed her a copy of the Russian paper *Pravda* with an obituary of Simeon.

On an assignment for Intourist Simeon had been travelling south through Georgia. During the long journey the passengers bought food and refreshments from local peasants when the train stopped at country stations. Simeon had drunk contaminated milk and contracted typhoid fever. At Tbilisi he was taken off the train and to hospital.

There, in the hot eastern capital of Georgia, he was recovering from the typhoid when his heart, already damaged by the extreme stresses of the years, had given in under the strain of the high fever, and he died.

The death of our loving, cheerful father so far away, and separated from us too long, was the greatest tragedy for us all, a tremendous sorrow. Somehow the remoteness of Russia from South Africa, even from London, seemed to make it more painful. We had all firmly believed

– I know I did – that one day, some time, somehow, he would return and we would all be reunited with the father who had already been absent from our lives for so many years. I had so longed to see him, just to see him again.

I can remember very little of all those growing-up years. My sisters could both recall much more, but my lack of memory has been a handicap to me all the years of my life, and as I only began writing this book after both of them had died I had lost the opportunity to ask the questions that might have enabled me to flesh out those times in all our lives. I have only snatches – more of feelings than actual memories – of his warmth and protectiveness; remembering, for example, how when we stood on a station platform, he would pick me up and hold me close, because the noise and rush of the incoming train frightened me.

But of the years when he was away, almost nothing. All I can recall is the sense of anxiety in our home connected with the problem of money, that somehow things were always difficult for us. I don't think I understood why he was away, nor why he did not return. For the first few years we believed his return was imminent. Gradually we became used to his not being with us; his return seemed more and more remote. Yet somehow I believed that one day he would be with us again.

Nor could I intimately share my grief with my sisters because we were so separated. I was at an age of adolescence when the intimacy I had always had with my mother was lost. Olga told me years after that she was eating soup when her host handed the notice of his death, and that from that time she always disliked soup. Vera suffered all her life from a sense of guilt for the hostile letters that she wrote as a teenager – influenced by Dora's attitude – upbraiding him for living away from us and not coming back. But they were both so far away at the time I heard of his death, and somehow I could not speak freely to my mother. All I could say as I wept was, 'I wanted to see him again; I just wanted to see him.'

And, through her own tears Dora said 'So did I.'

I think I now understand why, all my life, I have had a longing to be loved.

*

It was 1933. Now there was nothing left of our beloved father but a few postcards that had not been lost or discarded, the letters that Dora had kept; and a life insurance policy that only became payable in the event of his death. For that, Dora needed a death certificate.

So Olga went to the Soviet Union. She set out on what seemed a straightforward and limited mission to obtain the death certificate and to find out, if she could, more about the circumstances of our father's death. This should have been a brief episode in her life, but it ended in her living there for nearly twelve years.

I was struck by the strange way in which she replicates his experience. Both of them spent years of their lives in the Soviet Union against their own wishes, against their own intentions, although their attitudes were far apart. He went because of his desire to contribute to and help build the new socialist society; he stayed because he was not allowed to leave. Even if he had broken his allegiance to his party and abandoned the ideals that had shaped his life, he still could not leave without a visa, and there was no way he could reach the borders of that vast country or safety without one.

She went to fulfil a small mission; she was hostile to the regime, and had no intention of staying. She was caught by a web of circumstances that led in the end to her long sojourn – circumstances that were partly beyond her control but partly the result of how she chose to confront them. They imposed on her the necessity to make certain choices; she could have made different decisions, with a different outcome.

So this now is Olga's story, told by me but with her own interventions. She was twenty-one years old.

BOOK TWO

THE DAUGHTER

CHAPTER I

My Sister

WHEN I think of my sister I do not recall all the years when we grew up together and shared our lives. I think instead of those years we were apart – far, far apart. We three were separated geographically, for my home was in Johannesburg, South Africa, Vera lived in London, and Olga was living in Moscow. We were also totally apart in our experiences. I was more in touch with Vera, for we corresponded. But just as Olga had no knowledge of my life in that rich, beautiful country riven by an extreme oppressive racism, so I had no knowledge of her life in Russia in the Stalin era nor how she survived during the years of war.

We were completely out of touch. I did not even know her address. I assumed that she had remained in the Soviet Union out of choice. I had not the least inkling of the series of events that caused her to stay there for so long.

We three, who had grown up together, were now scattered in three different continents; and we would each have widely different experiences arising from the politics of those countries and how we confronted them.

I was seventeen when I went to South Africa with my mother, and it took me many years and a great deal of emotion to integrate into my new country. But eventually I did, and because I was deeply involved in the problems and politics of the country I came to consider myself a South African. She never became a Russian.

She did not fit in to the usual categories of foreigners who lived in Moscow during those years. She was not one of the regular expatriate communities – the journalists, embassy staff, trade representatives. She did not have any idealistic belief in the Soviet system, as did a number of Westerners who went to work in the USSR in the thirties. She had no confidence in a theory which, she believed, ignored the propensity for human greed. She soon became aware, in ways that touched her own life, of the underlying terror. Yet she lived there as the Soviet people themselves lived, and she shared the same hardships and privations of the war years. If she enjoyed any privilege it was that of being part of the professional and intellectual community. In all other ways the conditions of her life were the same as that of any Russian living in Moscow.

She was joined to Soviet society through her partner, Henry, who was working on the Moscow Metro; and later by her own job as a lecturer in English at the Foreign Languages Institute. Yet she never lost her feeling that in a way she was just a visitor. She never regarded Russia as her true home. She was inside Russian society but at the same time she was an outsider looking into the inside.

Her great ability was to adapt to whatever situation she found herself in, so she was an integral part of a shifting history; but at the same time she never went native; she was always in a sense a stranger and an exile whose home – and heart – was elsewhere. Her talisman was her British passport.

The later break-up of the Soviet Union and the re-ordering of the world's maps do not diminish the relevance of those years, the vital years when she lived there. As with the history of the First and Second World Wars and of Nazi Germany and the Holocaust it seems to take a gap of many years – sometimes decades – before what has happened in the USSR is written about in depth, personalised, assessed – in effect really recognised, remembered and understood.

Years later, long after Olga had returned to England, she joined a writers' class and began to produce short, episodic pieces about her experiences in those times. They do not comprise any sort of historical record, nor do they give a coherent picture of her life. They are brief sketches of aspects of living and working in Moscow, of months in a peasant village in the far north, and of people she knew. They are like close-up photographs; the background is missing or blurred, not in focus. It is the personal, the small events of daily living that make the experiences real to those who come after.

When we were reunited after she left the Soviet Union she rarely spoke of her experiences and not at all of Henry. He was the motive that brought her there, the one who shaped her life. We know he was there with her almost every day during all those years. They shared a one-roomed apartment in Moscow. He was her companion when they danced at the Metropol, when they swam in the Volga, when they were evacuated as the German armies stood at the gates of Moscow. Together they travelled in cattle trucks to the far north. He lived with her in their small room in that distant village through a bitter winter.

When she returned to live again in wartime Moscow, it was because Henry had been summoned back. He was there with her during those harsh and hungry wartime years; on the last holiday in the Caucasus they climbed the hill together to the cottage where the grapes were ripening. And he surely accompanied her to the station when she left on the final journey to Leningrad; stood there watching the train as it gathered speed and disappeared; believing, because he loved her and knew that she loved him, she would return.

But in all the episodes she wrote Henry is never mentioned. He was always there, but he never really appears. Except for one or two passing references, he does not appear in anything that she wrote subsequently; and she never spoke of him. When she left the Soviet Union it was as though she closed a door on those years of her life, and Henry was on the other side.

Being so far away in South Africa I did not know that after she had left him, Henry kept writing to Olga, and that she did not reply to him. Vera knew, because he also wrote desperately to her, asking why his beloved partner of so many years did not reply. When she told Olga about this, Vera told me, she simply burst into tears and cried, shaking her head; but refused to speak about it.

The Years Between...The Countryside

In the years after 1932 when we had the last news of our father in Moscow, enormous political and economic changes were taking place in the Soviet Union.

The socialist society that the Bolsheviks envisaged necessitated the development of a planned economy, built on the basis of rapid industrialisation in the towns and the collectivisation of agriculture in the countryside. But years of war and revolution had left both town and country devastated. Their industrial plants were obsolete, there was a shortage of raw materials and of skilled labour.

The first Five-Year Plan launched in 1928 gave priority to converting the Soviet Union from a country that imported machines and equipment to a country that produced machines. All industrial planning was centralised and every effort devoted to the development of heavy industry. Consumer goods, they believed, could come later. In fact from the launching of the Plan consumer goods began to disappear from the stores and the era of chronic shortages began. The most basic requirements – shoes, clothing, matches, everyday items – were difficult or impossible to obtain.

For the development of heavy industry the Soviets lacked experts in every field and had no time to train a new generation of officials, scientists, managers, engineers, technicians of all kinds. They issued a call to professionals of other countries to come and help build the new socialist society.

The confidence and optimism generated by the scale of these projects, especially in contrast to the idle industries, the decaying machinery and the misery of the dole queues of the capitalist countries caught the imagination of many in the Western world. Engineers came, at first from Germany, and then from America to supervise and help build the huge new projects. It seemed as though the West, with its disastrous slump, was in decline, while the Soviet projects were giving rise to feelings of hope for the future, a future when anything seemed possible. Many well-qualified professionals, inspired by a mixture of idealism and the chance to escape from the unemployment of the Depression responded to that call.

The most famous of these projects, the hydro-electric station on the Dnieper river, employed thousands of unskilled labourers, men and women, who excavated the huge dam with few machines other than spades; and it also employed a small army of American engineers, utilising American technology, with an American, Cooper, as its consultant. This project, and others such as the Turksib railway that linked Central Asia to western Siberia, spawned vast new industrial complexes, steel works producing cars and tractors, and the growth of new towns.

The Five-Year Plan necessitated a vastly expanded supply of food for the new armies of industrial workers in the towns. Eighty per cent of the population were peasants, the majority living at subsistence level. A new system of compulsory grain collections was introduced with quotas set for districts and villages. At the same time to develop large-scale farming needed tractors and machinery that could only operate on large tracts of land. So the small plots were to be consolidated and worked collectively. In the winter of 1929-1930 an army of 25,000 industrial workers were sent to the rural areas together with party officials and Red Army men to establish *kolkhozy* – collective farms.

These urban party workers and their leaders had no knowledge of the countryside, nor any understanding of the ancient traditions and superstitions that governed peasant life. They were there to carry out the decisions taken at party headquarters in Moscow. Their innovations were met with the implacable hostility of the peasants.

Stalin imposed a policy of 'dekulakisation' – the expropriation of the property of the kulaks who were the more prosperous and successful peasants, the owners of larger strips of land and of machines and animals. These policies of collectivisation were applied with ruthless brutality, not just to the kulaks but to all the peasants who resisted. They tried to hide their grain, to bury it; their homes and land were torn apart as the armies of urban workers, anxious to carry out party orders, searched for grain. And when it had been seized the peasants could no longer feed their animals, and slaughtered their livestock for food. Tens of thousands of peasants were evicted from their holdings and dwellings, the remaining animals seized. The way was cleared for collectivisation – and for a massive famine.

The process of collectivisation continued at an awful and incalculable price. The dying and the dead were piled onto carts and emptied into common graves. A vast army of homeless children – 'wild children' – encrusted with dirt, ragged, barefoot, with swollen stomachs wandered from village to village, begging, foraging for food, gnawing grass. What was planned as a great achievement ended as one of the greatest tragedies which left millions dead of famine, an estimated 6.5 million peasants 'eliminated', and millions more who managed to move to the towns, begging and dying on the streets where there was no food, no shelter. It left a stain on Soviet history. The countryside was devastated, agriculture fatally disrupted; grain production did not reach the level it had before collectivisation began until the late 1930s, and the shortfall of animals persisted even longer.

It was not until 1935, the year that my sister returned to Moscow, that bread became obtainable without ration coupons.

Henry

Some time in 1933 my sister joined a tourist group visiting Moscow and set out to see if she could obtain the official piece of paper that would certify that our father was dead. The journey took five days by boat from Southampton to Leningrad; and from there the tourists went by train to Moscow.

On the first day at sea she was approached by three young men. Two of them were English, Esperanto enthusiasts who were visiting the Soviet Union to find out if Esperanto, devised as a universal language, could be introduced there. The third was an American. He asked her: 'Do you play bridge?'

'Not exactly,' she said cautiously. 'I know how to play, but I am not actually a player.'

'You'll have to do. You'll just have to be the fourth. There's no one else on board who knows how to play.'

After the game she asked the American why he was going to the USSR. He drew a wallet from his pocket and took out a snapshot which he gazed at fondly. His girl-friend? Olga wondered. 'Isn't she beautiful?' he said. 'I want to build bridges like that.' It was a photograph of the Manhattan suspension bridge.

Henry was a qualified civil engineer, and his ambition was to build bridges. But neither he nor his sister Ray, who was a teacher, could find jobs. They had decided to respond to the Soviet Union's call for foreign experts, believing that in two or three years, when America's economy had recovered from the depths of the depression, they would return to jobs in their own country. Ray had gone ahead and was already in Moscow. She wrote to Henry to join her, knowing that a civil engineer would find work without any difficulty.

In the five-day boat journey to Leningrad there was plenty of time for my sister and the tall, good-looking young American to get to know each other. They played their not very serious bridge games, and danced in the evenings. They arrived in Leningrad and went on to Moscow.

Soon after they arrived there Olga became ill. The authorities wanted to send her to a sanatorium, but she resisted this very strongly. Finally they agreed she could stay in Moscow, as Henry had promised to look after her while she was ill. The authorities allowed her to extend her visit to four weeks instead of three. This is how their romance began.

Olga obtained the necessary death certificate and returned to London. She and Henry corresponded; and two years later, when he was on his way back to the USA to renew his passport, he stopped off in London to try and persuade her to marry him and go back to the Soviet Union with him. Early in 1935, she decided she would join Henry in Moscow.

Olga never spoke of her feelings for Henry. I can only assume she must have been strongly drawn to him, for she had no desire to leave England, nor was she short of suitors. She was the pretty one in our family. Our mother had been extremely attractive, and Olga had inherited her good looks. She was petite, with a well-proportioned figure; she had curly black hair, beautifully arched eyebrows, a fair complexion and rosy cheeks. She combined a lively and cheerful personality with an air of innocence, a certain helplessness, that aroused in the male psyche a desire to protect and care for her. It was deceptive; she was well able to look after herself, resourceful and adaptable in the unusual conditions she later encountered.

Their intention was to marry. Like my father, she believed that she was going to the USSR for a year – two, at the most; that when Henry's contract expired they would leave and make their home either in Britain or the USA. She had little knowledge of Soviet politics nor of the extraordinary events which were unfolding there, nor could she anticipate the profound effects they would have on her life. This was the beginning of my sister's twelve-year odyssey in the Soviet Union.

The Years Between…The Towns

She was entering a country foreign to her – foreign not only in the in the sense of spoken language and social customs and the experiences of her childhood and upbringing in England, but different in a wider context. A new country – more than a country, an empire of many countries, a world of its own, a world in transition, in monumental upheaval, a struggling, changing, challenging world. She was going from familiar territory, from the limited radius of a small island kingdom, into this place whose geography and history were largely unknown to her; and that was undergoing cataclysmic changes; of changes in values, of objectives, of the construction of the economy that were shockingly different from anywhere in the world.

Never before had industrialisation been undertaken so swiftly, so deliberately on such a vast scale, bringing revolutionary upheavals to peoples' lives. The famine in major grain-growing regions in 1932-33 had been followed by years of bad harvests. During the period of the first Five-Year plan alone more than ten million peasants had moved to the towns, a massive migration driven by the disasters that followed forced collectivisation; towns where there was a growing need for workers in the burgeoning industries; and where there was no place for them to live.

In our times the migration of peasants to the cities has been a feature of the changing face of Africa, Asia and South America; and we are familiar with pictures of the vast squatters' camps where people erect their own shacks of sacks, cardboard, corrugated iron, wooden crates. But this was not Africa. Shack-dwellers in Moscow would freeze to death before one winter had passed. Nor could the homeless sleep on the streets at night. So all available space in every building was divided and sub-divided. Sheila Fitzpatrick writes how Homo Sovieticus became accustomed to calculating housing quotients in square metres per person.[5] For those in the cities – Moscow, Leningrad – it was the era of communal living. The housing situation had not changed from the conditions that Simeon had described ten years before; if anything it had worsened as more and more people were drawn into the cities, while there had been little new housing development. The fortunate ones lived in communal apartments, usually one family to a room with shared kitchen and toilet facilities; a bath was a rare luxury.

Those of us who live in cities of the West find it difficult to visualise this type of urban living. Where did they keep their clothes? Toilet articles? How did people adjust to the lack of privacy, the need to wait for others before they could even heat a little water or use a toilet, to endure babies who cried all night in the next room, to wash napkins, to hang them to dry? Margaret Wettlin, an American who went to Moscow in the early 1930s and married a Russian theatre director, writes about some of these very simple, daily domestic problems.[6]

'I knew it was impossible to further handicap movements in that crowded kitchen by hanging wet diapers in it, yet I was deeply injured when the neighbours vehemently opposed my attempt to do so. "Where am I to hang them? They freeze out in the yard," I appealed in desperation.' She had washed them in her room, bringing kettles of hot water from the kitchen, throwing out the suds in the bathtub embossed with 'unspeakable gobs'; and so, in the one room in which she, her husband and the new baby lived, she had to string a line over the table and the beds with newspapers spread to catch the drippings.

Until 1918 the capital had been in St Petersburg (renamed Leningrad after the revolution), developed by Peter the Great into a beautiful city with palaces and great buildings such as the Hermitage, set among its numerous canals. It was on the edge of Russia, closer to the West in its architecture and culture, the home of writers and intellectuals. During the First World War in, 1917, the capital was removed to Moscow as a temporary measure in the belief that Moscow would be safer, and there it remained.

Olga arrived in Moscow when it was still very much a provincial town. The traffic in the streets consisted mainly of horse-drawn carts and carriages; there were trucks and vans, but cars were a rarity.

Moscow was architecturally nondescript. At its heart was Red Square where the church spires and the fantasy of twisted domes and turrets of St Basil's rose in splendid outline against the sky, unspoiled by the modern background intrusion of high-rise concrete blocks. Even in the centre of the city and sprawling out into the countryside there were still thousands of wooden homes, heated by the traditional wood-burning stoves.

Winter comes early to Moscow with light snow or rain that would freeze and cover the streets in ice; when real winter came the muddied snow was heaped along the kerbs. Between September and May the sun was rarely seen, a city of heavy grey skies, of darkness and restricting cold; a winter that forced people to retreat into whatever warm space they could find indoors.

*

We were born and had always lived in the suburbs in the north-west of London, whose huge population was spread far beyond the centre. In that sense although we were Londoners we were not city dwellers. Our home had a garden, a strip of lawn back and front, flower beds; and an added luxury – apple trees. The green countryside – Stanmore Common, Burnham Beeches – where we hiked with friends at weekends was within our reach. For my sisters and myself open space, trees, grass and flowers were essentials in our lives. After I went to South Africa with my mother, Olga and Vera had moved into a flat in the Vale of Health on Hampstead Heath. There they lived in the midst of a great open area, a piece of countryside in the middle of town.

From the time we were born we had lived in houses in which each room, however small, was delineated for a separate function; houses with doors that opened onto a garden.

Now, for Olga, all living was contained within one room, which had to undergo a daily transformation from a bedroom to a living room, and within its limited area embrace and conceal all the props of everyday life: clothes (including the bulky wear needed for a Moscow winter), crockery, bed linen; books, a typewriter, writing materials, a gramophone. A room three or four flights up in an apartment block, with a lift locked and guarded by one of Moscow's great tribe of formidable old women, who might not be there to unlock the gates.

Although living conditions were easing by the time Olga arrived and bread rationing had been lifted, the thirties was an era of chronic shortages. Everything was in short supply – clothes, shoes, every type of consumer good and basic household necessities from kitchenware to matches.

In the 1930s, people no longer talked about 'buying' something, but about 'getting hold of' it. The phrase 'hard to get hold of' was in constant use; a new term for all things that were hard to get hold of was 'deficit goods'. People went around with string bags in their pockets, known as 'just in case' bags, on the off chance they were able to get hold of some deficit goods. If they saw a queue, they quickly joined it, inquiring what foods were on offer after securing a place. The way to formulate this question was not 'What are they selling?' but 'What are they giving out?' But public access to goods through regular distribution channels was so unreliable that a whole vocabulary sprung up to describe the alternatives.

Olga's letters did not describe her living conditions; she was never a frequent or expansive letter-writer. She wrote that she lived in an apartment in the city, and we just assumed that it was a self-contained flat as we knew them. With her sense of pride and her secrecy about her personal life she probably felt it was demeaning for us to know the details of how she lived, how acutely she missed the gardens, the flowers and trees of our leafy suburbs with parks and open spaces always nearby. To compensate she would bring flowers to her room. Whenever they were available it was filled with flowers, a friend of hers told me.

Such living conditions were tolerable not only because everyone else they knew lived in similar circumstances; but in any case she knew they were only temporary and she would not have to live like this for long. She and Henry would soon be moving back to the world from which they had come; or so she believed.

Americans in Moscow

All foreigners living in Moscow had to be registered with the authorities. Henry and Ray were registered as employees of the government. Olga had to obtain separate registration as a visitor. Then they began arrangements for their marriage.

This, it seemed, was not a simple matter. The problem of two people marrying when each was a citizen of a different country, neither were Soviet citizens, and one was only a temporary visitor, presented insuperable obstacles to the officials. There were no printed forms for such circumstances. It was their first encounter with an implacable bureaucracy that never let reason override regulations.

Eventually, after filling in countless forms and after many interviews with officials, they abandoned the attempt, considering themselves husband and wife, even without an official document. We did not know that they were not legally married, and nor did their friends. But it was through these difficulties Olga was able to retain what she believed was a guarantee of protection – her British nationality and passport.

Because of her conviction that her stay in Moscow was going to be limited, she made no serious attempt to learn Russian. She felt she only needed to learn a few Russian phrases, enough to familiarise herself with the location of her building and the surrounding streets, to be able to ask someone the way if she got lost; to learn where and how to shop, to be able to calculate in roubles and kopeks instead of pounds, shillings and pence. And to master the system of queuing three times for whatever she bought – first to order the cheese, bread, sausage, or whatever; then to take the slip to the cashier who would work out the charge on an abacus (admiring the nimble fingers speedily moving coloured beads back and forth along their metal rods); then to return with the cashier's slip to show she had paid, and collect her order.

Soon she found friends among the Americans working in Moscow to show her around. They were teachers, engineers and other professionals who came to work in the Soviet Union, usually influenced by socialist ideals, people like Henry and Ray whose own parents had emigrated to America – the new world – to escape from poverty and persecution in countries of Eastern Europe. They were thoroughly American, but retained some affinity with the cultures from which their parents and grandparents had come.

It was natural for these middle-class Americans in Moscow to gravitate towards each other. They became Olga's friends and companions in finding her way around the city. A pretty face, a ready smile and a great deal of charm was also of help in adjusting to her new life.

Bernie was a young man whose father worked in the meat industry. He himself was passing time between completing his studies and starting work. The other Americans called him Big Bernie, and then told Olga: 'You wait until you've seen the rest of his family. They're all big, and their apartment is big too. They love having parties with lots of food.'

'But all I remember of what he showed me,' she said, 'were the kiosks on the street corners where we were always stopping to buy ice-cream or *piroshki*; so that we were always eating. And as eating was prohibited in art galleries and museums that made it impossible for us to enter them. I think this is what he intended.' Another friend who had time to spare to accompany her around Moscow was Stan, who had been a watchmaker and was now the manager of a watch factory. He and his wife Zena had left America some years before, filled with the zeal of true revolutionaries. They had both applied for membership of the Communist Party but for some reason Zena was accepted while Stan was not. Thus Zena had become a person of some standing. So while Zena had maintained her ardour for the system and did not seem to notice the hardships and differences between theory and practice, Stan gradually lost some of his revolutionary ardour and began to hanker for the car and apartment he had left behind in the States.

This was not hard to understand. Zena and Sam had not simply come to find work, but to assist in the building of an entirely new system of society. They believed they were pioneers in an experiment that had never been undertaken before. So many of the problems and difficulties they encountered arose from the backwardness of the Russian empire during Tsarist times. They could accept the mistakes and anomalies because their eyes were firmly focused not on the errors of today but on that fine future for which they and their comrades were working and sacrificing. In such a situation you are disciplined not only by your own idealism but also by your loyalty to those who share your belief. The group both contains your doubts and reinforces your faith.

Zena was on the inside, busy and involved, a lively, capable and active woman. Stan was outside the political group, the ones that discussed things and made decisions and felt that they were changing the world – everything for the future. A chasm of expectations, of hopes, of interests was opening up between them. For once you are outside the magic circle the perspective changes. The inconsistencies give rise to doubts that sully the ideals. And doubts give rise to questions; and questions mean you start measuring what you are supposed to believe against what you actually see.

At that time the working week in Russia was six days except for those who worked in factories and heavy industry; they had a five-day week. Zena had a six-day week, but for Stan who managed a factory it was five days, so he had an extra day off each week while Zena was working, and was free to take Olga round Moscow. Stan's great interest was antiques and old books. They walked everywhere and gradually Moscow buildings and streets became familiar to my sister.

Deep snow-shrouded winter, icy winter came with its meagre grey days and long hours of darkness. Henry had warned Olga that she must bring very warm clothes and boots from England; and, suitably protected, she did not seem to mind temperatures lower than she had ever experienced before. But even so she was unaccustomed to the severity of the cold, as she realised when Stan accompanied her on her first winter in a search for a Christmas tree.

The Soviet Union – having discarded religion – did not celebrate Christmas. Instead it broke the darkness of their long winter on January 1, when they celebrated the New Year with Father Frost, who bore a striking resemblance to our own Father Christmas. Parties were held on New Year's Eve, and January 1 was a holiday. Stalls and small fairs were set up in the city streets, mainly for the children, with ice-cream sellers (Russians consumed masses of ice-cream, even when the temperature plunged) and a special issue of tangerines, the first in the season.

For us, as children, Christmas was a time of great delight, giving us endless occupations in the short dark December days; designing our own Christmas cards, making presents for our parents and small surprises for each other; decorating the main room; and hanging out our stockings on Christmas Eve, to find them in the morning crammed with small parcels. Always with some sweets and a tangerine – the first of the season – in the toe.

Best of all was the tree. Whatever the origin of the custom it was the green growing tree that was for us the symbol and meaning of Christmas. On those cold, endless English winter days when the light faded in the early afternoon and pea-soup fogs often obliterated the streets, the curtains were drawn against the dark; in a corner of the room the wavering glow of real wax candles, spiralled in white, pink and red in little metal clips; trails of silver tinsel across the branches and coloured balls of the utmost fragility that would crumble into spiky fragments if handled carelessly; sweets and chocolate money; the fun of wrapping and decorating.

Although celebrating Christmas had no religious significance for us, we always had a tree, even when we were older. And all three of us continued the tradition for our own families; even in South Africa when Christmas comes in mid-summer and the only intimation of snow would be balls of cotton wool in shop windows. Often we were on holiday by the sea at Christmas time, and once on the hot sands of the Cape peninsular, a beach umbrella, every spoke garnished with tinsel and dangling with wrapped gifts, served as a tree.

Still steeped in the nostalgia of past Christmases, Olga was determined to have a tree for December 25. She was not trying to recreate the Christmases that we had enjoyed as a family; it was more a desire to recall the flavour of those days; the setting up of the basic symbol – the tree – would help to retain her continuity with the past. She saved the coloured and foil papers from sweets and wrapped them around nuts to hang on a tree. She bought some small decorations from a peasant selling them in the street. Accompanied by Stan she haunted the street markets in search of a small tree, and eventually managed to find one.

As they were walking along the street a man confronted them, talking excitedly, pointing at Olga's face. 'Stan looked at me,' she said, 'seemed startled; and suddenly bent down, seized a handful of snow and started rubbing it in my face and on my nose.' She could not understand this eccentric behaviour, and protested vehemently. But Stan, agitated, said: 'No, you must let me. It's all my fault. I did not realise it was so cold, your nose is white with frostbite. Do you feel anything?'

'Oh!' she exclaimed. 'And I thought it was just that I was getting used to the cold.' Soon feeling returned, and her nose started tingling. It seemed strange to her that to stave off frostbite you rub the affected part with snow. She was learning to adapt herself to the conditions imposed by the climate.

The Metro

Henry never did get to the building of the beautiful bridges he dreamed about. 'Bridges in Russia were considered security risks,' Olga said. 'Armed guards stood on all of them, and no foreign engineer was allowed to work on their construction.'

Instead, he was asked to work on the building of the new underground system in Moscow, the Metro. When he protested that he was not trained as this kind of engineer he was told: 'But you've ridden on one, haven't you? We've never even seen one.' So he was with the group of engineers who pioneered the building of the Metro and who constructed the very first station. It is Mayakovskaya, named after the famous revolutionary poet, Mayakovsky, who was very popular in the early years of the revolution, but later committed suicide.

Olga always maintained that this station was the best in the Metro. It is indeed a beautiful station, still regarded as the jewel of the Metro.

There is no doubt that the Metro was of fundamental importance to Stalin, not only in the practical sense of providing Moscow with swift, cheap, reliable transport but also symbolically with 'palaces for the proletariat'. It was he who insisted that the building underground did not cease, even during the most desperate years of the war, when the Soviet armies were in retreat. The use of the Metro as war shelters was embodied in its construction and saved many Moscow lives during the German bombing of the city.

The building of the Metro began in the 1930s, when life for all Muscovites was at its most spartan. Yet from the first it was considered the most important of all the State constructions. The transportation of the necessary materials and of steel and cement were given highest priority.

During 1934 alone twenty-one per cent of Moscow's annual budget went into building the Metro; and of this a great part went to the construction of the beautiful stations. The Metro was not only an essential means of transport for a rapidly growing city, but also a proud public statement of what Soviet society could achieve.

Each station was of individual design, using the finest materials – bronze, brass, rare woods delivered from the Urals, Siberia, the Caucasus and twenty-three types of marble; using the skills not only of engineers, architects and masons but of sculptors, painters, glass-makers and others who worked in the decorative arts.

Construction on the first three lines began in 1932, 1935, 1939; the fourth was only begun after the war in 1945. As a result the stations reflect not only the economic circumstances in each period but also the political climate of the times with changing official attitudes towards arts and aesthetics.

Despite growing restrictions on the visual arts, when the first line was being built they were still under the influence of an avant-garde, with its freedom of new ideas, innovation and exploration. Mayakovskaya exemplifies this. It has a broad central concourse separated from the platforms on either side by slender columns clad in deep pink rhodonite and stainless steel, the material of the machine age, of the industrialisation on which the new society would be founded. The metallic arches support thirty-six elliptical domes, each one of which is finished with a different mosaic. Looking at them, head strained back and neck extended, you see in each one a miniature mural set against a blue sky. The Soviet artist Dieneka who designed them was said to have been influenced by Tiepolo. There are planes, parachutists, gliders; a mother holding a child, a tree in blossom; always a blue sky and white clouds, serenity and peace.

The floor is inlaid with black marble squares which are reminiscent of the geometric abstractions of the artist Malevich. The combination of red and black marble with the stainless steel gives the station a clean, uncluttered, modern look.

It is all these features of Mayakovskaya's design that so clearly show how the revolution had released an exciting new experimentalism in the arts and what the arts were beginning to achieve before the clamp-down on modernism.

In 1935, when the second Metro line was begun, the time of the avant-garde in art and architecture was already over. The official art of socialist realism replaced the modernist aesthetic of the first line with baroque crystal chandeliers and monumental marble statues of workers, soldiers, peasants. The theme was of relentless positivism and heroism emphasised by size.

The third line, begun in 1939 and completed in 1944, was built during the terrible suffering and sacrifices of the war, its very existence a memorial to the tenacity and resistance of the people. The fourth line, completed shortly after the death of Stalin, is the most flamboyantly ideological; it is its own memorial to the grandiose ideas of the dictator.

In the thirties the contrast between the beautifully designed, scrupulously clean, bright and shining underground stations, and the drab dark streets of Moscow onto which the elevators disgorged their passengers was extreme. It was as though the Soviet authorities were presenting the stations as an exemplar of what socialism would bring – marble and crystal, beauty and light for everyone.

The Moscow Metro is still swift and efficient, its stations still clean and beautiful. The luxurious stations with their huge underground avenues were show places, but had no benches for travellers. As trains arrive at one-minute intervals, perhaps it was not thought necessary. But as Victor Serge remarked in *Memoirs of a Revolutionary*: 'We know how to build subterranean palaces, but we forget that a working class woman coming from work would like to be able to sit down beneath all the rich-hued stones.'[7]

Henry started work on the first construction in 1932. Members of the many different nationalities of the Soviet Union took part in the construction of the first metropolitan route, the largest enterprise that had been undertaken in the Soviet Union. By 1934 its work force had reached 75,000.

The Metro staff became a small nation in itself. It had its own clubs reflecting the interests of the Metro workers. There were a hundred members in its literary society and several newspapers were published. 1,500 Metro workers competed for the titles of chess and checkers champions; and twenty-five athletic clubs grew up at the Metrostroy tent cities.

Henry worked on the construction of the first three lines. Despite all that happened afterwards, he must surely have known pride and satisfaction in his work as a pioneer in constructing the Moscow Metro and in Mayakovskaya.

The Age of Utopianism

I was lucky to have arrived in Russia at the tail end of a period of revolutionary fervour that lasted with diminishing force, from 1917 to 1936. Later events have blotted out the memory of its vital antecedent… But I must bear witness to this vibrant period because this alone reveals the extent to which hopes were betrayed.

Margaret Wettlin, *Fifty Russian Winters, An American Woman's Life in the Soviet Union* (Pharos Books, 1992)

Olga's arrival in Moscow in 1935 was towards the end of this 'vibrant period', when the imposition of Stalinist orthodoxy was beginning to bring an end to diversity and experimentation in the arts and just before the era of mass arrests had begun. Despite the difficulties and sacrifices that confronted everyone in their daily lives, the vast advances in developing industrialisation and in education were opening up new prospects for society as a whole.

The Bolshevik projects for 'literacy, numeracy, cultural awareness and administrative facility' were welcomed. 'The exhilaration of learning, common to working class people in other societies undergoing industrialisation was evident in day-schools and night classes across the country. Despite all the problems, the Soviet regime retained a vision of political, economic and cultural betterment.'[8]

Thousands of schools were being built and the USSR was becoming a literate society, not just in Russia and the Ukraine but in the most far-flung parts where the majority were illiterate. There was compulsory schooling and a universal obsession with study. Pedagogical institutes were being built to train a generation of young teachers, not only in schools, but also in polytechnics, night schools, factory clubs for adults.

Books were sold cheaply, newspapers cost ten kopeks. There was a huge leap in education that was bringing about a virtual end to illiteracy. By the late 1920s there were three million high school students; a decade later eighteen million. Children of illiterate peasants were becoming academics, political leaders, scientists.

In the cities the training of experts in diverse fields of science and in performance arts such as music, opera and ballet was reaching high standards. Perhaps a society poor in consumer goods found compensation in less material rewards: in books, poetry, music, theatre and ballet. Moscow was being rebuilt with provision for inexpensive facilities for relaxation – cinemas, sports clubs, 'Houses of Culture'. There were public parks, symphony concerts.

The theatres and their directors became world famous, their methods studied and imitated. Stanislavsky created the Moscow Arts Theatre; Meyerhold's theatre with no curtains and constructionist scenery made the stage look like a Kandinsky abstraction; Okhlopkov was the founder of the first theatre-in-the-round. The Bolshoi (big) produced opera and ballet, and the Mali (small) was the national theatre of the classics. And the Moscow Arts theatre was Chekhov's theatre.

Moscow had trolley buses and trams; but they were hopelessly overcrowded and not enough to serve the ever-increasing population. The construction of the Metro was an essential part of the city's development and it also made the theatres accessible to the people of Moscow.

These were giant advances in transforming the old Tsarist empire into a modern, literate society. They spurred the belief not only in the Soviet Union but also among many people throughout the world, that the Revolution had put in place the building blocks for an entirely new society that would, in time, transform not only the economy and social relations but human nature itself. Visitors from the West shared in this belief in a new Utopia; like the American writer Lincoln Steffens they had 'seen the future and it works'. What they did not see was the developing stranglehold of Stalin's dictatorship, the removal and soon the disappearance of all rivals, the growth of the power and activities of the secret police and Stalin's paranoia which would lead millions to suffering and death in the gulag.

Dancing at the Metropol

I try to reconstruct what my sister's life was like at that time, to bridge the distance and years between us; to reconcile the contradictions between her personal life and the cataclysmic context in which it was being enacted.

Perhaps for Olga and Henry and their friends, for a short while it was the best of times; or at least the last of the best. 1936 was for her a time of exploration, of making new friends, of tasting a new culture, of adjusting to different social customs. Moscow was home to many foreigners. There were the official diplomats at the various embassies, business people from trade organisations, journalists from many countries and agencies. But my sister's friends were a different social circle. There were not only Americans and others who had come to work for the Soviets. Moscow had also become host to refugees. Hitler had been in power for three years, and the lives of all communists in Germany and surrounding countries were in danger. Many had escaped after imprisonment and torture to seek asylum in the Soviet Union – from Germany, Austria, Rumania, Hungary and other countries of Eastern Europe.

Olga and Henry had friends among foreigners like these who were living in Moscow. And through their love of the theatre they came to know actors and other young professional Muscovites who were happy to sit around and talk with Olga; they found it a good way of improving their English and her pleasant personality won her friends in this diverse crowd.

Gradually the climate began to change. At first she and Henry were enjoying their social activities and their circle of new-found friends. They were young, full of energy. They went dancing at the Hotel Metropol, at that time *the* place to go, close to Red Square in the centre of the city. It was a very grand hotel, built in the *belle époque* style in the early 1900s, adorned both on the outside and the interior with Vrubel mosaics. Although by then it had an air of neglect, a dowager dressed in faded satins, it was still impressive, with its heavy mahogany furniture and spacious rooms, the high ceilings hung with crystal chandeliers.

Particularly in Moscow in those years, when consumer goods were scarce, the range of foods and clothes limited and austere, dancing at the Metropol brought a touch of luxury, even decadence, to the heart of the grey, drab city. For Olga and her friends going to the Metropol was like going to the Ritz in London's West End.

'In many ways it was a hard life,' Olga once said, 'but it was culturally rich and rewarding. Ordinary people read voraciously and they loved intellectual discussions.'

The change came gradually. The signal for change came less than three months before my sister arrived in Moscow. It was the shooting in Leningrad of a man called Kirov, a murder that was the signal for a conflagration that would engulf the whole of the USSR, that would touch people at all levels and leave no one unscarred.

The Killing of Kirov

Sergei Mironovich Kirov was the head of the Communist Party organisation in Leningrad, a member of the Central Committee of the party and of the Politbureau. He had been in dispute with the Politbureau on a number of issues, but despite this he was believed to be the man closest to Stalin, the one most likely to succeed him. At the Seventeenth

Congress of the Communist Party in February 1934 he had been elected to the Central Committee. The count had revealed substantial opposition to Stalin, while Kirov had only three votes against him. On December 1 Kirov was shot dead outside his office.

The assassin was a young student, Leonid Nikolayev, who was known to be at loggerheads with the party's leadership. But his personal motives soon ceased to be the main issue. A circular from the Central Committee of the Communist Party was immediately sent to all Party branches throughout the USSR declaring that Kirov's murder was part of a widespread conspiracy to destroy communism and wreck the country; and calling on all party organisations to engage in a full-scale rooting out of all 'enemies of the people'. Stalin asserted that wreckers, spies and assassins had insinuated themselves into party posts, and that Trotskyite groups were aiming at the restoration of capitalism. A wave of arrests scooped up all those in the Party hierarchy who formerly were thought to have been in the opposition to Stalin, together with tens of thousands of suspects at local level. It was the beginning of the time of terror which would destroy the lives of millions.

The trial of the alleged 'Leningrad Terrorist Centre' was held before the end of the month. The accused were all revolutionary pioneers, leaders who had played an important role in the formation of the new society. Nikolayev and his co-conspirators were tried in camera, sentenced to death and executed. In January, Zinoviev, Kamenev, Tomsky, Rykov and other leading members of the party, dubbed the 'Moscow Centre' were accused of conniving in Kirov's death. They were tried in camera and given sentences ranging from five to ten years. This was the first big trial in which old Bolsheviks, potential rivals to Stalin's supreme authority, were being eliminated. The purge of the Party had begun. But more than that, the purge would embrace the highest and once most powerful as well as the most obscure and insignificant.

In 1936 Kamenev, Zinoviev and others were tried again, this time on charges of treason, in the first of a series of show trials. They were sentenced to death and shot.

Kirov's closest associates had been amongst those accused of complicity in his assassination. All his former aides and assistants perished. It seems that those who had supported him most strongly were now accused by Stalin of having conspired to kill him, while people totally unconnected with Kirov or Leningrad were accused of being accomplices in his murder on the grounds that they 'shared the views of terrorists'.

Kirov's bodyguard, Borisov, died shortly after Kirov's murder in a car accident. Then all those connected with the car accident were themselves killed.

Later Gernrikh Yagoda, head of the secret police, the NKVD, who was in charge of these arrests was himself arrested, brought to trial, and sentenced to death.

Many historians and writers have since examined the question of who killed Kirov. Unless one accepts that those put to death for his murder were indeed the guilty ones – that his murder was all part of a vast conspiracy embracing hundreds of thousands of Party officials and members, the evidence points to Stalin himself.

The killing of Kirov 'has every right to be called the crime of the century', wrote Robert Conquest. 'Over the next four years hundreds of Soviet citizens, including the most prominent political leaders of the revolution, were shot for direct responsibility for the assassination, and literally millions of others went to their deaths for complicity in one or another part in the vast conspiracy that allegedly lay behind it. Kirov's death was in fact the keystone to the entire edifice of terror and suffering by which Stalin secured his grip on the Soviet people.'[9]

There can have been very few people in the Soviet Union who would have had any intimation of the real significance of Kirov's murder, nor of what was to follow, Certainly my sister could not have known the impact it would have on her own life and Henry's when she arrived in Moscow a couple of months later.

Two Plays on One Stage

When I think of those times, when I think of my sister, young and popular with her stimulating new friends, I see her life as a theatre in which two different plays are being performed at the same time on the same stage. Sometimes you can hear the voices of the actors in the play in front of the stage, sometimes those in the play at the back.

Which was real, which was the truth?

The truth was that the vast majority of the people were peasants, their endemic poverty and backward conditions made harsher by the famine and loss of livestock brought on by forced collectivisation. The truth was also that schools and higher education were gradually extending to remote republics. The scrubbed and innocent faces of the young pioneers with their white shirts and red scarves had their own reality; educational and cultural facilities for children were becoming available in towns and cities throughout the USSR. In summer the children were going to camps in the countryside. And working mothers were supported by crèches and nursery facilities in factories.

The truth was that industrialisation was spreading rapidly, that scientific education was expanding; that children whose parents were illiterate and unskilled and who never had an opportunity to change their lives were training as musicians, dancers, scientists, specialists in professional fields.

And the truth was also that the concentration on heavy industry left an urban society permanently short of the basic necessities of city life, of food, clothing, shoes, everyday essentials in the home such as matches, pens, pencils, paper; so that a large part of each person's life was spent in searching, queuing, buying on the black market at inflated prices (often what had been illicitly removed from factories and stores) and living on expectations that socialism would build a better life – patience, patience; it was all going to change.

Yet there was another reality below the surface optimism. A framework of persecution and terror was being constructed to enable a paranoid dictator to remove every obstacle to his absolute power by banishing and killing an unimaginable number of people, imposing silence and subservience by the creation of fear.

Perhaps there are always two sides, two different ways of interpreting reality. Perhaps if you believe in something strongly enough it is possible to go on believing even when it contradicts reality. For you believing is reality, it is the truth. Witnesses who lived through the prisons and the camps told how, even in the very depths of their sufferings, some loyal communists clung to their belief that if Stalin only knew what was happening, he would intervene to establish their innocence and restore socialist justice.

And there is the difficulty of adjusting to what you believe and what you see – a country forging ahead, striving to lift itself out of backwardness into the modern world, devolving a new economic system, developing a strong industry, caring for its children; while there are a contradictory events – something else taking place that you do not understand; something inexplicable, frightening, bewildering.

People living on the edge of disaster try to retain a semblance of normality in their lives. They busy themselves with ordinary routine things. They convince themselves that whatever may be happening to others it won't happen to them. What have they done? Why should they be afraid? For everything that appears to be wrong they convince themselves there must be some logical explanation.

My sister would have seen herself as a bystander to these black events happening around her. She and Henry and their friends would be cast in the first play, the one about living ordinary lives – working, shopping, eating, meeting with friends, going to the theatre, living in a community. The second play, with the sinister plots and a fatal ending is not happening to them. It is taking place on a different stage.

But it is taking place at the same time.

At first it seems to be in the background, a murmur of indistinguishable voices, irritating perhaps, a distraction, but not really a part of the play in which they live their ordinary lives. But gradually the voices of the actors in the second play become louder, more insistent. Inevitably this dark drama starts to move to the front of the stage; there is confusion, the players are all trying to speak at the same time. And soon the strident voices of the actors in the second play are overpowering the voices of those in the domestic drama.

And then the time comes when the men in hats and overcoats, carrying briefcases, come to the front of the stage; and the two plays merge.

Sasha and Larissa

With her limited knowledge of the Russian language, Olga did not think of looking for a job. However, one day her friend, Sasha, asked her to come in to his office twice a week for a couple of hours to vet his English correspondence and to help decipher his telegrams. Sasha was the husband of Larissa, a young Russian woman who had once lived with us in our home in London.

She came to live with us when we were still at school. One day our family doctor had said to our mother: 'There's a young Russian girl over here working. She's terribly lonely. She doesn't speak any English. Do you think you could perhaps take her into your household for a time? She seems to be afraid of everyone and everything.'

So Larissa joined our family as a late-acquired older sister. She was tall and lanky, with very long legs. She had light blue eyes and pale, fly-away hair. My two sisters started to teach her English. They had diffi-culty in explaining things with which she was unfamiliar, such as that bananas don't go into soup. She nearly drowned in Hampstead ponds one day because she did not understand when they told her it was deep, and she insisted she could swim – which she couldn't. And they con-stantly worried that she would not be able to find her way home from her job in the City. She lived with us for quite a long while, even stay-ing with us when we moved house. Then she married the director of the Russian firm where she worked. Sasha was tall and quiet with a husky voice and slow manner of speaking. They moved into a flat and lived there for a couple of years until he was recalled to the Soviet Union, and they returned to Moscow.

Larissa never lost touch with our family and was delighted when Olga arrived in Moscow. So it was through Sasha that Olga began to work. Then she was persuaded to take on more work teaching English.

Watchdogs and Minders

One day Henry's sister Ray, who was teaching English to all sorts of im-portant people, said: 'Wouldn't you like to teach English?'

'Oh no; I wouldn't know where to start.'

'I'll show you.'

'I couldn't! I don't even know any grammar.'

But Ray persisted.

'You, with your real English accent – it won't matter. After our American voices your students will be happy just to listen to you.'

So I started with my first student who apparently only wanted practice in conversation. She was young, and seemed to me not to be in need of any practice at all. She herself was a teacher of English and spoke quite flu-ently. I asked her about her name, Era, and she told me that her father, in true revolutionary spirit, had optimistically named her after the new era which was bound to come.

She was about my age, pretty, with dark hair and eyes and a pale skin. She wanted to have her lessons late in the day, explaining that she had a bad heart and usually slept very late. We arranged that she would come first with all her difficult questions and after that we would just sit and talk.

The first question she asked was: 'Please can you tell me the difference between the gerund and the verbal noun?' I was thankful that the phone rang, and I rushed to answer it. The telephone was a communal one hanging in the hall and used by all the tenants. It was Stan, asking if I was free the next day to go out walking with him.

When I came back to my room I explained to Era. 'That was just my watchdog.'

She looked surprised. 'Watchdog?' 'Yes. All foreigners have someone who checks up on them. Stan checks up on me.' Immediately I said it I realised from the expression on Era's face that she must be my watchdog. Perhaps Stan was as well, part of a system of keeping a check on the checkers in an administration that didn't trust anyone; perhaps I had been mistaken about Stan – it was only my assumption. Certainly Era was my watchdog until she left for Armenia with her husband.

*

Olga was thus already aware of the unrelenting check-up that the Soviet system had installed to monitor all its citizens, and particularly those who might be considered spies – all foreigners living in the Soviet Union.

The surveillance was unbelievably extensive. One writer comments: 'I recently came across a document in the Party's archive suggesting that in Leningrad alone in 1934, a cadre of 2700 intelligence "residents" ran a circle of ten regular "informants". A further network of 2000 "special informants" was attached to factories, schools and government departments, with each informant expected to gather information from "casuals". Moscow had a network twice that size, and Stalin was informed that in the USSR as a whole there were at least half a million regular informants.'[10]

The NKVD collected information on public opinion from informers standing in queues outside shops, at *kolkhoz* markets, listening to workers complaints in the factory cafeteria; from letters in the press, from meetings of professional organisations and from conversations in private homes.

Margaret Wettlin describes how she herself was 'chosen' to report on three friends and how she believed it was an honour to think that in this way she could assist her adopted country. Her belief that she was merely being patriotic was undermined only when she found out that others were also reporting on the same people. Only when one friend she was convinced was completely innocent was arrested did she begin to have doubts and refused to continue her reporting.[11]

Two Summers

Leaving the city in summer for a dacha in the countryside was – perhaps still is – almost a religious ritual for Muscovites. The firmly-held view was that it was an absolute necessity for everyone to get to the countryside, to the fresh air and sunshine, and eat berries and mushrooms and fruit to prepare themselves for the long, cold winter ahead.

A favoured few had their own dachas in the forests around Moscow. Many foreign embassies had their own dachas – the American one was on the banks of the river Istra, a favoured location – but most people rented dachas for the summer, or rooms in peasant houses. The wage-earners would stay in Moscow during the week, going to the country for the week-ends to join the wives and children who would often spend the months from June to August or even later – depending on the weather – in the country. Teachers and professors would return in September, the beginning of the academic year.

When summer came Olga and Henry's friend Mark urged them to join him for a holiday on the river Volga. The Volga, one of the world's greatest waterways, is deeply woven into the history and cultural life of Russia. Their destination was Kalyzin, a village on the banks of the Volga not far from Kalinin. They travelled there by a local train, crowded with peasants carrying huge bundles, so that they had to struggle to get seats. As always in small towns the station was some distance from the village and there was no transport. Finally they found a peasant with a horse and a two-wheeled wooden cart to take them to the village.

Where the Volga passed through Kalyzin it was wide and calm; and just beyond the village there was a bend in the river where it became deep and swift-flowing. Here the river had pushed its way through sand and clay, ever seeking to broaden itself. The sediment eroded from the right bank by force of the water formed sandbanks and beaches. In the curve of the bend, below a steep bank, there was a beach of fine silver sand. For holiday-makers this was the 'good side' of the river.

Mark told them that all the accommodation on that side was already full, but they should try to find a room in one of the peasants' houses on the other side. In the morning a ferry would bring them across to the beach.

The peasants' houses, decorated with fretwork around the windows and doors, were strung out in a row along the dusty street. The peasant who offered them a room in the house at the end of the row looked as though he had stepped out of the book of Russian fairy tales which we had when we were children. He had a ragged grey beard and wore a linen blouse belted at the waist, his trousers tucked into long felt boots.

He showed them the room and began to speak to Olga rapidly in Russian. Mark explained that she did not understand what he said because she did not speak Russian. At first the old man would not believe it. He was totally mystified by this strange disability. Mark explained to him that she was a foreigner, English, and spoke no Russian at all.

The old man was amazed. 'What a shame!' he exclaimed. 'How come? Why didn't her parents teach her when she was small?'

There was no electricity in the village and no running water; but their landlord was proud to show them his indoor lavatory, an earth closet with two holes in the floor. The days were hot, and when the wind blew from behind the house they were sorry that the closet was not in the traditional place at the bottom of the garden. They washed in the yard where water was stored in old kerosene tins. Their landlord was intrigued by their elaborate washing and teeth-cleaning operations, all in full view of the village street.

There was not much food in the village, but they could buy bread, eggs, and sour milk. In the morning they took the ferry across the river to join the other holiday-makers on the silver beach where peasants would bring currants and berries for sale; and later in the day they would wander into the forest to search for mushrooms.

'There were beautiful forests there,' Olga said, 'as in most parts of central Russia.' She was always content to walk in the forests among the silver birches, their trunks slender and dainty as dancers, poised amongst the shadows of the dark firs. Violets and small white flowers clustered on the forest floor. They walked barefoot on the moss, the soft grasses and flowers as they searched for edible berries and mushrooms.

They would take boats for the day and go off down the river. It was a joy going downstream, but hard work coming back. There were places where they found it easier to get out and pull the boat, the current was so strong. Logs floated down from a lumber camp in the upper reaches of the river. Sometimes they would sit astride them, racing downstream.

The perilous race took them a long way down the river, and then they would have to swim against the tide as far as they could, or walk back upstream along the bank.

There was an old crenellated monastery at this place, mostly in ruins, but very picturesque, with an interesting wishing wall. 'You shouted your wish, and then after a few seconds it came echoing back to you.' Olga's Russian friends used to love to take her there, delighted to hear the English echo when she called across to the wall, as though the wall itself was capable of speaking in English as well as Russian.

The river was wide and golden when the sun went down; a gentle, soft twilight, after their sun-drenched days; evening light filtered through the birch trees, the sound of voices carried across the water before intense darkness covered the village.

Kalyzin no longer exists. The ruined monastery was destroyed by the Germans; then, after the war, the village was drowned by the Uglich reservoir, built to make the river more navigable at that point for the increasing commercial and holiday traffic.

The next year, in the summer of 1936, Olga fulfilled one of her ambitions when she and Henry went travelling around the Caucasus.

Georgia, bordering on the Black Sea, now an independent nation, has always been a country with a strong national character of its own. Its people had a different cultural background, a different history, and a completely different temperament, born from the warm and generous south. Although its neighbours are Iran and Turkey, Georgia is more of a Christian than a Moslem country.

In the long hot summers life in Georgia was lived out of doors. In May the land was full of blossom from the fruit trees: peach, apricot, cherry, apple. It was a land of vineyards, of cypresses, of lilac, laburnum and bougainvillaea. The vineyards stretched up the hills to where the forest line began and the excellent wines, together with shashlick and other foods were offered to any stranger. In the country pomegranate, fig and mulberry trees grew wild, and in the towns fruit trees were planted in neat rows down the streets. Beyond were the high mountain ranges topped with snow.

In Tbilisi the air was soft and warm, the wide streets shaded by the trees. Through arched gateways they glimpsed cobbled courtyards with fountains. Grapes hung in heavy bunches in the hotel garden. 'Take your pick', they were told. At sunset they heard the Moslem call to prayer, and at night listened to the Tiflis Orchestra. In the dining room a bottle of Georgian wine arrived at their table with a note of welcome.

For one week they took a Black Sea steamer travelling as far as Batumi and stopping at villages along the coast. They travelled back by car along the famous Georgian military highway that stretched right across the Caucasus to Tbilisi.

Time slipped away in the languid days of the southern summer. When the train they were waiting for was late they were told: 'No train? No matter. It will come later.'

Leaving the Caucasus was like leaving a land of peace and golden sunsets to enter a land of darkness, a night of terror. For of all the years of arrests and great show trials that lay ahead, that year, 1937, was the worst.

CHAPTER 2

A Fatal Year

I n January there was a second big trial of old Bolsheviks and former leaders: Pyatakov, Radek, Sokolnikov and fifteen others. The trial was held in public and reported in the press. Foreign observers attended the trial, and watched in bewilderment as these old stalwarts of the revolution confessed to crimes against the Soviet state. The fact that now, in an open court, they did not repudiate confessions that could have been extracted in prison cells impressed observers. The American writer Lion Feuchtwanger commented, 'If this is a fabrication, then I don't know what's genuine.' For him, although much was obscure, inexplicable, the alternative to accepting their validity was unthinkable.

Ernst Fischer was the representative of the Austrian Communist Party in the Comintern (the international organisation of Communist parties that had been founded by Lenin). He wrote subsequently that the way in which the permanently maintained atmosphere distorted consciousness was truly terrifying. The most absurd statement, the most implausible lies begin to take effect if repeated day in, day out. 'Arrests and accusations on such a scale cannot be the result of pure arbitrariness – and on whose part?… But to carry these thoughts to their logical conclusion was something of which nobody was capable unless he dared to think that Stalin was at the origin of a methodical madness... a thought beyond imagining.'[12]

The accused were permitted to have lawyers, and Pyatakov was defended by a lawyer named Braude. It was a very strange defence in which Braude did little more than confirm the State's allegations, while pleading for clemency in sentencing.

I doubt whether Olga would have read the reports in the Russian newspapers, and if she did the name 'Braude' would not have meant anything to her. But only a year or two later she would have a brief, unpleasant encounter with Braude.

The first two trials of former leaders heralded the mass purges that began at the top and filtered down to scoop up an estimated nineteen million victims in the end. Between the years of 1934 and 1938 when the purge was at it most intense it was as though a fever raged over the whole of the Soviet Union. No one was immune, no government department, no public body, no professional organisation, no section of society. All were subject to the fatal virus that spread from leading people to encompass their children, their families, their friends, their associates. And, in the end, just anyone to make up the quota of arrests that were required from each geographical region, from each area, from each organisation, from each section.

Soviet military science in the 1930s was considered to be among the most advanced in the world. In 1937 the Red Army was the first to have a mechanised corps. At the head of this modern strategical thinking was the famous Mikhail Tukhachevsky; in that year Tukhachevsky, together with the flower of the Red Army command were charged with treason and executed almost immediately. His wife, sister and two brothers were shot, their children sent to NKVD settlements.

The Soviet Commander of the International Brigade in Spain, General Kleber, 'the hero of Madrid' in the battle of Madrid, was shot, as were other military victims from Spain.

The armed forces lost their best, their most able leaders: three of the country's five Marshals, thirteen out of fifteen Army Commanders, eight out of nine Fleet Admirals, fifty out of fifty-seven Corps Commanders… and so the list goes on and on.

There was no logic and there was no compassion. Many of the wives, sons and daughters of these men were also arrested and were shot or sent to labour camps where many of them died.

Some parts of the country suffered more than others – those places to which Stalin was particularly antagonistic. In the provinces Leningrad suffered huge losses; the purge affected the entire political and industrial leadership. In the Ukraine where there was always a strong nationalist feeling, Stalin was suspicious of all those with influence. In one sweep the whole political leadership disappeared, and in their turn their replacements also disappeared, thus effectively destroying the Party in the Ukraine.

It was a time of prolonged fear for ordinary people. Anyone with contacts abroad, representatives of foreign firms, employees at legations, engineers and people associated with production were suspected of sabotage. Certain groups were particularly vulnerable: Jehovah's Witnesses, priests, national minorities living in Russian towns, people with foreign contacts, such as philatelists and Esperantists. The purge spread abroad. Soviet diplomats were recalled and shot, as were members of the Comintern, representatives of countries where the party was illegal, such as Germany, Yugoslavia, Italy, Poland; in their own countries there was no democratic voice, nobody to raise objections.

The most visible victims were foreigners who were working in the Comintern. Many of these were men who had been given refuge in the USSR from persecution by their own governments, particularly Nazi Germany. In 1937 Heinz Neumann, a former leading German communist then living in Moscow was arrested, and three other leading members of the German Communist party disappeared. Other foreign victims were those who had sought sanctuary from the terror in their own countries. (After the Nazi-Soviet Pact in 1939 many German communists, including Jews, were arrested as undesirable aliens and sent over the border into German-occupied Poland – into the hands of the Gestapo.)

Stalin's paranoia also extended to foreigners who had come to work in the Soviet Union. Every foreigner, even those who had come to work for the Soviet government at its request, became suspect; even those who had been accepted into the Communist Party. To Stalin all were potential spies who could have been planted by the Americans, the Germans, the British – the whole capitalist world was opposed to socialism. The foreigners could have been trained to act as though they were devoted to the Soviet cause, only in order to betray it. In the widespread and increasingly indiscriminate disposal of human beings a few foreigners were of little consequence.

Some of the foreigners who had come to give their expertise to the Soviet Union returned to their own countries in those years before the war. Amongst those who stayed the Americans and British who had retained their own nationality had some safeguard; once their arrests became known their embassies might intervene on their behalf. Those from European countries where there was no democratic authority had no one to speak on their behalf.

The arrests filtered down, the net spread wider. In the pervading secrecy and suspicion it was easy for people to denounce anyone against whom they had a grudge, or whose job or home they wanted to take over. Once someone was arrested anyone who worked with them, belonged to the same group, or was associated with them – as well as family members – felt threatened. They put their heads down and avoided any contact with the relatives of the arrested person.

One American victim was Stan, Zena's husband. He simply disappeared. Although Olga had never shared Zena's political certainties, and in a sense, like Stan, was still an outsider in Soviet society, she had formed a close friendship with Zena. As soon as she heard of Stan's arrest, Olga phoned Zena.

Zena said, 'You know, you shouldn't be phoning me, should you?' Olga said: 'Yes I should. I'll come and see you.'

'No, don't come. We're being watched.'

Olga said Zena's case was very, very sad and she was so brave. 'They had a nice apartment right next to Lubianka,' she said, 'and one of the people working there, possibly investigating her husband, had his eye on that apartment. I'm sure that was why he was arrested. They tried to arrest her, too, but she managed to avoid it. But she lost her home.'

My sister never completed her story about Zena, and in the end I do not know what happened to her; only that Stan never came back from the camps. But my sister did write about one German who had escaped from the hands of the Gestapo – her friend Probst.

My Friend Probst

I met him at a friend's flat. He was lively and animated, danced extremely well, and was happy to air his English, which he spoke fluently. He knew I had not been in Moscow long, and he asked me to go skiing with him. 'But I've never been. I don't know how.'

'Oh, that's all right. I'll show you.'

He took me to the Lenin Hills, then still known by their old name, the Sparrow Hills. On the way he told me how he had gone skiing in the mountains all over Europe – Switzerland, Austria, and in his native Germany. It was his great love, and he spent all his holidays skiing. The Lenin Hills have short, steep inclines, though beginners start on the straight. We did, too. But soon Herman could not resist the slopes. He said they were only little ones, 'nothing like the mountains'. For me, they were formidable, but I didn't want to be left behind. So I simply sat on the backs of my skis and slid down, following him.

When we left the Lenin Hills we had to wait in an unheated trolley bus for two hours for some 'demonstration of workers' solidarity' to be over before traffic got back to normal. At the end of our journey, when I tried to stand up, to Herman's great amusement I found I had frozen solid to the seat. 'That's all the snow you collected sliding down the slopes of the Lenin Hills. Another demonstration of solidarity,' he teased.

On our journey back to town he talked nostalgically of his home in Berlin. He was a Jew, a Communist, and had worked as an interpreter for the Russians, so his arrest by the Gestapo was not unexpected. He had been so beaten up in prison that he had lost one kidney and the other was badly damaged. The Russians eventually exchanged him for a prisoner they held who was wanted by the Germans. They had given him a pension, and looked after his health, but he missed his home and family and longed for news of them. He had left a young wife and baby son in Berlin. For her own protection his wife had divorced him, and now he no longer heard from anyone at home.

From time to time he disappeared. In those days we did not ask too much about someone who was missing, particularly a German, but Herman would come back – brown and revitalised – after a health cure in some Southern sanatorium.

We used to go dancing to the hotels frequented by foreigners – the Metropol and the National – a little risky, as foreigners were watched, but fun. There he would meet his old friends from Berlin. During the months their numbers steadily diminished as they were arrested. But Probst remained – vital and joking, full of fun, and always ready for a party, a show, to go dancing or skiing.

One day a stranger telephoned me. She said she was a nurse in the Butminsk – a famous hospital on the outskirts of Moscow – and that Probst was there as a patient and he asked if I would visit him.

I went to the hospital. It was summer, and the gardens surrounding it were filled with bright flowers. Inside the hospital was cool and dark. The walls were painted in a dingy green, and as soon as I saw Herman I realised how ill he was. His vitality was gone. I knew how he hated the drab clothes Russian women wore – the shapeless dresses, thick stockings and heavy shoes. So I had put on my smartest English dress, even wearing a hat and gloves. But he, who always noticed and remarked on every detail, even of make-up, made no comment on my appearance. He was despondent, and talked gloomily of all his German friends who had been arrested. He had heard the news of the most recent victim – Willie, young and newly married, in whose flat we had first met.

He said sadly, 'Even Willie. I could believe perhaps that Pete was a traitor, or Georgie, or Fritz. But Willie! We fought the Nazis together, we were beaten up in jail together – he didn't talk. I shall never believe it of Willie.' Suddenly he was in great pain. A nurse came and asked me to wait in the corridor outside while she gave him an injection. When I went in again he was lying still, with his face turned towards the wall. I sat down beside him and held his hand. And for me, he died then, though news of his death came officially some days later.

Socialist Realism

The purge struck the intelligentsia with particular force.

The attack on the highly creative but unorthodox movements in theatre, films, painting, music, literature and poetry had already begun in the late 1920s, although their work continued into the 1930s. But with the arrival of the purges every branch of the arts was to be shorn of its revolutionary experimentation and subsumed into the orthodoxy of an academic classicism in the name of 'socialist realism', an art that would present to the people representations of themselves as their rulers would like them to be. Everything had to depict Soviet society in positive terms. Labour was heroic, peasants and workers in field and factory must be shown to have triumphed over nature and industry.

Art now had to serve the cause of preconceived ideas. In literature, as in the visual arts, there could be no doubts, no dark side, no ultimate defeats, no unresolved conflicts. The work of those writers and painters who did not conform went unpublished, their work not shown. Poets and novelists were silenced, many suffered arrests and exile. Artists whose work is now acclaimed world-wide were reviled; some of them emigrated. The works of Kandinsky, Chagall, Malevich, Tatlin, were locked in basements where they could never be seen, together with a vast collection of impressionist paintings confiscated from private collections. In 1936, the Politburo ordered paintings of 'a formalist and crudely naturalist character' removed from the Tretiakov Gallery.

In the theatre the best-known victim was Vsevolod Meyerhold, a name revered by actors and producers everywhere for his innovative work. In 1938 the Meyerhold Theatre was liquidated as 'alien to Soviet art'. In June 1939, Meyerhold had made an outspoken attack on the theatre of socialist realism; he was arrested the next day, cruelly beaten, and died in prison in 1940.

The writer, Osip Mandelstam, made the fatal error of writing a little epigram about Stalin which was read to a small circle of friends. Someone must have spoken about it. He was arrested, then exiled to a provincial town. He was allowed to return to Moscow for a short time, then arrested again in 1938 and sentenced to five years' forced labour in the Far East. Already ill with a nervous complaint, he died.

The NKVD surveillance of the intelligentsia was intense. The purge extended to scientists, historians, academics in all disciplines. Leading figures in every branch of science and culture disappeared and died in prisons or in the camps.

Fortunately, as far as can be judged, many works were never destroyed, only locked away; and the wonderful collection of Impressionists and Futurists have since been displayed world-wide. And the clampdown did not extend to classical music and literature which remained widely available and enormously popular. Many contemporary English and American writers were translated and published in Russia. Henry's sister Ray was now sharing a flat with her friend Natasha, who was a translator of English literature into Russian. Their flat was lined with books by Graham Greene, Ernest Hemingway, Somerset Maugham, J.B. Priestley, John Galsworthy, dos Passos, Erskine Caldwell and others, as well as the classics.

But the annihilation of the most talented and capable in every field became a tragic legacy for the future. No creative work comes out of a vacuum. The artist in every field builds on the works of the past, incorporates what others have revealed, takes the foundations and brings them into the present, projecting their ideas into the future. The work of great artists of the past provides the necessary structures on which the next generation of scientists, writers and artists must build. These works were being removed from sight. It was the death-blow to originality, experimentation, to all creative work.

The Innocent Women

The charade of democracy was played out side by side with the terror of the secret police, the NKVD. On the eve of the first All-Union elections, December 12, 1937, the couple who were Henry and Olga's first Russian friends became victims of the purge.

When Henry first joined his sister in Moscow he had been able to rent a room in an apartment block where she was living. Two of the other rooms were occupied by Grigorii Belen'kii and his wife Kseniya and their two children, a son and a daughter, Leonid who was thirteen and Irina who was eight. Henry and Olga became very friendly with this family.

Grigorii was arrested first, and his wife Kseniya was arrested two months later. Irina was eleven, and her brother, Leonid, was sixteen. The two children who were left without parents had to get permission to remain in the family rooms. One room of their apartment was boarded up by the NKVD, and the usual procedure had been to send the children away to orphanages. But their grandfather, who lived far from them, became their official guardian; and a neighbour whom they called Aunt Maria, although she was not an actual relative, did all she could to help the lives of the two children, who stayed on in the room together.

Olga and Henry kept in touch with the two children. When Irina was in her teens, she used to walk several city blocks with food to cook on Olga's stove, as the room she shared with her brother had no facilities for cooking. And then she would walk back through Moscow's streets, carefully carrying the hot food. A lasting bond was formed between Olga and Irina and sixty years on I was to meet Irina and her husband Vladimir when they visited England.

For a year after the arrest of their parents Irina and her brother knew nothing of what had happened to them. Leonid and his grandfather wrote letters to various high-ranking officials, but nobody replied. Later they were told that their father was an enemy of the people and had been sentenced to ten years hard imprisonment without the right to correspond with his family. Many years later they found out that he had been shot only two months after he was arrested. Years later still people came to understand that ten years hard labour without the right to correspond was in fact a euphemism – the sentence was death. And sixty years after Irina would learn from newly-opened archives of that time that her father was shot because he was a 'Mongolian spy'. Mongolian? We look for logic; but there is no logic. Yet somehow the lack of reason increases the pain.

As the purge spread to embrace more and more, officials determined to fulfil their quotas of arrests dispensed with even the pretence of a trial.

Irina's mother was kept in Butyrskaya prison for several months. She was never brought to trial, never had an opportunity to call witnesses, to make a defence. She was simply told that as the wife of an enemy of the people she had been sentenced to eight years in a labour camp.

The camp was Pot'ma, in the Mordovian republic. Once she arrived there she was permitted to write to her children once a month. At the end of the second year the children's grandmother managed to get permission for them to visit her.

They arrived in Pot'ma on a small local train. When it stopped a group of people got off the train and began walking along the rails without saying a word to each other. It seemed obvious that they, too, were going to the camp, and Irina and her brother and grandmother followed them. They had not gone very far when their suitcase, which was old and very heavy, because they had packed in as much food as they could get hold of, burst open; they had to stop to pack it up again, and tie it together with a rope.

When they had finished they realised that they were alone; the other people had disappeared. They continued walking along the track for some time until they came across a local woman. They asked her where the camp was. She said: 'Do you mean the camp where the innocent women are held?'

They stayed in Pot'ma for three days, living in a small wooden house in a room they shared with three or four relatives of other prisoners in the camp. When I met Irina all those long years after she still remembered that revealing phrase: 'the innocent women'. She told me: 'I will never forget that awful room – with strangers; and the warders – who brought our mother – sitting in a corner watching us. I remember that Mom asked us to walk outside at a certain time of the day, and go along the paling protected by barbed wire and watch-towers, because other women, who knew that her children had come to visit her, wanted to see us.

'When we did what she asked, we saw a large group of women who rushed towards the fence. They cried as we came near to them, and shook the fence, and shouted that we should tell their children that they had done nothing, that they were honest Soviet citizens.'

How could they comprehend what was so senseless, so unjust? They still believed that their arrests were some terrible mistake and that the great Stalin could not be aware of what was happening. For they knew themselves to be innocent of any wrong-doing against their country, and they still desperately wanted their children to know that they were loyal citizens.

Later Irina's mother managed to pass on to Irina and Lenya tiny slips of paper which she had smuggled out of the camp. They had on them names of other women, and their telephone numbers.

Blood and Gold

That summer Moscow was exceptionally hot. I entered the hallway which was always cool, even on a hot summer's day. As usual the old woman who guarded the lift was not there to open the door with the big key she kept under her voluminous skirts. So I started to walk. That's when I first noticed the blood, a trail of it leading up the stairs.

I walked up, my eyes riveted to the ground, carefully avoiding the fresh-looking red spots. They stopped outside the door of the flat where I was living. I shivered with a presentiment of danger, and hesitated.

The moment I pushed the door open I regretted it. The narrow hall was filled with people who looked like thugs. My neighbour, Zoya Michaelevna, was standing pale and distraught. She muttered under her breath: 'It's not you they want.'

Then I saw that two of the men were in the uniform of the Security Police. One of the men, clearly in command, asked me who I was and what I was doing there. After I explained that I was an English teacher, a temporary resident, just renting rooms in the flat, I was allowed to go to my room where I sat on the edge of a chair and waited, wondering apprehensively what was happening outside. Soon there was a knock on my door. The intruder apologised for disturbing me, but would I please show him what things in the flat were mine. These they left alone, but silently and systematically went through everything else, turning Zoya Michaelevna's room upside down, looking on the tops of cupboards, poking into recesses, peering under carpets.

The telephone rang. I heard a rough voice say curtly, 'She's not here,' and the click of the receiver. I thought, 'That won't satisfy Henry. He'll try again.' And of course he did, several times. Finally they called me, warned, 'Speak Russian, and don't say anything about us.' But I couldn't speak Russian. I'd forgotten it all. Henry feared the worst – an arrest – and said, 'I'm coming over.'

There was a ring at the doorbell; an actor friend on his way to an evening performance bringing some theatre tickets. He blanched when he saw the crowded flat, then became agitated when he found he was not going to be allowed to leave.

A student came in to collect a book, a neighbour to borrow some potatoes. Both were reluctantly forced to join us in our tense wait. I could stand the strain no longer, and went into the kitchen for some water. The searchers were still busy; emptying out all the boxes of cereal, rice and flour; clearing saucepans off the shelves. I wondered what they could be looking for.

There was a sound of the rending of wood, a sudden exclamation, and one of them came into the hall carrying a heavy-looking brown slab. The others rushed to look at it, then settled down to wait, all eight of them, sitting silently in a row on cases in the hall, smoking foul-smelling cheap tobacco which they rolled in newspaper. I had to step over their feet to go back to my room.

There was another ring at the bell, and in walked Tamadze, who was staying with Zoya Michaelevna on one of his little business trips to

Moscow. Even his jaunty Georgian moustache wilted when he saw the trap he had walked into.

After that, the searchers went, taking Tamadze and Zoya Michaelevna with them, and I and my friends were free again. 'What,' I asked, 'was that dirty-looking slab they got so excited about?' 'That "dirty-looking slab" as you call it, was a bar of gold.' And the blood that had given me the eerie feeling that something was wrong? Oh, that was my friend Talik, the little boy from the flat upstairs, who had been playing football in the yard and had run up with a nose bleed.

Soviet Citizens

As foreign workers, Ray and Henry had to have their residents' permits renewed from time to time. Now when they went for renewal they were told that according to a new government decree all foreigners except accredited newspaper correspondents and those in the diplomatic service would have to take out Soviet citizenship or leave the country. Olga, it appears, was not subject to the same order as she was still regarded as a temporary visitor.

For foreigners working for the Soviet government it was a moment of choice. Walter Friedman, also from New York, had already applied for citizenship but his wife Clara hesitated. She filled in a form and handed it in; then she and Walter had doubts about what was happening around them. After discussions they decided that it would be better for her to return to America for a year or two.

Clara went to the office the next day and asked for her form to be returned. The woman she spoke to went away for a long time. Then she came back. 'You are too late,' she was told. 'You are already a Soviet citizen.' So Clara no longer had any choice; her future was fixed. And her three daughters were all born in Russia where she was still living when I met her in Moscow in the 1990s when researching this book.

Ray had been born in Vilastock in an area that had passed between Poland and Russia before her parents emigrated to America. Henry, several years younger than his sister was probably born in New York, where their parents went to live when they emigrated to America. They had both grown up in the USA as American citizens.

In Moscow Ray had a variety of jobs and she loved her work. She was teaching at the university, giving private lessons in English to some rather important people, and writing textbooks. She enjoyed it all, and the students were very appreciative. When she was confronted with the choice of becoming a Soviet citizen or returning to America, she decided to take out Soviet citizenship. For her it seemed a logical choice. But Henry was faced with an abrupt choice – become a Soviet citizen, or be deported immediately.

It had never been his intention to make a permanent home in the Soviet Union; he knew that Olga did not wish to live there, and had only joined him because she thought it would be for limited time. Yet somehow Henry was persuaded that he too should become a Soviet citizen.

I can only speculate about the reasons that made him take such a drastic decision. Perhaps he did not wish to leave the work on the Metro so abruptly. Clearly, foreigners felt themselves to be under threat. Ray probably thought this would be a temporary protection for them, a guarantee of their loyalty. But they do not seem to have adequately weighed up the long-term consequences of their action.

Looking back after this long passage of years, it is difficult to judge; harder still to feel the sense of uncertainty and confusion of those who still believed that they shared their ideals of a socialist society with the Soviet government. At that stage, like the vast majority of others, their faith in the government and in its objectives had not been destroyed. While many felt disturbed and even bewildered at what was happening; they still believed that there were rational reasons for the events around them, that eventually it would all be explained.

Perhaps Henry thought that taking on Soviet citizenship was, in a sense, a device that would enable him to go on working there for a while; that he could still conform to the regulations and that when his contract expired he would be free to leave. No, say my Russian friends, it is difficult to believe that he was so naive at that time. It is more likely that he was pressurised to decide on the spot, that he was confronted with having to decide there and then. They say that, like Clara, he became a Soviet citizen without having a chance to think it over; nor was he able first to discuss it with Olga. Whatever the reason, she was faced with a *fait accompli*.

She was angry and felt betrayed. By this act she felt he was committing himself to a future contrary to the one they had planned together and imposing a pattern of living on her that she did not wish to share.

It was at this point that she decided to return to England. She told Henry that she wanted to visit her family. She was not making this a definitive break; she wanted to test her own feelings. She felt that away from Henry, away from the Soviet Union she would be able to judge what was most important to her, what course her life should take. She was longing to be back in England, even for a while.

At least, that's what she told me later. Perhaps she just could not accept the thought that she might have to leave Henry. Perhaps she hoped some other solution might present itself. But Henry agreed that she should go for a visit. She began to make arrangements to leave and applied for an exit visa. She decided that she would leave in the New Year – definitely in the New Year.

The Accident

In the New Year there was an accident underground at the Metro station where Henry was working. He suffered complicated leg fractures and was hospitalised. The hospitals provided medical care, but were not well served in other ways. Patients needed their relatives to bring in food, to provide clean clothes, and often to help attend to them while they were still in hospital.

Ray was in full-time employment, and Olga felt she could not leave Henry as long as he was hospitalised. She postponed her departure and decided she would stay until he was up and mobile again. She became fully occupied with attending to him, going to and from the hospital every day; and also dealing with the inevitable bureaucratic difficulties of obtaining a subsistence allowance, for his salary was not automatically paid in full while he was unable to work.

Of necessity she was becoming more fluent in Russian – certainly in understanding, if not in speaking. She began working part-time at Zaochnyi which ran university correspondence courses. The students came in twice a year to have practice in speaking and to take their exams. She was liked by the students because she spoke clearly and well.

Henry's fractures took a long time to heal, and it was six months before he left hospital. He was on crutches and still needed a lot of help. 'You know how things drag on when you are looking after someone who is not well,' she said.

But now she could think again about going back to England. It was the summer of 1937. They were going to a dacha in the country for the summer, and after the holidays were over, she decided, she would leave.

Holiday Reminiscences

We had decided to spend the summer in the country near Moscow. Ray was reading the proofs of her book; Betty, her sister, who had come to the USSR on a visit from America, was helping her. Henry was learning to walk on crutches after his accident and a six-month stay in hospital.

The place we chose was so undeveloped that it had not yet been given a name; it was simply called '42nd Kilometre'. The wooden dachas had been built in the midst of a pine forest. Wild strawberries grew in the grassy patches of the uncultivated garden plots, and mushrooms sprang up

116

overnight at the foot of the trees. In the morning we went fishing, and in the hot afternoons we lay under the tall pines which shaded us from the blazing sun.

Natasha, who shared a flat with Ray, and who was a leading translator of English literature into Russian, was visiting. She wanted help with her current translation... Hemingway's 'Death in the Afternoon'. 'How do you translate "rich bitch" and keep the flavour?'

She told us that when she was given Steinbeck's 'Cannery Row' to translate, it was wanted in a hurry, so the first half was given to a translator in Leningrad, while Natasha worked on the second half in Moscow.

The Leningrad translator had sent her portion back to her with a note saying that she liked the book, but could not understand where the title came from – perhaps it was in the second half? She had translated 'Cannery Row' as 'A Quarrel between Canaries'.

We laughed; and Natasha gave me Mayakovsky's poems to read 'to test your Russian'. I started slowly on an easy one. 'What is "good" and what is "bad"?' We did not notice the two little men who came through the gap in the fence where a gate should have been. They were wearing town clothes – dark suits and hats – and carried brief-cases. They asked curtly for Ray. She got up quickly and went into the dacha with them. We fell silent. Betty said, 'They're a long time. I'll go and see what it's all about.'

Now it was getting late, time for our 'domestic' to leave for town to buy provisions for the following day. I helped Henry to get on his crutches and we went onto the veranda, leaving Natasha lying silently on the sweet-scented prickly pine needles.

On the way I stopped to speak to our 'domestic' and give her money and instructions for her shopping. She seemed anxious to leave.

Inside the dacha the floors were scattered with paper and books, and the two men were busy searching in drawers and cupboards, throwing down discarded documents. Ray was pale; she looked tense and shocked. To my question she muttered, 'I've been arrested...'

One of the men shouted to her to be silent. He was putting papers in his *case; and soon they left, walking out through the gap in the fence, this time with Ray between them.*

We watched her get in the car they had left standing on the dirt road beyond the cottages. And that was the last we saw of her for eight years.

A Visit

As in times of plague people shunned the affected families for fear of contagion.

'When Ray was arrested most Russians shunned us,' Olga said. 'We didn't blame them. The same thing happened to all arrested people – their friends were afraid of being watched and interrogated, and kept away. So I didn't phone Larissa; and we remained in the dacha in the country for the rest of the summer, where in any case we had no phone.'

One day, coming back from a walk in the forest, Henry and Olga were surprised to see Sasha and Larissa coming down the lane. They, in turn, seemed to show surprise at meeting Olga and Henry. They said they were just out for a day in the country. 'What a coincidence,' Olga remarked afterwards, 'to have chosen this little-known place, and this lane close to our dacha.

'But of course they had come to see if we were all right, and also to try, in their own way, to warn me that it would be advisable for me to return to England.' It was an act of real friendship. So many people at this time tried to shut themselves off from facing the truth, a denial that in a way made them co-conspirators with the persecutors.

Larissa proved shortly afterwards that she was well aware of what was happening, and knew what precautions one could take.

In her searing book about her years in the gulag Eugenia Ginzburg, a loyal and devoted member of the Communist Party, describes how she was called up for questioning and then dismissed from her job as a teacher. Her mother-in-law, a simple peasant woman, urged her to 'run as fast as you can' to her old village in the country. 'Out of sight, out of mind, the further away the better.' The old woman had experience of secret police in another era and tried very hard to persuade Eugenia to go away.[13]

But Eugenia felt that as a communist she could not run away. She knew she was innocent, and that she had to prove her innocence. Her loyalty and belief in the Party did not save her from eighteen years in the camps. This was the reaction of many loyal party members; convinced that the arrest of a spouse was a deep mistake and would be rectified, they rejected appeals by relatives and friends to disappear for a while – and remained to find the 'mistake' extended to themselves. Guilt by association had become an inevitable part of the process.

When the NKVD went to arrest someone, if they did not find them, they did not try to ascertain where they were. They filled their quota with someone else. Margaret Wettlin writes about her friend Katya who had learned that if people marked down for arrest disappeared in time they were rarely tracked down; and she knew also that when a man was arrested the secret police would come back for his wife, sometimes weeks, sometimes months later. In this way Katya saved the life of a friend by hiding her in her home when the husband had been arrested.

Larissa, too, saved herself by disappearing. It was not long after she and Sasha had gone to the country to give Olga a guarded message that she went to visit her brother in Leningrad and stayed with him for a few days. When she came back to her Moscow flat Sasha was missing. The front door of their flat was sealed with the seal of the NKVD. That should have made her go to make enquiries at their offices. But Larissa was far too aware of what that would mean, and she fled, moving from place to place, staying for short times with different people. Much later, when she felt that the quota of arrests for that period had been filled and that the danger of her own arrest had passed, she returned to the flat and went to the NKVD to claim her belongings.

But she could not find out what had happened to Sasha, and she was never able to trace him. She believed he must have been sent to one of the severe penalty camps where it was said no privileges were allowed and from which no letters came. But why should Sasha, a comparatively minor state employee, be subject to severe penalties? Many believed that these severe penalty camps did not exist, and that the rumour of them was put out as a cover for prisoners whose records had been lost, or who had died under the strain of the harsh treatment, the lack of food and clothing. Or who had been shot soon after their arrest.

So there was never any news of Sasha. Tall, quiet, soft-spoken Sasha. It is unlikely that he survived for long, and only after many years was he 'rehabilitated' – posthumously.

Choosing the Victims

Why Ray?

In March of 1938 the third big show trial took place, the biggest, most important trial of all. By this time the remaining members of the opposition and any semi-independent voices among Stalin's own supporters had been crushed. Now Bukharin, Rykov, Krestinsky – these three who had been members of Lenin's Politbureau, the very backbone of the Bolsheviks, engineers of the revolution, were charged together with eighteen others.

Bukharin was popular and had many supporters. For this reason alone Stalin saw his existence, and that of others who did not fully support him, as a threat to himself and to the whole machinery of state power that he had built up. He had to eliminate them. He would maintain his unchallenged authority by imposing a culture of fear.

By the time of Ray's arrest almost anyone could become a victim. Ray had been teaching government and army officials who were now disappearing into the jails and the labour camps; or were simply being eliminated. Her close relationship with some who were accused of sabotage or treason now jeopardised her own position.

Towards the end of 1938 the arrests had reached extreme limits. Economically, politically, even physically, the machinery of government in all its aspects had become overloaded and could no longer function. Even the inquisitors, even the jailers, were being jailed in their turn. The whole system of arrests and interrogations, of the prisons and the camps, of the personnel needed to keep it functioning, was becoming now too vast to be sustained. In any case the real objective had been achieved: all potential opposition to Stalin had been removed, leading opinion makers in every sphere of life had disappeared, and the whole population was stultified and silenced by fear.

But to search for an answer in particular to 'Why Ray?' is in itself illogical. We want to make sense of what was happening, we want order, logic, reasoning. This is not how state terror works. The very lack of reason invests the operators with their power. To believe that each individual act – such as the arrest of Ray – must have a reasonable explanation is to endow those responsible with logical thought and rational action, which would, in turn, give legitimacy to the Stalin era.

'When Ray was arrested,' Olga said, 'I decided I would not leave at least until we knew what was happening to her. So I stayed.'

Forty Years Later

Many, many years later – in fact it was four decades later, long after Olga had returned to England and I had been forced to leave South Africa and was living in London – I joined her on a week's trip to Moscow, over the New Year. By then Stalin and Stalinism were dead. Henry had died some years before, but Ray was still alive, and she and Natasha still shared a flat. Olga and I went to visit them.

We took a train to a suburban station and walked along icy and empty streets. According to the Russians it was quite warm for that time of the year, only some degrees below freezing, not extreme. I found the air so icy that I had difficulty in breathing.

We came to a dark apartment block, under an archway. The doors were shabby and peeling.

Ray and Natasha, both now retired and living on small pensions, shared a flat with one bedroom, a bathroom with a shower, a tiny kitchen and a living room with bookcases that held hundreds and hundreds of books; worn, used books that had been read and read; and copies, both in English and Russian, of the many that Natasha had translated.

The building was an old one, and in the flat the plaster was peeling off walls and ceilings. There was central heating through old fashioned radiators, but they did not give off sufficient heat; and the electric power was very low. The two women kept themselves warm with rugs.

But as always when visiting Russians, a feast had been prepared for the guests; salad, fish, caviar and *piroshki*. No matter how acute the shortages were nor how cash-strapped our hosts, wherever we went they would set out a lavish and appetising spread. Their hospitality was expansive. We were always made to feel welcome and honoured.

Later, having earlier eaten the delicious snacks, we sat down for a proper meal: *shchi* (cabbage soup) with sour cream, potatoes and *kasha* (porridge), with butter and more sour cream.

Ray was in her seventies, small and rather frail. Natasha seemed sturdier, a square woman with iron-grey hair parted in the middle and drawn into a small bun.

While she was talking to Olga I went into the kitchen with Ray who was preparing the food. I asked her about her years in the labour camps. After she had served eight years she had been released, but later, during the terrible resurgence of post-war arrests she had been re-arrested in 1948 together with hundreds of thousands of others. She was finally released for the second time in 1956.

I told her that I had read Eugenia Ginsberg's two compelling, amazing books about the camps (*Into the Whirlwind* and *Beyond the*

Whirlwind) and she said: 'Then I don't need to tell you anything. It is all there. It could have been my experiences that she was writing about.'

'Everything? The extreme cold, the lack of food, the hardships, the shaving of your heads?'

'Everything. Except that they not only shaved our heads but all our hair. When I was arrested there were 120 of us in a small cell built for twenty-five, sleeping on pallets on the floor, so tightly packed in rows that if you wanted to turn over at night you had to nudge your neighbours to turn over as well.

'There were terribly heavy restrictions and rules. We were given two sewing needles between all of us, to mend our clothes; but no thread. The needles were passed around and we would draw threads from sheets. One day when we were called out for exercise, which was only five or six turns around the yard, I was in a hurry and so rushed that I left the needle behind with a thread in it. This was found, and all books were stopped as a punishment.'

'But why? How could you mend without thread?'

'They said it might have been a secret signal to someone.'

Ray said they lived like this for more than a year while their cases were being considered. Then they were loaded into cattle trucks for their long journey to the camps.

'Sometimes the train stopped for days at a time. We were not permitted to open the doors, even if the train was in open countryside. You could cut the air with a knife. There was a hole in the floor for a latrine.'

They travelled this way for weeks.

Ray's destination was Vorkuta. It was in Siberia, on the borders of the Arctic Ocean. For two thirds of the year the temperature was below zero Celsius, and could drop to fifty-five or even sixty degrees below zero. For a hundred days the *khanovey* – the wind of winds – blew across the tundra.

Ray survived the extreme cold, the hard physical labour, the starvation and scurvy, the cruelties. What saved her was that she had someone to send her parcels with vitamins. They did not always arrive, but some did get through.

She spoke without bitterness, with a wry, literate sense of humour. Her deepest anxiety had been for the safety of her brother, with a feeling of her responsibility if he too should be arrested.

At the time of her first arrest Ray had almost completed a new textbook for students of English: *Advanced English 2*. Olga and Henry arranged for teacher friends to finish it. But Ray was now a non-person and when it was published her name had been erased from the book; instead the authors were cited as Karr, Weiser and Louise Todd.

This was part of a policy of creating non-people. A.N.T. Tupolev was the creator of a type of plane called ANT. When he was arrested the plane was re-christened. A physicist had completed a paper together with four collaborators, and had lectured on it to the Academy of Sciences; when the paper was published it appeared under the names of the only two who had not been arrested.

I met Louise Todd in Moscow in 1997 when I was researching Olga's past. When I was introduced to her I was struck not only by her English name but by her very English appearance. She was a relation of a well-known Rhodesian, Garfield Todd. She was tall and slim, her grey hair neatly drawn back. It was only when she spoke – fluent English but with a definite Russian accent – that I realised she had been born and brought up in the Soviet Union.

Louise's mother came from New Zealand. I do not know what brought her to the USSR, but there she formed a relationship with a Russian man, and Louise was born. Her mother's lover left her; without any money she was unable to return to New Zealand with her small daughter. Then came the war, and so travel was no longer possible.

Louise had grown up and studied English and become a teacher and translator. Her name, and that of two other Soviet citizens were put on

Ray's book when it was published, but later – in 1947 when Stalin's campaign against 'cosmopolitanism' had begun – the book had been banned.

We visited other friends of my sister. Her main teaching years had been the war years, and for this reason, with only one or two exceptions, her students had all been young women – now mothers and grandmothers. I tried to imagine them as young people in their late teens and early twenties together with Olga in that far time – it all seemed too remote, too many years in between.

Another visit was to Tidinov, a close friend who had been an actor in the Moscow Arts Theatre. Olga said he was good to her. During the war, when Henry was working at night and she was alone in the flat with no electricity, no light and little heating, he would come and sit with her in the dark to keep her company.

I spoke to Grisha who had been another of her students and later, when he qualified as a teacher in English, a colleague. At his home there was a wonderful feast. Two kinds of yeast bread like little cakes, one filled with cabbage, the other with cream cheese; tinned fish, cods' liver, mushrooms and paprika salad, followed by duck and rice, and then a meringue pie.

'Your sister was so brave,' her friends all told me. 'When everyone else was scared to go to any authority, she would go, and demand to find out about Ray.'

'I wasn't brave,' Olga said. 'I was crazy, absolutely crazy. I thought my British passport protected me. I thought because I was born in England and had a British passport and had never been a communist, was not politically motivated, that I led a charmed life and could do what I liked and the British would look after me. I thought I could leave any time I wanted to and nothing would happen to me. But of course it wasn't so. But I only found that out years later.'

Olga visited Ray and Natasha and her friends in Moscow several times, always returning laden with gifts. I have one of these, a small wooden table painted black with traditional patterns of orange and gold, as a reminder of her life, and of those times.

Butyrka

After her arrest at the dacha in the summer of 1937, Ray was taken by car to her Moscow apartment which was searched. She took a few items of underwear and a handbag. She was suffering from shock, and not thinking clearly, for though she was only wearing a sleeveless summer dress, she did not take any warm clothes.

It was some coincidences that brought me Ray's own description of what happened to her after her arrest, told in a lengthy interview that she had with a journalist. This in turn had been made possible by profound changes in government in the Soviet Union

In March 1985 Mikhail Gorbachov was elected General Secretary of the Communist Party of the Soviet Union. He set about a programme of *perestroika* – in effect what he himself described as a policy of restructuring and of animating social and economic progress. It was the beginning of the breakdown of the long and disastrous Stalinist era and made possible much greater freedom for the press. A group of journalists decided to interview victims of the Stalin regime.

Olga's friend Irina Vosolova made contact with a young historian and journalist, Lazarevna Shcherbakova, who came to interview her about her brother Leonid; and then Irina took her to meet Ray with whom she had a lengthy interview.

Shcherbakova did not publish these interviews, but permitted Irina to translate them from Russian into English and pass them on to me.

Ray had been brought to Butyrka, the central prison in Moscow, where she was stripped and her body searched. Then she was taken to a cell.

It was originally meant for twenty-five but now nearly a hundred women were packed in so closely that there was no place for her to sit down.

A woman of about twenty-four beckoned to me and said, 'Come here,' and she moved a little to make room for me.

She was beautiful, with wonderful hair and large eyes. Her name was Ida. She told me that she was worried about her two-year-old daughter whom she had left with her parents. She was married to a young Canadian communist who had come to Russia to study; he had been sent to Rumania, where he was arrested. She had had no news of him since his arrest. She had learnt a little English from her husband and as time went by in the cell, I offered to teach her English. We had no pencil or paper, so with a match I would write English letters on a cake of soap.

After a month I was interrogated for the first time. The officer in charge said, 'You have got back to your business, haven't you?'

'What do you mean?'

'We have been informed that you have resumed teaching English in your cell.'

'Is it forbidden to teach English in prison? I'm a teacher, it is natural for me to teach. Lenin studied foreign languages when he was in prison.'

The interrogator made no comment.

A woman in the cell asked me about my case. I had not seen her before. I told her that I came to Russia to teach English, and that I was accused of being a spy. 'Don't worry,' she said, 'you'll be sentenced to five years.' 'Why should I be sentenced to five years? How can an innocent person be sentenced to five years?'

'Unfortunately, this is what is likely to happen.'

I was told by others in the cell that this woman had many times disappeared and then returned to the cell. She was a lawyer, and the other women felt that probably, after her arrest, she had agreed to assist the secret police.

There was a Bulgarian woman who had come to the Soviet Union and had been arrested. She was good-looking, full of energy, and proud of being a communist. She kept saying, 'I don't understand anything. People in Bulgaria are sometimes arrested by mistake, and in two days they are released. I have been here for three months. They say I have done something wrong. Don't they see that I am a communist, I have always been on the side of the communists.'

Ray had long, thick hair which was difficult to brush, and she did not have a comb and had to borrow one. One day, when they were being led to the toilet, she saw a man cutting a male prisoner's hair. She obtained permission for him to cut her hair. He said he had never cut a woman's hair, so he gave her a man's haircut.

Ray was told she was allowed to receive fifty roubles a month from a relative in two separate instalments. She could buy things from the prison shop. She bought cigarettes and matches, some bread – about 300-400 grams; and the shop also sold *kasha*, tea, onions, and very bad quality cucumbers. That was all.

Prisoners were allowed to borrow one book from the library each month.

Books helped us a great deal. Sometimes we were lucky to get really good books. Anything was liable to cause punishment. For breaking a rule, we would not be allowed to take books from the library. Once, when I came back to the cell from the washroom, I left my soap there. All the women in our cell were punished by being deprived of books for a month. 'You left the soap on purpose,' they said. 'It was a sign for those who came to the toilet.'

The toilet was a problem that made me suffer very much. We had to empty a latrine bucket used by ninety people. I was very grateful to Ida. She would do it for me when it was my turn.

There were six or seven holes over which we had to squat. We were allowed about twelve minutes. Because of lack of exercise we suffered very much. We felt wretched and humiliated. Some women tried to exercise in the cell. The moment they started raising their arms or bending, the door opened. 'What are you doing here?' Exercising looked suspicious. It might be something dangerous, a conspiracy.

I was told to come for interrogation. A man of about thirty-five began to question me.

'You are accused of espionage. Tell us everything.'

'What country do you think I was spying for?'

'For England, of course.'

'Why do you think that? I have never been there.'

'What do you mean by saying you have never been to England? You teach English, don't you? You used to have a foreign passport. Then why do you say you have never been to England? What passport did you have?'

'American.'

'And you didn't used to be an English citizen?'

'No.'

'Oh, I see. It doesn't make any difference.'

The interrogation lasted about an hour. Ray refused to speak about things she didn't know about. In a month she was called for again. Once more the officer failed to make her speak. Why could she not admit she was guilty? She said that as she had not committed any crime she had nothing to confess to. Two months passed, it was autumn, and she was called again. She was told to stand up, and that she would have to stand until she had answered his questions. She stood for three days and three nights. Hundreds of times she was asked to speak, but refused. She told him again and again that his accusations were made up, she didn't know what he wanted her to speak about.

'Stop your fucking speeches!' he shouted.

I had never heard the word 'fucking'. My Russian was limited.

She was watched all the time, questioned, shouted at. She was not allowed to go to the toilet. She became dizzy and fainted. When she regained consciousness she found they had poured water over her; she was lying in a pool of water. They dragged her to her feet and she stood for about ten minutes, then collapsed again.

She told her interrogator that she could not stand any more, her blood vessels would break. He said 'They have already broken.'

She was taken to a basement cell – solitary confinement. There was a bed, and she slept a long time. When a man came with some bread and hot water, she said she did not want it.

'Take it,' he said, 'don't refuse it. You will need it later on.'

At that moment I heard the voice of a human being. 'Take it… You will need it later on.' He was right. I did eat the bread later, and drink the water.

My legs were in a very bad condition.

She was taken to a hospital for some time. Eventually she was taken back to the big cell. Ida looked after her, washed her clothes and mended them with a thread pulled from her towel. She was unable to walk for a long time. She received money regularly and shared what she bought at the kiosk with other women who had no money.

She loved poetry and knew many poems by heart, which she recited to the women.

I like listening to people, many found it important to tell others about themselves. People are in need of sympathy.

Sometimes she would be called again for interrogation. She was told she would be shot. She said she was not afraid of anything he could do, and would never write about things she had never done.

He told me that both my brother and his wife had been arrested. I asked him if he would tell my parents what had happened. He said 'Your parents are also arrested.' I knew he was lying, because my parents were in America.

Ida told Ray that her interrogator had said: 'You will soon see your daughter.' Ida felt she was going to be released. Eventually Ida was told to take her things and come. None of the women in the cell knew what had happened to her. But some time later a chance meeting in a bakery between Olga and Ida would shed some light on her release.

My leg became worse. I was unable to get up. I was given an old basin as I couldn't go to the toilet. The woman lying next to me took it to the toilet. I gave her my portion of bread. She needed it badly, she was suffering from hunger.

When they stopped questioning me I felt better. We often recited poems to each other. Eventually they forced me to sign a paper without reading it. I was no longer asked any questions, but I did not tell them anything. I was told: five years.

The winter was over. It was May 1939. Ray and other women prisoners were being sent from the prison to the camps in Siberia.

It was not easy to part with some of the women in the cell with whom she had become friendly. She gave one friend, a meteorologist, who had left earlier, a small gift; after she went Ray found a pair of wonderful woollen stockings that her friend had left for her.

We were going north, but nevertheless we saw that spring was approaching. We went by train for some way, then by boat. On the train I slept in the lower bunk, because I could not climb to the upper one. Zelma Fedorovna Ruoff slept on the bunk above me. She was German but she had lived in Russia a long time, and Russian was her mother-tongue. She was very well educated, had read a lot, and knew and appreciated Russian poetry. Later on, in the camp, she slept on the bunk above me, and sometimes would lean over and ask: 'Ray, dear, do you remember the second line of the third verse of this poem?'

They were taken to Vorkuta and housed in wooden barracks.

There I met criminals and 'urkas' for the first time. My dressing gown that had been sent from home was stolen. A little later my gloves were stolen. It was very cold and my hands were frozen. I was lucky to have a little kettle. One of the urkas near me asked to borrow the kettle, which I lent her. When she returned the kettle I told her my fingers were swollen and hurt because my gloves had been stolen. 'Where did you keep your gloves?' 'Under my pillow.' 'That was foolish.' In the evening she brought me back my gloves. 'You did not refuse us when we asked to borrow your kettle.'

The doctor at the camp – he was also a convict – said that because of her leg, she should be given work which she could be done seated. At first she had to straighten used nails with a hammer. *(Frankly speaking I did not do it well.)*

She was told to make baskets out of willow reeds, sitting in a barn, on the floor; with no light except candles.

The working day began at six, and lasted until it was dark. We could not stand the way the urkas talked. Their language was nauseating even when they joked; it hurt us, drove us to despair. But later I understood that they found it just as unbearable to associate with political prisoners. I overheard two urkas speaking in the washroom – they did not see me enter. One of them said, 'These political prisoners are disgusting. I hate to live so close to them.'

It was autumn, and it was already very cold. Five long winters in Vorkuta lay ahead of her.

Queues

For the family of an arrested man, the period of waiting was taken up by routine steps… such as obtaining money, and standing in line with packages. From the length of the lines we could see how things stood in our world: in 1934 they were still quite short.

Nadezhda Mandelstam, *Hope Against Hope, A Memoir* (Collins Harvill, 1989)

In 1938 the Moscow queues were long.

Relatives were not told where the one who had been arrested had been taken. In Moscow the way to find the prisoner was for the wife (at first it was the wives although many of them would themselves in turn become victims) or nearest relative to go to the 'Information Centre' opposite the Lubyanka prison at 24 Kuznetsky Most. Then they would begin a round of the prisons in search of information: to Sokol'niki, then to Taganka, then to the office of the Butyrka in a small courtyard; then to the Lefortovo military prison; and back again. The largest prison was the Butyrka, where Ray had been held. At the height of the purge it held 30,000 prisoners.

Those prisoners who had not yet been convicted were entitled to receive fifty roubles a month; so when you reached the head of the queue, you would ask the official to accept the money and a parcel for the prisoner. If refused the likelihood was that your relative was not in that prison. This was not a sure sign, but if the parcel was accepted it could be assumed that you had located the right prison. Sometimes it was necessary to do the round a second, even a third time.

There is a much-quoted episode in the writings of the poet Anna Akhmatova:

'I spent seventeen months in lines outside Leningrad prisons. One day someone recognised me. Then a woman standing behind me with blue lips… woke from the stupor in which we were sunk, and spoke into my ear (for there we spoke only in whispers): "Can you describe all this?" "I can," I said. Then something like a smile slipped over what had once been her face.'[14]

Henry, although not yet fully mobile, was back at work. Olga was only working part time. Her life became a round of standing in queues, of waiting outside the offices of officials who might have information, of trying to find out where Ray was being held, whether she would be brought to trial, what she would be charged with. Hours, days, weeks of standing in queues, of waiting to see, of pleading with those in authority.

Lidiya Ginzburg wrote: 'A queue is an assembly of people, doomed to a compulsory idle and internally isolated communality. Idleness… is just misery, punishment (prison, queue, waiting to be received)…Very few people read in a queue, even a newspaper… The psychology of the queue is based on a tense, wearing anxiety to reach the end; this weariness excludes everything else that might relieve it. The mental state of a person standing in a long queue is usually not fit for any other occupation.'[15]

Years later, long after Ray had served her sentence, Olga wrote about one of the days she had spent in a queue.

Braude

After the war, when the trials of the German war criminals were due to start in Nuremberg, radio speakers blared out the details. Among the names of eminent lawyers taking part was a name I involuntarily echoed: 'Braude!'

Ray looked at me and said nothing. (Dear Ray, in all the years she was my big sister-in-law, she only asked one awkward question, and that was months later.) But I explained:

'I went to see him, to ask him to take your case.'

Ray said: 'His wife was in prison with us; in the same cell, in the Butyrka prison. She was a blowzy creature who sat apart from us all.'

'How could the wife of a man like Braude be in prison?'

'That's what surprised us. We wondered if she was a stooge. She was still there when I was sent to the camps.'

My mind went back to the day when Natasha had come round with the news: 'There's a lawyer who takes up old cases for exiles. He seems to be able to get them reviewed. They say he's even managed to get some sentences reversed.'

We discussed how to interest him in Ray's case and it was decided that I should go and plead with him. I protested: 'In my bad Russian!' But no-one else could go. Natasha wasn't family. It was too risky for Henry, but my obvious 'foreignness' should protect me.

I went to see Braude. It was one of those biting winter days in Moscow when the cold seems to creep through your buttonholes, the moisture freezes stingingly in your nostrils and the day ends at three o'clock in the afternoon. I had wanted to be inconspicuous and look like a Russian. Hopeless. The frost was too severe and I had to be warmly dressed, and my cold-weather clothes were clearly foreign. I didn't wait for a tram. I'd freeze. Besides, a brisk walk would steady my nerves.

Braude had his office on the third floor of a tall old building, one of a row that had once been elegant but now looked shabby and neglected, with peeling stucco and no paint. Inside it was dingy but warm, with the familiar smell of old Russian buildings in winter – no ventilation, too much smoke, and too many people in too little space. The lobby was crowded, and the stairs too. So many people were sitting and standing on them that there was hardly room to walk through. As usual no one would move, and there were grumbles and angry retorts from those who were asked.

The outer door of Braude's office was open, and his secretary was sitting in the small ante-room. A few chairs were all occupied by men and women waiting to see Braude and the line extended beyond the door and down the stairs to the first floor. I joined the seemingly endless queue.

The whole day was spent gradually moving up the stone stairs to Braude's office, looking at the sad faces of the men and women who were waiting to plead for their beloved ones, and listening to their pathetic stories. Every few minutes another applicant emerged from the office, came slowly down the stairs and the next in the queue went in.

Hours passed; the windows were dark blue, then black squares in the dirty grey walls. At last I was outside the door. The person before me was inside for only moments. It was my turn.

Braude, a middle-aged man with a hard expression, was sitting at a desk placed directly facing the door. He was writing, and I stood and waited for him to finish. He looked up and asked briefly what I wanted.

I started to speak and he went on writing – I told him of Ray's arrest, of her months in prison with no charges against her, of how she had been sentenced without trial to eight years in a labour camp, of her illness, and how unfit she was for a life in the Arctic. He didn't help by asking questions, but let me go on until I finally faltered and then stopped and waited for his verdict. Did he believe it was all a mistake? Would he take up her case? Could he bring her back from the Arctic Circle, if only for the trial she never had?

He didn't seem to have taken any notice of me, and I felt furious. We had pinned so many hopes on my interview. I had stood all day waiting to see this man and now I was here he had hardly even noticed me.

Finally, he stopped writing. Slowly he looked up at me – from my white fur hat down to my white boots and back again to my flushed cheeks. Then quietly, in an emotionless voice:

'Are you always faithful to your husband?'

Zachem?

By the end of 1938 the purge was losing momentum. With the trial of Bukharin and others no one was left at the top who could possibly challenge Stalin.

I asked myself and others, what for?' said the Soviet author, Ilya Ehrenburg. 'No one could give me an answer.' *Zachem?* – Why? Was found written on cell walls, carved into the sides of prison wagons and on the planks of the transit camps. It was the over-riding question from which other questions arose.[16]

Why, when they stood up in an open court, did men like Bukharin confess to being spies and agents of foreign capitalist powers and why did they not repudiate their false 'confessions' openly when they had the opportunity?

Why had these men, themselves at the top of the political ladder, become subject to the will of one man, who was himself neither the most popular nor the most intelligent of the Soviet leaders, who Lenin had warned the Party against in his last will? The question why? merges with another question – how? How was he able to concentrate such total power in his hands alone? How did he manage to build up such a vast army of men – police, interrogators (who themselves were aware of the falsity of their interrogations) and all those others associated with operating this fearful murder machine, to take part in the macabre fiction that their victims were all part of a conspiracy to destroy the Soviet regime, under the direction of the British, Americans and others? Then the most basic of questions arises: How did these men go home to their wives and children each night – as in Germany did the administrators and operators of Hitler's 'final solution' – how were they able to live with themselves?

And why, when Stalin had finally removed and put to death almost all of the old Bolsheviks, had consolidated his supreme position and surrounded himself with acolytes, did he then choose to continue his destructive purge against millions of others, relatives, co-workers of those he had eliminated, ordinary people who were not in a position to do him any harm or to challenge him?

Robert Conquest writes of the incredibility, the problem of understanding how these old Bolsheviks with impeccable revolutionary credentials, who had been imprisoned under the Tsar, who had fought in the civil war, getting up in an open courtroom and confessing to a plot to murder Stalin and others, declaring themselves to be agents of foreign powers, condemning themselves for 'contemptible treachery' – calling themselves not only murderers but fascist murderers. He suggests they must have yielded to pressures that were not only physical but psychological, and were the culmination of a whole series of submissions to the Party.[17]

In the trials of the old Bolsheviks, apart from prolonged interrogations – cold, hunger, bright lights, sleeplessness, torture and other physical mistreatment – there were bribes. Bukharin, desperate at the end and aware of his certain fate, agreed to 'confess' if Stalin would save the life of his wife and son. Their lives were spared – but his wife was arrested, and his infant son eventually sent to an NKVD orphanage.

There must have been other such bargains made. But these promises were rarely honoured. The families of those executed were almost always shot, the youngest children taken to orphanages.

We should not forget that there were many who never confessed, or who repudiated their confessions when the torture ceased; but these were never brought to court and to a public trial.

In 1935 Bukharin, who had been denouncing Stalin's 'insane ambition' was asked why, in that case, the oppositionists had surrendered to him. He replied with considerable emotion: 'You don't understand, it is not that at all. It is not *him* we trust but the man in whom the Party has reposed its confidence… He has become a symbol of the Party.' And a year later he said it had become 'difficult, if not impossible for us to live' but felt saved 'by faith that development is always going forward. Like a stream that is running – if one leans out one is ejected completely; the stream goes through difficult places, but still goes forward.' Party discipline, the absolute submission to the party leadership had instilled this attitude; the party loyalists could see no possibilities of changing things, no future except within the party. The party was supreme, and Stalin had made himself the embodiment of the party. His old comrades had underestimated his ruthlessness, his determination and his cunning.

There was also the attitude of capitalist countries. There were indeed Western spies. The Western powers *did* desire the overthrow of socialism and were prepared to resort to any means to achieve the return of a capitalist society, so that the Soviet regime, Communist Party members and others felt themselves constantly beleaguered. The choice was a stark one between two systems, capitalism and socialism. This is why many communist leaders from other countries who worked in or had contacts with the Comintern, and who became aware of what was happening, kept quiet. The revelation of reality would condemn not only Stalin, not only the Soviet regime, but – in the eyes of the world – socialism itself. In a sense it meant repudiating their whole past, shattering their own lifetime beliefs. To them the fault was not with the concept of socialism; and they believed that as long as they stayed in their posts they could help to change the situation within their leadership. It was no new dilemma, and arises – less starkly – within our own democratic societies: stay within a government or organisation where you believe you can help change things, or isolate yourself and become totally powerless to effect change.

There was the personality of Stalin himself. E.H. Carr writes that his strength lay in the rigid management of the party machine which controlled appointments to key posts; his approval was a sure avenue to advancement. Thus he gathered round himself a body of faithful henchmen whose political fortunes were linked with his and who owed him unquestioning personal allegiance. He was regarded by ordinary people as the man who led all the new industrial enterprises; and he did have a complete commitment to the industrialisation and modernisation of the economy which appealed to Marxists; and a commitment to a revival of Russian power and prestige which appealed to the army, to bureaucrats and the technological elite, and to all survivors of the old regime who had entered into the service of the new.

But in addition to his lust for total power, absolute control, there was his cruelty: he was a pervert, a sadist who enjoyed humiliating others, deceiving them, pretending to be generous, kind, forgiving one day – and having them shot the next morning. His pleasure was found in his certainty of supreme power, his capacity to exercise it over all others, in playing with others and then destroying them; a monstrous cat whose mice were human beings.

While Stalin's portrait always appeared side by side with Lenin's, Carr writes that he was completely different to Lenin. Stalin had a form of vanity totally alien to Lenin: it demanded absolute obedience and the recognition of infallibility. He could permit no covert criticism; no expression of dissent was allowed to appear in the party press or journals. He became a remote and isolated figure, exalted above ordinary mortals. Unlike other dictators, familiar both in the past and in modern times, who use their power to amass enormous personal wealth, spending millions on palaces, clothes, luxuries, Stalin had no desire to live ostentatiously. He dressed in a plain brown military coat and lived unpretentiously. But he fostered the cult of the personality; his picture appeared on every hoarding, his bust was carried to the peak of every Soviet mountain by alpinists, he was decorated with every medal. On his fiftieth birthday in 1929 he was lauded as unsurpassed. He was supreme. And it was enticing; he became the glorious leader, commanding love and loyalty that was injected into children from their nursery school days.

Many victims of his cruel purges believed to the end that Stalin himself did not know what was happening, that those others who were responsible were keeping him in ignorance.

Robert Service wrote: 'The Jews and gypsies that were exterminated by Hitler knew that they were dying because they were Jews and gypsies. Stalin's terror was more chaotic and confusing: thousands went to their deaths shouting out their fervent loyalty to Stalin.'[18]

And finally there are the people, those among the people who see and know but must deny what they see; some because of fear for themselves, some because to recognise, to admit, would rob them of the structures on which they have always built their lives. If you have lived through many years of deprivation and hardship with the conviction that all sacrifices are for a finer future, for greater happiness for all, how can you face this great emptiness, the loss of all you lived for? To what can you then cling? It is easier to deny reality. It is easier to stay together than to go against the tide. And the intimidation was total, the price of protest too high, a threat to life itself. So through their silence, their turning away people become complicit, they become participants in the process.

*

Towards the end of 1938 the arrests were slowing down, but they did not cease. And by then an immense primitive industry had been developed that guaranteed employment for torturers, jailers, informers, stenographers, van drivers, executioners, grave-diggers and camp guards, all of whom now had a vested interest in the continuation of arrests and in the gulags.

Rumours of War

That was a grim time, the winter of 1938 to 1939, not only in the Soviet Union. The British Prime Minister, Neville Chamberlain, with his moustache and bowler hat and black umbrella waving a piece of paper proclaiming 'peace in our time' had, fatally, brought war nearer to the West. His piece of paper in fact gave a free hand to Adolf Hitler to go ahead with his plans.

Hitler's bid for German expansion had opened in March 1936 when he sent his armies into the Rhineland.

The Rhineland was a demilitarized zone under the terms of the First World War peace settlement, and Hitler was intent on its reintegration with Germany. When some 60,000 German soldiers and armed police entered the Rhineland, Hitler waited for Britain and France's response. Neither country took action. Many British politicians argued that the Germans were simply recovering their own territory. France did nothing.

Thereafter Spain became the touchstone. In 1936 a military uprising against a newly elected democratic government in Spain was headed by the fascist General Franco and supported by Germany and Italy. Germany's Condor Legion, units from the budding *Luftwaffe*, used Spain as a testing ground for new bombing techniques – valuable experience for use in the world war to come. Britain and France deprived the legitimate government of the means to fight Franco by placing an embargo on the supply of arms; only the USSR supplied arms to the government. Sensing the significance of the defeat of democracy in Spain the refusal of Western democracies to take a stand against fascism could only be explained as a preference for a fascist dictatorship over the idea of support for a left-wing government – even if elected. Political allegiances were polarised and hardened. And Hitler, unrestricted, felt that he could push forward with his territorial ambitions.

The feeling of impending disaster hung over Europe, but nobody seemed to be able to make a move to divert it.

Early in 1938 German troops entered Austria as part of their overall plan for a Greater Germany. Austrians welcomed the Germans, and the

Anschluss - annexation - of Austria opened the doors for German ascendancy in Eastern Europe.

Hitler now used the excuse that a fifth of the population of Czechoslovakia were German to turn his attention to incorporating the Sudetenland into the Greater Germany. Chamberlain's 'peace in our time' was an agreement to acknowledge Czechoslovakia's redrawn frontiers. The Czechs had become expendable.

An attack on Poland now seemed imminent. Hitler had a non-aggression pact with Poland, but abandoned it. A stupor seemed to pervade the West, a dark feeling of the inevitability of a terrible war. Poland stood between two powerful, military nations – Germany and the USSR. The only nation standing in the way of the conquest of Poland was the USSR.

My sister must have been aware in a general way of the danger of war, but she could not yet read Russian newspapers nor follow the local radio; and she was not focused on the external drama – there was enough tension and anxiety in her own, personal life.

She had not anticipated spending so many winters in Russia. Even in good times they were too long, too harsh. By late October winter had begun. By December and January it seemed as though there never was, never could be, any other season in the world but winter. The sun rose faintly after nine, and the light was already fading by two in the afternoon. In the brief days bereft of sun, the unceasing curtain of snow, the falling light, the icy winds – the very pulse of life was numbed.

February was the darkest month, the longest to endure, when the thought of two more months before the coming of spring was almost unbearable. Everyone longed for spring, and spring came late to Moscow that year. The sombre clouds did not lift until well into April. Piles of snow, soiled and grey, clung to the streets.

When summer came Ray was finally sentenced – without trial – to five years in a labour camp. Now Olga felt there was nothing more she could do by staying. Made more anxious by the prospects of war in Europe, she began to make arrangements to go on her long-postponed visit to England. She needed to wind up her teaching jobs and obtain an exit visa. Inevitably there were bureaucratic delays.

In August the Soviet government felt they were getting nowhere in their talks with the West. Poland continued to be intransigent about not permitting Soviet forces to enter Poland – for how else could the Russians guarantee support against a Nazi invasion? – and Britain's dilatory attitude brought the threat of invasion very close. Stalin abandoned his search for collective security and shocked the world by signing a non-aggression pact with Germany. It committed both countries to settle differences through negotiation; and to neutrality should either country become involved in war with third parties.

What was not revealed at the time was that, in addition to the published text of the agreement, there was a secret protocol that partitioned Poland – western Poland to Germany and eastern Poland to the Soviet Union. In effect the secret clauses gave Germany a free hand to invade Poland while the Soviet Union stood by.

A Birthday Party

When summer finally arrived it was hot and oppressive. At the beginning of August Olga had obtained her visa and was ready to leave, but some visitors arrived from England, and she delayed her departure to show them around Moscow. When they left she was ready at last for her own departure.

The day before she was due to leave was her birthday. Her friends organised a joint farewell and birthday party for her at the Hotel Metropol. Some of them were going to the Caucasus on holiday the next day. 'Why don't you come with us?' they urged.

'But you know I'm leaving tomorrow.'

'A couple of weeks won't make that much difference. Come and join us! You can always leave two or three weeks later. And when will you be able to see the Caucasus again?'

It was like a challenge to ignore the sombre situation, an invitation to be reckless and light-hearted; to carry away with her the sun, the scents, the many gifts of the Black Sea in summer.

She left for the Caucasus with her friends the next morning. Her birthday was August 31. The year was 1939.

On September 1 Hitler invaded Poland. Two days later Britain and France declared war on Germany.

*

The train journey to Novyi Afon took three days and two nights. 'We had no news of the outside world on the train,' Olga said. 'It was packed with holiday-makers. And we arrived at Afon at midnight and had to spend the night on a bench in pitch darkness waiting for the dawn, so that we could see to find our way to the monastery.' The monastery, set in spacious gardens, was now a holiday house.

The long summer was just nearing its end, the golden time when grapes hung ripe to be picked.

An avenue of laurel trees ran up to the monastery – they called it 'lovers' lane'. There were cypresses and olive groves and a waterfall. At night they danced by moonlight in the monastery garden to the music of an accordion. The popular tune of that time was: *We'll meet again in Lvov, my love and I.*

'All passenger trains were taken off and there was no way of getting back from the Caucasus. I couldn't have got to Europe anyway. I would have had to travel round the world the other way, to the far east and from there gone across to America. I didn't know if it was possible, or if I could have got back to England.'

CHAPTER 3

Warm Clothes and Vitamins

THE money that prisoners received always had to be divided into two parts, each sent separately; a small amount was always added, or more usually deducted, by the authorities from the money. According to Olga this deduction – or occasionally addition – to the amount sent was to prevent any coded message that might be conveyed through the sending of a re-arranged number of roubles.

By this time the numbers of prisoners had risen exponentially. The whole machinery connected with the camps was becoming clogged. You have to think of the vast distances from the authorities in the centre, in Moscow, to the arctic wastes of Siberia, and that Siberia was a region unable to supply even itself with many of the fundamentals that humans needed to live or to exist.

Everything had to be brought by train; not only the prisoners themselves but also those who would guard them and those in charge of the guards. With so many prisoners, such extensive camps, the scale of what was needed to sustain this huge new population with the basics of life was enormous. There had to be huts for the prisoners, houses for those in charge. And not only housing for this vast population but tools and building materials, machinery, hospitals.

So many people were trying to send food from Moscow to their relatives in Siberia that a ban was placed on the despatch of parcels from the Moscow area. Olga and Henry had been sending parcels to Ray. How could she manage without the warm clothes and vitamins she so badly needed for her second winter in the Arctic labour camp?

Then Olga and Natasha heard that a certain number of parcels could be sent from Vladimir, an ancient town about 200 kilometres away. It was a direct ride in a local train. But they had been warned that only twenty parcels a day were accepted, so they would have to be amongst the first in the queue when the Post Office opened.

They devised a plan.

Parcels

We had met at the Northern Station, leaving home at dawn and walking all the way as we were too early for public transport. And we each carried a ten kilogram parcel.

The journey had been agony. The train was packed and the heat stifling. I sat with my eyes glued on the ragged old peasant sitting opposite me. Did he know there were lice crawling on his jacket? Fascinated, I watched a large one reach his neck and disappear inside his collar, followed by a small one. But he paid no attention.

We realised the people in the crowded train were also taking parcels to be posted, and that we could not run with ours; so Natasha would go ahead to establish her place in the queue, and I must somehow transport both parcels to the Post Office before her turn came.

'You're sure you can manage?'

'Yes,' I lied, 'I'm sure I can.'

Natasha jumped from the train before it stopped, crossed the line, and ran off down a dusty footpath towards the town. With difficulty I manipulated the two heavy parcels off the high train onto the bare boards that were the platform, and tried to find help in transporting them to the Post

Office. Desperately I saw the train steam out and the crowd of passengers disappear in the direction of the town.

'Carry your parcels?'

Two little boys came up to me. They looked about nine or ten years old, undersized, ragged and dirty. One was covered in festering sores, the other looked far too small even to lift such a heavy load, and I realised with a shock that he was blind. I said: 'They're too heavy for you.' But to prove me wrong the little blind boy picked up one of the parcels and started to run with it. The boy with the sores picked up the other, and we were off. It was a nightmare. The blind boy kept stumbling on the uneven path, but when he fell he clutched the parcel tightly and I could not take it from him. The other boy ran on ahead. I dared not hold him back, I was afraid to touch him. But I was equally afraid that if he ran too far he would run off altogether with the parcel, which was worth far more than the money I would give him for carrying it. So I ran between, calling the first one back and picking up the little one when he fell down.

I felt Natasha had the better of the bargain, until I got to the Post Office. There had been a fight to get in, but she had managed it, and there she was, red-faced and dishevelled, but well up in the queue. Ours were the last parcels to be accepted that day, and we left the Post Office clutching the precious receipts in our sticky hands, with the queue behind us arguing, cajoling, and finally cursing when they found they were not able to send their parcels.

The heat hit us as we walked out into the street, and we tried to find the market so that we could get something to quench our thirst. But the wooden stalls in the market place were empty. There was nothing left to buy; everything had been sold and everyone had gone; and we, too, left the town to walk back to the station.

Months later, one of the parcels was 'returned to sender', with the bottle of vitamin juice smashed inside a sheepskin boot. And months later still came the letter from Ray that said, among other news:

'The matches were particularly useful this time.'

By arrangement, the fourth item on the list of the goods that we had sent was a 'special'. And so we knew that the thirty-rouble note, neatly folded under the false bottom of the matchbox, had been found, and was welcome.

Ida

The unknown voice asked 'Is that Olya?'

'Yes; who is that?'

The woman at the other end of the telephone ignored the question and asked, 'Is Henry's leg better?'

'Yes.'

'Is he *free*?'

'Yes, he is – please, tell me who you are.'

'I've come from where Ray is,' said the soft voice. 'Listen to what I am telling you. When Henry goes to give money next time, tell him not to send two lots, just one. One only. Give just half of it in one go.'

'But why? It won't be enough for her. How is she? Where are you? When may we see you?'

The caller did not reply to Olga's urgent questions. 'If he gives only one lot of money, Ray will understand and know that he is all right. Do as I say.'

'Please,' Olga pleaded, 'tell me where you are. We'll come anywhere if you can't come to us; or meet you anywhere!'

'I can't explain. Don't forget, only one payment on the first of the month. I'll phone you again.'

Henry handed in the single packet of money. A small amount was returned as usual.

And Ray sent a card from her camp on the Arctic circle: 'When I received the one amount after Ida had left I felt everything was OK with you.'

But Ida never phoned again.

And then, totally by chance, they met her.

They had gone to a shop in Gorki Street that was always tremendously crowded because they baked bread and piroshki on the premises and sold them piping hot. Henry negotiated the three long queues that operated in all the shops, from counter to cash-desk and back to counter again to show the receipt and collect the bread. Olga stood to one side, watching the crowds, and waited.

She heard someone say her name: 'Olya.' She looked up. There was no one she knew in sight – it must be another Olga, she thought. Then she heard the soft voice again, and near her saw a young woman looking directly at her. She was exceptionally lovely, with large violet eyes, dark curly hair and a Russian pink and white skin. Now she had caught Olga's attention, the stranger nodded her head towards Henry, who was in the queue to pay for the bread. She said, 'He looks so much like his sister!' And her eyes filled with tears.

Olga asked, 'But why did you never get in touch with us again? We were so anxious to see you. How could you let us worry so much when you could have given us news of Ray?'

By this time Henry, holding the hot bread, had joined them. Olga said, 'It's Ida.' and he knew at once.

Ida looked around nervously. 'Let's talk outside,' she said.

Out in the street she said, 'I couldn't get in touch with you. It's better so. And I can't see you now.'

'But why?'

Finally she said, 'The man who was my investigator visits me. It's better for you not to know where I live, or to see me again. If ever I can, I will contact you.'

Dora in 1915 with Vera (left), Olga (right) and holding Hilda.

Hilda, Vera and Olga picking wild flowers.

Simeon - taken in the USSR.

Vera and Hilda wearing Russian head-scarves gifts from their father.

Petropavlosk, May 1927.

Simeon in Kamchatka.

Olga in 1935 - just after her arrival in Moscow.

Olga and Henry.

Olga with the author's daughter, Toni, in South Africa, shortly after she left the USSR.

The Postcard

Today we heard from Ray; the first direct news we have had since she was sent to the camps. There was a knock on the door of my flat, and when I opened it a woman was standing there; I did not know her, but her face seemed vaguely familiar.

She asked: 'Does Henry live in this apartment?'

'Yes.'

'Is he in?'

'He's at work. I'm his wife.'

'A postcard has been sent to our flat; we think it may be for him. Do you know anyone in Vorkuta?'

'I'll come with you to get it.'

The woman stood for a moment. 'Well, let's say in half an hour,' she said.

Was this some kind of trap? She did not live far away. Why didn't she bring it with her? Perhaps they thought we would pretend it wasn't for us, reject the card.

In her flat there was another woman who looked at me intensely and then held out the postcard. Unmistakably it was in Ray's good American Palmer writing. But the numbers on our address had been changed – crudely, even in a different coloured ink. Someone had wanted it to be collected, wanted to watch the reaction of the recipient.

It was essential for me to remain calm, not to express any feelings. I mustn't make any comment, or discuss the case.

I said: 'Thank you, thank you very much,' and turned to leave.

I could feel them looking curiously at me, but I controlled myself, not even trying to read the card. I opened the door and let myself out of the flat. But on the landing I went to the window overlooking the courtyard and started to read Ray's card.

It was from the far north, beyond the Arctic circle. How many months had it taken her to get there, inadequately clothed, and without any money.

She wrote her address, and said: 'When I received the money after Ida left I knew Henry's leg was better and you were all right. But now I can't believe that. Clearly you were not there when they came for my things; I didn't receive the clothes I put on the list, only old things that were no good for me. What happened?'

The writing was minute. I went closer to the window to see more clearly. What she wrote was so pitiful that I started to cry. The door opened again, and I was drawn back into the flat. The two women looked at me sympathetically. 'Is it your sister?' they asked.

This time I felt that whatever their role, they knew what it must be like for those in the camps. But I dared not lower my guard and say anything unwise.

A Distant War

Early in 1940 a Captain Fielding from the British Military Mission in Moscow came to look for my sister. Her family were worried because they had had no letters and no news about her for a long time. Sir Stafford Cripps, then British Foreign Secretary, had been approached and asked to make enquiries about her. She had been listed as a British citizen at the Embassy, and she should have been warned to leave the country at the time of the impending war.

Captain Fielding apologised for the omission, but told her it was not possible to send her back now, as it was too dangerous. He promised to keep in touch and let her know if there was any possibility of a passage to England.

The German *Blitzkrieg* swept over Europe. Early in the year the frontiers of Holland, Belgium and Luxembourg were bombed. In just seven weeks the Panzer divisions had invaded Luxembourg; in five days the Dutch surrendered. The German armies broke through the Ardennes forests into France.

The Panzer divisions occupied city after city. British, French and Belgian armies were driven back into a pocket at Dunkirk. In June 1940 the German divisions entered Paris. The English Channel was the last barrier between the German armies and Britain.

In the summer of 1940 the *Luftwaffe* were ordered to clear the skies of British aircraft as the first step in Operation Sealion. Now the war was being fought in the air.

The *Luftwaffe* had twice as many planes as RAF Fighter Command. From late 1940 to May 1941 London suffered continuous heavy raids in an attempt to bomb the UK into submission. Over 1,000 tons of high explosives were dropped on the square mile of the City in one raid. Schools, shops, houses as well as many famous buildings were damaged or reduced to rubble. Other cities and ports were also bombed. But the Blitz failed in the face of the growing strength of anti-aircraft defences and the ability and sacrifices of Britain's night fighters. Hitler turned from a severely wounded but unbeaten Britain to take on the USSR.

My sisters and I were now divided not only by the vast distances between the countries in which we three lived, but by the course of the war. I worried about Vera whose home was in London. We wrote to each other regularly; I knew when bombs had fallen near her home, and she told me of her fear. I knew when, in her job as a teacher, she was in charge of children who had been evacuated to the country, and who wet their beds and cried all night for their mothers. But I knew nothing of Henry's accident and Ray's arrest, nor of Olga's wish to go to England. I believed that at least she was safe since the Soviet Union was not at war.

In Moscow the war must have seemed like a distant roll of thunder over Europe whilst the Nazi armies had headed relentlessly West.

In August, at the height of the battle of Britain, Olga and Henry went on their summer holiday to a village outside Moscow.

Pushkinia was a peaceful place. The garden of the house where they stayed ran down to a lake where they could swim. Streams that fed the lake were rich in fish.

It was a hot, calm season. They would spend the day catching fish, silver in the sunlight; frying their catch by the side of the sparkling water. The streams and lake supplied them with fish the whole summer.

We were so widely dispersed. For us in South Africa the war was very far away. We followed news of it, but it did not impact on our lives. In December – high summer for us – I went with friends for a holiday in one of the most beautiful coastal districts: Plettenberg Bay, in the Cape. The house we shared was on a slope leading straight down to the sands and sea, with an unimpeded view of the curve of the whole bay, the wide white beach, the rocks to the right and the distant mountains on the left. There were no other houses in such a wonderful position. It was a paradise, still undiscovered and undeveloped.

Southern Africa was so far from the war, so far from Moscow, so far from Vorkuta.

Sylvia

Sylvia was very young and very pretty and crazy about dancing. She was a dancer, not the kind she really wanted to be; but in the days of the American depression there was not much demand for ballet dancers.

Her father was a window-cleaner, employed by a contractor to stand on a platform of pulleys, cleaning the windows of the office block skyscrapers. He couldn't afford to pay for Sylvia's dancing lessons, so she made hats during the day and danced in the clubs at night when she could; and dreamed of dancing in the ballet.

Her greatest wish was to go to the Soviet Union, for wasn't Russia the home of ballet? So Sylvia saved all her money and finally succeeded in amassing enough to pay for a trip to the Soviet Union. Moscow was her aim. The first night she could she went to the ballet at the Bolshoi Theatre, and the rest of her holiday was spent in trying to arrange to stay on in Moscow. This she finally succeeded in doing, and when the group of tourists with whom she had been travelling returned to New York, she remained behind. Still in her teens, she was now a resident of Moscow.

She managed to join ballet classes and she studied during the day and danced on the stage at night.

But Sylvia was fated not to be a ballerina.

One night, on the uneven floor of the open-air stage where she was dancing, she tripped and fell awkwardly. Her ankle was broken, and set badly; and although after some months she walked without a limp, her life as a professional dancer was over.

America had not yet recovered from the depression. Sylvia's father was out of work himself, and so Sylvia stayed on in Moscow, going back to her old standby – making hats.

At that time the American expatriate colony had a dacha, a house in the country where they spent the hot summer weekends; and which they used in the winter months as a centre from which to go skiing in the forest. Sylvia sometimes went there on her free day, and here she met Walt. He was one of the best-known American newspaper correspondents, intelligent and full of fun, and considerably older than she was.

They went skiing together, to the ballet and opera, and after some months they married. Sylvia knew that Walt had been married before, that his wife Rosa was in New York, and that he kept in touch with her. What she didn't know was that Walt was an alcoholic. For about six months their romance flourished, then Walt went off on a drinking jag. He was gone for a week, and when he returned, still drinking, Sylvia simply didn't recognise him as the Walt she had married. He was unkind, morose, retreated from the world, and unable even to work.

War was imminent. It had already started in western Europe, although Russia and the United States were not yet involved. However, in those times in Russia foreigners had to behave themselves, and Walt was recalled to the USA. And although officially divorced, Walt went back to Rosa. He always did after a cure. She understood him, and could live with him when he was drunk or ill. Sylvia was too young and inexperienced to accept Walt in this state. It frightened her, and when he was recalled to America she remained in Moscow.

For Walt the episode was over, but for Sylvia it was not. She was pregnant. Now, more than ever, she was determined not to go home, to be a burden to her unemployed father.

So she took a job in a workshop in Moscow, and as she had no flat and could find no accommodation in the city she rented a room in a wooden house outside town.

The baby was born, and Sylvia insisted on registering its name as Walter. There is no 'W' in the Russian alphabet, so in Russian the child was called Ualtaire, or Voltaire. An added difficulty was that it was a little girl.

Every morning Sylvia took the baby to the crèche, travelled in the crowded trains to work, collecting her baby again on the way home in the evening. The room she rented was tiny and cold; in the winter there was often no light; and there were mice, and the usual Russian vermin – bedbugs – to contend with.

'Why don't you go home?' we would ask her, 'At least, write to Walt and tell him.' But she was determined to manage on her own. She never complained, and the baby, who had rosy cheeks, bright dark eyes and curly hair, grew and developed.

When little Walter started to speak, it was naturally in Russian. By this time Sylvia, who no longer seemed so young and rosy herself, spoke Russian nearly as well as English, and seemed completely Russianised. When the ballet or theatre was mentioned it was clear she had not lost her keen interest. But she was fully occupied keeping herself and her little daughter going, and could not take time off for such pleasures.

*As the war came nearer still and life became harder we tried to per-
suade Sylvia to go back to America. She knew that Walter was still with
Rosa.*

*'I can't go back,' Sylvia would say. 'Look at me; nobody would recognise
me. And I have no money.'*

*The war in Europe was spreading, more and more countries were
involved. And life became harder than ever in the Soviet Union. Foreigners
were mistrusted, and no one needed fancy hats.*

*Finally Sylvia, whose father had written to her urging her to come
home, decided she would really go. It was impossible to travel across
Europe. She would have to take the trans-Siberian railway to Vladivostok,
cross to the West coast of America, and then travel overland to New York.*

*I went to the station to see her off. She stood there saying, 'I feel Russian
really. I don't want to go.'*

*With the usual complete lack of sex discrimination in the Soviet Union,
for the two week journey across Russia she and her baby were sharing a
compartment with a young Red Army man. I wondered how she would
manage.*

*'Don't worry. I will look after them,' the Red Army man said to me as
he lifted their cases into the compartment.*

*A few weeks later a card came from Sylvia. 'It's been a lovely journey.
Quite romantic. I am thinking of staying in Vladivostok.'*

The Foreign Languages Institute

There was no possibility now of Olga's long-deferred trip to England.
The course of the war was uncertain; she had no choice at present; it
could be years – if ever – before she would be able to return. With her
usual pragmatism she accepted and adapted. She was welcomed as a
teacher in English at the Moscow State Pedagogical Institute for
Foreign Languages. The Institute had over a thousand students, and the

English faculty was the largest. Larissa was also teaching there; she taught the first course. Olga's students were generally in the final year of study where they were already fluent in English, so her lack of Russian was not important.

In addition to her usual classes Olga had been asked to teach two mature students, Deans of other Faculties. They both spoke several languages and were quick to learn. The classes went well until another beginner asked to join their classes.

He was a problem. He knew no Western languages, and as he came from the Ukraine, his Russian was hard for her to understand. He simply couldn't keep up with the other two, but it was made clear that she could not refuse to teach him. So he had to have separate lessons on his own until he could join the other two. Larissa and Olga used to meet in the staff room, where they helped each other with any teaching problems. Now Olga explained the difficulties she was having with her new student.

'I just can't teach beginners,' she explained.

'Who is it?'

Olga told her his name.

'Ooh! Is *that* who you're teaching!' Larissa showed her how to start with beginners and how to demonstrate with actual objects. As her confidence grew she was able to enjoy her work at the Institute.

*

Larissa said: 'I want you to come to the dacha in the country with me. I want you to meet some very good friends of mine.'

On the way there she told Olga quietly: 'I've given up hope of ever seeing Sasha again.' And when they arrived at the dacha: 'I want you to meet Nicolai. He wants to marry me.'

Nicolai was younger than Sasha, not as tall nor as distinguished looking. Fair-haired and blue-eyed, he was very good-natured and liked to sing romantic songs, accompanying himself on the accordion. Although he could not speak any English he and my sister became good friends.

State Examinations

Now it was the actual day of the State examinations, the final exam for graduating students. The examining commission sat all day. It was midsummer, very hot, and by the afternoon the examination room was unbearably stuffy. There were cigarette ends in all the saucers, and a fly was buzzing on the window.

Students came in one by one in alphabetical order. Each picked a ticket and was given a text to prepare for the exam which took nearly an hour. The last student on the list was Yantsova. She had been waiting all day in the corridor outside. All the students waited outside, pouncing on each one who had finished the exam, trying to see which questions and authors could be eliminated.

I could see Yantsova had prepared herself for this important occasion when she had to appear before the State Commission of Professors and justify her years of study. She looked unusually neat and tidy. She was small and dark with a sharp face and lank hair, and was the student no one wanted to get close to. Whenever they sat in the lecture hall or classroom the other students put their books and school bags on the seats next to them so that there was a certain distance between them. She smelt, and had lice. Her father was chronically ill, and she was the eldest of a large family living in one room in a wooden hut, without water or sanitation. She travelled to college by train every day, leaving home and arriving back again in the dark.

The author on her exam ticket was Dickens. That was lucky. She had chosen the Christmas Carol for her book review that term, mainly because it was the shortest she could find on the list of recommended books. I remembered the way she had come to me with 'special' questions before presenting her report to the class. She had asked:

'What part of the body is a fancy?'

'It's not a part of the body.'

'Oh yes it is. It's in my book.'

'Fancy?'

'Yes. It's somewhere near the stomach.'

She showed me the passage in her book.

'I know what "corporation" means, and "abdomen" and "livery", but I don't know what part of the body a "fancy" is.'

I looked at the book. Dickens had written 'Scrooge had a little of what is called fancy about him as any man in the city of London, even including – which is a bold word – the corporation, alderman and livery.'

Now Yantsova spoke about Dickens, read her passage which was from 'Great Expectations' and somehow managed to answer most of the questions put to her by the Professors of Linguistics, Grammar, Stylistics and English. But she was not doing herself justice. Only the bold students did at exams. Her pronunciation was abominable. It was hard to understand what she was saying. I heard Professor Smirnitsky mutter: 'Why didn't she do translation?' The students who couldn't master the difficult English sounds usually ended up in the translation faculty where they only needed a thorough understanding of the language. We had a language laboratory, but Yantsova could never use it. She had too far to travel, and had to leave early every day to get home.

Finally it was the Phonetician's turn to question her. He said: 'Have you read "Pickwick Papers"?'

'Yes.'

'Do you know the sounds Sam Weller had difficulty in saying? Which ones did he always confuse?'

There was a gleam in her eyes.

'The double-you and the vee.'

'Can you give us an example?'

'Yes, he said "werry vell" instead of' – with a tremendous effort she said it correctly – '"very well."'

The Professor of Phonetics sat back in his seat.

'That's all. You may go.'

The Examining Professor said, 'Her accent is appalling. How can she teach?' The Professor of Phonetics answered: 'Ah yes, but she knows it all, and that's what matters.'

Yantsova had passed.

A week later the students had their graduating ceremony. The group Yantsova was in presented me with the usual huge bunch of sweet-smelling peonies. They also presented me with a grandly ornate Victorian vase they had gone to great trouble to buy at a commission shop selling antiques.

Was it feelings of compunction for their treatment of her that made the students choose Yantsova to make the presentation, or had they drawn lots and Yantsova was the lucky one? She made a little speech that she had prepared and carefully memorised, and ended with a lovely mix-up of prepositions:

'This is to express our gratitude for you to all that you have done to us.'

BOOK THREE

THE WAR

CHAPTER I

Lunch at Bella's

O N a radiant morning in June, 1941, Olga and Henry set out to walk across Moscow. They were going to Sunday lunch with Bella, who lived over the other side of town. Having a meal with Bella was an enjoyable event, for she lived with her mother who was just about the best cook in Moscow.

Originally her mother's home had been in Riga; but after the 1914-1918 war she had gone to Moscow with her husband, bringing all her household treasures with her, valuable china, glass and cutlery.

Her husband had died, leaving her with a baby daughter, Bella, and she did dressmaking to earn a living. Now Bella was a student about to graduate as a radio engineer.

Bella's mother not only provided wonderful food, she also believed that her precious china and linen should not be stowed away, but that they should be used. Every invitation to lunch was a special occasion.

Bella and her mother lived on the other side of the Moscow river, but Olga and Henry had decided to walk because it was such a lovely day. Their route took them down Gorki Street, Moscow's main street, and across Red Square. The people of Moscow were strolling across the cobbles and along the river bank enjoying the summer sunshine. The Byzantine domes of St Basil's sparkled in the sunlight.

As they came close to the Town Hall the music from the loudspeakers attached to the lamp posts all the way down the street ceased suddenly, and a voice blared out: 'Attention! Attention! This is an important announcement!'

They stopped to listen. All along the street people stood motionless, fearful and unbelieving as the voice boomed on.

Barbarossa

War came to the Soviet Union with deadly and devastating suddenness. A massive force had been assembled on the Russian borders and Hitler's attack, code-named Barbarossa, was launched in the early hours of June 22, 1941. The first Panzer divisions crossed the border at 3.30 a.m. The main *Luftwaffe* assault began soon after. The attack on Russia was an essential part of Hitler's plan to supply Germany with the *Lebensraum* - living space - for German settlement, and also to destroy 'Jewish Bolshevism'. Russia had been supplying oil, cereals and many other essential materials to Germany, but now Hitler was determined to have complete control of the wheat from the Ukraine, the oil from the Caucasus, and the slave labour to work for those riches for Germany.

Preparations for this huge operation had been going on for months. More than three million German troops and other pro-Axis armies were massed along the borders from Finland to the Black Sea. Such an assembly of troops, tanks and aircraft could not be concealed. In addition the Soviet authorities had been receiving warnings of the coming attack from a variety of sources: from their own agents in Germany, who sent reliable reports; from both Britain and United States at the highest level – the State Department in Washington had warned the Soviet Ambassador six months before that Hitler was preparing to strike at Russia, reinforced by warnings from Britain; from German deserters; and even from the German Ambassador in Moscow. Yet when Barbarossa was launched the country was totally unprepared for the onslaught.

Stalin had ignored all these warnings. He distrusted Roosevelt and Churchill even more than he distrusted Hitler. He did not believe that an attack by Hitler was imminent, or that it would come without a formal declaration of war. He sent messages to his commanders not to be 'provoked' into retaliatory action even after the invasion had begun, even as the German planes had begun their bombing raids.

Not only were they taken by surprise, but in addition the Soviet forces had been immeasurably weakened by the purge of its most experienced leaders. Now, despite a massive build up of their armed forces, they were facing the greatest war of all time stripped of their most experienced leaders at every level.

The Russians faced a three-pronged invasion aimed at Leningrad in the north, Moscow in the centre, and the Ukraine and Caucasus in the south. Germany had embarked on what was to be the greatest land war of all time, fought with tens of millions of soldiers and enormous quantities of military weapons; a war that would also encompass millions of civilians and the devastation not only of innumerable towns but also the laying to waste of vast areas of countryside.

The first three months of war were an unmitigated military disaster for the Russians. The major part of the Russian airforce was wiped out in the first few days. In the first three weeks 6,000 aircraft were destroyed and 3,500 tanks. During the first fortnight a million Red Army soldiers were captured or killed in a series of spectacular encirclements. By the second week of July some of the German generals thought the war was as good as over.

Information provided to the British government by its Joint Intelligence Committee and Chiefs of Staff led them to believe that the Wehrmacht's *Blitzkrieg* campaign would lead to the capture of Moscow within three to six weeks, and the bulk of the Soviet army would be an-nihilated. They believed that Hitler's attack on the USSR could only provide a breathing space of at the most up to eight weeks before he turned his forces to the attempted invasion of Britain. The amazingly rapid German advance to the outskirts of Moscow confirmed this gloomy prognosis. Stalin appealed to the British to open a second front in Europe, but they considered the shoring up of their defence of the Near and Middle East a better strategy for the defence of Britain.

Within weeks German divisions had swept through the Baltic re-gions and entered Belorus and the Ukraine. The capital of the Ukraine had been captured and the great coal and metallurgical region of the Donbas was over-run. Lightning advances and great wheeling manoeu-vres outflanked Soviet defences and trapped a million Red Army men.

Less than two months after the invasion Smolensk was captured; and in early September the Germans reached the outskirts of Leningrad, cutting off its only land link with the Soviet Union, leaving the only connection across Lake Ladoga. It was Hitler's intention to destroy the city and its population by shelling and starvation. The siege of Leningrad had begun.

Within two and a half months German troops were close to Moscow. In October the Germans launched the first stage of their Operation Typhoon – the offensive that was intended to be the knock-out blow against Moscow.

When the War Broke Out

Before rationing was brought in there was a run of food in the city shops; not perishables, but anything that could be kept – flour, cereals, fats, sugar. Long queues formed and by noon the shelves in most shops were empty.

Molotov broadcast an appeal to the public not to save food, saying there would be enough for everyone. But the little old grandmother in the flat above mine came down to see what stores I had acquired. She was horrified.

'You must buy food. You must have at least ten kilograms of sugar, ten kilograms of fat, ten kilograms of flour and cereal and hard sausage!' She went into details.

'But,' I protested, 'Molotov said…'

'Take no notice. I've lived through three wars and a famine, and you must have at least ten kilos…'

Each day she would come down to see what I had bought, and under her insistence I did buy, not ten kilos of everything, but still a fair quantity of food, and finally she was satisfied.

Moscow under Siege

The city prepared itself for the siege that it knew would come. Drastic food rationing was introduced in July, with differentiation for various groups: those employed in heavy industry, the mines and the army, and children were at the top of the scale; later, people employed in important war industries including scientists and technicians were added; manual workers, white-collar workers and dependants came next. Able-bodied adults who were not working received no ration at all.

Lighting and heating was limited, with meters that allowed only a small amount for each apartment. Defence squads were organised in every apartment house and every block of small houses.

The whole face of the city began to change. Trucks with sandbags rumbled through the streets of the city, windows were boarded up and sandbags protected many main buildings. Familiar buildings disappeared under constructed and painted camouflage. The golden domes of the Kremlin churches were concealed under grey cloth, and other buildings in Red Square covered with canvas that had been painted with large splashes of black and yellow with images of small houses.

The Mali theatre was clad in old stage scenery from Ostrovsky's play, *The Forest*, while the Bolshoi theatre was hung with canvas painted with false doorways.

Social patterns changed swiftly. All men not working in essential industries were mobilised into the forces; women replaced them in the factories and offices. Then all children were evacuated from Moscow to country houses belonging to trade unions and other official organisations, and sent to various places on the Volga and further afield where it was thought they would be safe. But the German advance was swift and relentless. As the civilian populations fled the children were moved on again to safer areas. In this way parents who stayed in Moscow lost touch with their children; many would never be reunited.

Moscow lay in the heart of Russia's forest belt. Among the thick clusters of pine and birch, searchlights were laid in concentric circles. Anti-aircraft batteries were buried in the ground and covered with branches. Silver balloons were placed in readiness to raise a curtain of steel cables as a barrage.

The air blitz on Moscow came a month after the invasion began; German aircraft dropped bombs on Moscow for the first time. Accompanied by an anti-aircraft barrage, the sky was criss-crossed with spotlights. Basements in large blocks of flats had been prepared to provide air raid shelters; but the main shelters were the stations of the Metro, which had been built to serve as self-sufficient, fully prepared bomb shelters with steel doors and air filters.

Arthur Ling, in the magazine *Architectural Design and Construction* wrote: 'The Metro stations are not only bomb proof. They make the most beautiful air-raid shelters in the world.' Film projectors installed in the stations showed propaganda films. Together with the basements in the city blocks they provided immediate shelter for eighty per cent of Moscow's population.

Olga and Henry's apartment building had an air-raid shelter in the basement. But if an air-raid warning went off while she was teaching at the Institute Olga and her students had to rush for the nearby underground station – Park Kul'tury.

The normal courses for the students at the Language Institute were over for the year. The full-time students had taken their exams; now it was the turn of the out-of-town external students. Olga was an official examiner, and responsible for the issue of examination tickets and the protection of the papers with the exam questions. When the sirens went she gathered up all the papers and with the students rushed for the shelter.

The platform was crowded, and we were directed into the dark tunnel. Here the only place to sit was on the rails. We all hoped they had remembered to turn off the current, and sat down gingerly in our flimsy summer dresses.

One day the sirens went in the middle of an exam. I collected all the question papers, and off we rushed. In the tunnel the papers were the obvious things to sit on. No one could see them, and they kept our clothes clean.

I have a mental picture of my sister sitting very straight-backed in the darkness of the tunnel, the papers safely tucked under her buttocks and those of her students; she has a self-satisfied smile on her face, pleased with the double purpose the exam papers serve.

Evacuation

The Soviet Union's great industrial areas were centred around Moscow and Leningrad, and in the central and eastern Ukraine. With the eastward retreat of the Red Army a tremendous amount of essential and heavy industry was lost – steel-rolling mills, coal and aluminium, tank and aircraft factories, much of the country's capacity for electric power and railway freight.

The occupied territories also accounted for a large proportion of the food supply: grain harvests, cattle and pig herds, and virtually all the country's sugar-production capacity.

In August, as the German advance continued, the government began to evacuate heavy industry from Moscow and other threatened areas.

Dismantling of the plants went on day and night, often under the bombing, and the evacuations took place under appallingly difficult conditions, with great hardship. The uprooting of huge industrial plants, together with the men and women who worked in them, was a fantastic undertaking posing enormous and complex problems of organisation and transport. The size of the operation can be judged by the fact that one industrial plant alone – the steel mills of Zaparozhstal – needed 8,000 railway trucks to evacuate the entire plant and its workers. The evacuation of 100 aircraft factories took one million ten-metre trucks.

Nearly half the evacuated factories went to the Urals; the rest to the Volga region, western Siberia, Kazakhstan and central Asia.

The main railway lines were already clogged with troops on the move, with Red Cross trains bringing the wounded from the battle areas, with floods of refugees who were driven across the country as town after town fell to the Germans; and now with the wagons transporting the equipment of the vast industrial plants and the workers, who were being evacuated with their industries. It was the end of summer. Winter was approaching in the frozen regions of the north, and temperatures would soon be sub-zero for months on end.

At the end of their journeys accommodation had to be found for the workers in small towns and remote areas that could not provide what was needed for those who went with the factories. Under these conditions armies of technicians started immediately on the re-assembling the plants. Few of the factories had any heating, but once production re-started it never stopped. The workers showed incredible human endurance, working twelve, thirteen, even fourteen, hours a day, and often having to walk miles to work.

For the millions of people on the move, whether soldiers, industrial workers, or those driven from their homes and seeking to escape the Panzer divisions, there was often no accommodation and little food. The refugees, on foot, in carts, by train or car when available, struggled from town to town, travelling for days and weeks as they were swept before the Nazi tide. Mothers with exhausted children spilt out of trains into unknown towns to spend nights on station platforms or on seats in the parks. Wherever the refugees sought shelter any possessions no longer absolutely essential – clothes, watches, wedding rings – were bartered for food. For the duration of the war millions were always hungry, and untold numbers died of starvation.

It was as though the countries and the peoples of the Soviet Union had been stirred by a monstrous whirlwind that displaced industries, armies and families, dividing and scattering them in unimaginable confusion.

Journey to the Urals

In January of 1941 the whole Metro project had become a company called Metrostroy. Now, with the Germans outside Moscow, the engineers working on the Metro were told that they were to be evacuated to the Urals.

They were to be part of a 'Metrostroy Project'. It seems likely that the main intention was simply to keep them safe. They had been working on the third Metro line which had been begun in 1939, and except for the months when Moscow was under siege and they had been evacuated to the Urals, the work would continue ceaselessly day and night throughout the war.

Henry and the others of the Metrostroy Project, as experienced and skilled engineers, would obviously have been of great use in the military forces. The fact that they were not conscripted into the army shows the immense importance that Stalin attached to the building of the Metro – an importance that over-rode their vital value to the beleaguered armies.

The families of the engineers were evacuated with them. But Olga's marriage was not legally binding so her name was not automatically included on the list. Those in charge of the project took a helpful view and arranged for her to be put on their list as the night watchman. 'Once we got there they crossed me off the list, so as a result I didn't get any bread rations; but it got me out of Moscow with Henry when the Germans were very, very close.'

All the information they had was that they were going to somewhere in the Urals, close to Siberia. For how long? For all they knew it could be weeks, months, or years. Impossible to think beyond the practicalities imposed by the immediate necessities; there was not time to speculate. They were told that they could take one trunk and hand luggage. Into the trunk would have to go the clothes they would need for winter in sub-zero temperatures; but also practical items that might become essential for living in that distant and unknown place. So the trunk also contained kitchen utensils, plates and crockery.

They took a small selection of books and eight records that would go with their portable gramophone.

Among the books selected was an edition of Shakespeare, two collections of prose and poetry, a book by Somerset Maugham and collected stories of O. Henry, as well as a detective story and Evelyn Waugh's *Scoop*. The records were a mixture of classical music and popular tunes: a violin concerto played by Kreisler, a record of the famous Russian tenor, Chaliapin; Benny Goodman, and tunes to dance to: *Little White Lies, Parlez-moi d'Amour, Let's Put Out the Lights and Go to Sleep*.

They left Moscow on a brilliant August morning. They had no idea of their destination, nor when they could return, or if they would ever be able to return to Moscow. The only thing they knew was that with the relentless German advance they would be heading north.

There was the utmost confusion on Moscow's Northern Station with crowds milling around and nobody to give information and directions. But Olga and Henry had been given the number of their wagon, and as they came towards it a hand beckoned from one of the wagons and a smiling face invited them to come over. It was a Metrostroy manager named Grynsburg who had saved places for them and who helped them load their luggage into the cattle truck in which they would be travelling.

There were no windows in the wagon and the view through the sliding doors was partially obscured by heavy packing cases. While the men began moving the cases Olga sat on a pile of bare planks that she felt was her place and looked at her new acquaintances.

It was obvious who was in charge of the wagon, and that he was used to giving orders. Grynsburg spoke briskly with a sharp voice and only relaxed when he was with friends. His uniform was smart and new and he wore the soft black leather boots issued to officers.

Now he was busy arranging the disposition of the heavy crates, pulling them aside so that they would not block the doors. It was extremely hot, and they needed all the air and light they could get. Olga wondered why he had saved places for them in his truck. Was it out of the goodness of his heart or because he had been told to? Perhaps he chose as travelling companions those with no children or elderly relatives to make the journey more difficult. But more likely – because all foreigners were suspect and were constantly under some sort of supervision – it was his task to keep an eye on the foreigners, his duty to report their behaviour and their conversations.

The Grynsburgs were a family of three. They seemed to have masses of luggage. Olga thought: weren't we supposed to be limited to one trunk? But perhaps some of the crates surrounding them contained office files or engineering equipment.

His wife Sophie, dark hair pulled back Russian-style into a low bun, seemed to have dressed for a different occasion. Her brightly-patterned silk dress and high-heeled shoes were more suitable for a passenger train going to some southern resort than a cattle truck travelling to the hostile north. She wore heavy white make-up, and lipstick that seemed too thick and greasy in the heat.

The third member of the family was the daughter, Lucia, about fifteen. She looked at Olga's foreign clothes, but was obviously too shy to start asking questions so soon.

This family and this truck, furnished only with the wooden crates and bare boards, was their home for two weeks on a journey that normally would have taken two days.

They purchased food from the peasants whenever they stopped at a station, and Grynsburg would arrange for sufficient water for drinking and for washing. There were no toilet facilities, so the passengers in need had to jump off the train whenever it stopped.

The whole of Russia was on the move and troop and ambulance trains had priority:

Because this was wartime they never had any kind of schedule. You never knew where you were going, and if they stopped you didn't know if it was for half a minute, half an hour or half a day. And you had to rush off to relieve yourself, and then the train would start and you would run back. It was terrifying.

But we lost people. A mother would get off when the train stopped, to look for water to make tea, and the train would go, and she would lose her family. And very often they never found them again, never found out where the train finally went. And sometimes the train drivers themselves didn't know – the train might be diverted half way through its journey.

Once when the train stopped Sophie Grynsburg got off to see someone in one of the other trucks. And the train started unexpectedly – she got left behind. Grynsburg was sleeping, and when the train gave a jerk and started to move we woke him and said your wife's locked out. I'll never forget her running in her high heels trying to catch the train. And he showed great presence of mind: he made sure he grabbed his jacket with his documents, and then he jumped off.

Lucia sat there and cried and cried because she thought she would never see her father and her mother again.

But he was someone quite high up and he managed to get on a military train that actually went ahead of us. So we met up further along the line in a day or two.

Olga concluded that Grynsburg, who appeared to operate separately from the Metrostroy engineers, was someone in the secret police.

Moscow Realities

The Moscow they had left was full of contrasts.

Industry was re-keyed to war production and the Hammer and Sickle factory was working day and night turning out thousands of tank obstructions – 'hedgehogs' – that were placed in the outer ring of the city's boulevards. Yet fourteen theatres were open, invariably crowded, showing opera, Shakespeare and modern plays. Chekhov's Three Sisters was on at the Arts theatre. The front of the Bolshoi Theatre had been damaged by a bomb, but at the beginning of September the ballet season opened in the theatre annexe with the youthful Lepeshinskaya, later to become a prima ballerina, ethereal, light as swansdown, in the lead role in *Swan Lake*.

An escape from reality? The reality was the war but ballet at the Bolshoi was also a reality, a different kind of truth. Death came with Panzer divisions surrounding the city and with the planes bringing their bombs. But *Swan Lake* at the Bolshoi was an assurance that Tchaikovsky of the peerless music and Lepenshinskaya whose divine dancing gave it a visual form were more powerful; in them was an immortality that would outlast the destruction, the death. It was an assurance that the time of the tanks would come to an end.

*

There were other contrasts. Although strict rationing was introduced and a time of great scarcity of foodstuffs had begun, the Soviet authorities adhered to their policy of lavish entertainment of their important guests. A huge luncheon was given by Lozovsky, deputy Foreign Minister, on September 15 for the members of the foreign press corps who had just arrived to report on the war. Alexander Werth, who was the BBC correspondent in Moscow, described the scene. The big dining room in the Moskva restaurant was decorated with murals of the Caucasus and Crimea. There were bottles all the way down the table and butter moulded into the shape of horses. Vodka flowed freely. This was typical of the receptions held throughout the war for important delegations from the Allies. There always seemed to be a special reserve of luxury food, wine and spirits, even during the times of utmost stringency.[19]

The day after the dinner at the Moskva selected correspondents from Britain and the USA were driven out of the city to visit the front. A few days after they returned the German offensive against Moscow began. On October 6 the Germans broke through the Rzhev-Viazma line and advanced on Moscow. A week later, as the evacuation of official organisations began and rumours spread that the Germans were entering a suburb of Moscow, discipline disintegrated and on October 16 the hitherto stoical city was overcome with panic.

CHAPTER 2

Omoutninsk

THEY finally learned that they were going to a small town in Udmurtia, a small, undeveloped republic on the European side of the Ural mountains. Omoutninsk lay in a shallow valley where the river Viatka passes through a vast lake. Beyond the lake were the deep impenetrable forests of the north.

As they came nearer to their destination people at the stations where the train stopped would ask: 'Where are you for?' And when they were told 'Omoutninsk' they would groan, shake their heads, sometimes cross themselves, and mutter: 'That God-forsaken place!'

When they arrived, they discovered what they meant. Omoutninsk was the last stop on a branch railway line that continued to the labour camps in the north. Beyond, there were the great forests, but no other towns or villages.

Omoutninsk was more like a sprawling village than a town. There were some two-storey buildings – the Town Hall, the hospital and party headquarters, but the dwelling houses were really simply log cabins; some quite old, leaning drunkenly to one side.

My sister's impressions were of poverty and ugliness. The streets were pot-holed, the wooden cabins drab and decrepit, and the people seemed to her to be grim-looking in their patched clothes.

Most of the houses stood in small plots of land where their owners grew potatoes and some cabbage. Few other vegetables could be grown so far north, and no fruit. As in most places outside the major cities there was no gas, no electricity and no piped water. Most respectable houses had a well in the garden, though some wells were shared by groups of houses. And near the wells, in the garden plots, were smaller log cabins with no windows. My sister thought at first that they were garden sheds. But she was told proudly by the owner of one, that it was a bath house. Ultimately she too would have a bath in the log cabin bath house – but not until Christmas.

The train arrived in the late afternoon. The *nachal'niki* – the superiors, the heads – said they were going off to look for accommodation, and told everyone to stay on the train until they returned. When they returned those left on the train realised that the heads had obtained accommodation for themselves, and they, the less important people, were to stay on the train for that night.

Nobody could tolerate the thought of another night on the train, so they went looking for places to spend the night. Olga and Henry, together with the Grynsburgs and a Latvian cook and his wife who had been brought along to prepare food for the Metrostroy workers, found an empty house.

They became squatters. They shared out what little furniture there was, and each family had its own room. There was food from the central supplies, and cooking was done on a *kerosinka*.

At first the arrangement worked well. But summer in that region was short, and there was no wood for heating; as the temperature dropped the evacuees realised that they could no longer stay in the shared house without supplies of wood for the winter and not enough stores of food. The squatters had to find their own alternative accommodation.

The wooden houses were sprawled around the lake, spread out over a large area. Olga and Henry went looking for a well-kept house with plenty of logs in the yard – and a cow. The cow was essential. Poorer peasants with no cow had no milk.

The climate imposed its harshness on the lives of the villagers. Spring, summer and autumn were brief, winters were long and fiercely frozen. The soil was poor, unsuitable for agriculture. They were close to Siberia, in a locality where for months it was not possible to obtain any fresh produce. Whatever was harvested or purchased at larger markets was carefully dried and stored for the winter months. The peasants had basements under their homes, where they kept their stocks frost-free in winter.

The room they found was very small, but the house was comparatively clean, there was plenty of fire-wood and as the cow had recently calved, there would be milk all winter. They agreed on a price for the room plus one mug of milk a day.

While the men were busy with their project at a site somewhere in the forest, the wives – Muscovites all – formed their own social group and became Olga's new friends. The clothes, smooth skins and well cared-for hair of the city women were the outward marks of the huge divide between themselves and those among whom they now lived. The peasant women, formed by lives of heavy physical work, were short and dumpy, their heads always covered with a scarf, their legs sturdy and shapeless in their thick woollen stockings.

The project itself was not in the village; it was some distance away along the train line. Until the autumn rains began Olga would sometimes go on the train to the site of the project with the men, and while they worked, walk by herself in the forest, looking for wild strawberries, raspberries and mushrooms; and as autumn drew on, for hips; all of which could be dried and kept for the harsh winter when fresh foods and vitamins were unobtainable.

It was a drastic change in life-style. 'But in a way I liked it there,' she said. 'It was very beautiful. The forest was lovely. The conditions were very difficult, but then it was wartime, and we were safe from the bombs. We were out of danger. I suppose I was happy-go-lucky.'

*

Autumn turned the village paths to quagmires. The streets became impassable. Boots were sucked off your feet as you struggled through the mud. The only way to get anywhere was to walk along the single-track railway line. Even the engineers could not get to the site while the rains lasted, so the project was suspended while they waited for the frost.

The main problem for all the evacuees was how to obtain food.

Preparing for Winter

In Omoutninsk I remembered the little baboushka who lived above us in Moscow and made me lay in supplies of food when war broke out. Now I had to queue for a ration of bread. It was the one food that was issued – 400 grams of black bread, baked with the addition of potato peelings; and from the grit in the bread, it seemed the potatoes had not been washed.

One day there was an issue of salt, two kilos of it after a six-hour wait in the queue, in the open frozen snow, by the kiosk from where it was being distributed. We took turns in waiting, keeping places as each of us had to thaw out for a while.

Life in the north of Russia is always hard. During the short summer there is little time for the peasants to prepare for the long cold winter. They try to grow enough potatoes and cabbage in their garden plots to last until spring. In bad years the potatoes don't last till spring, and the poorer peasants are forced to eat their seed potatoes.

If they have a cow then enough hay must be cut and dried in the forest clearings to last till the snows melt in May. Mushrooms and berries are gathered, then dried and kept for the winter. In the forest they cut wood, heaping the logs in neat piles and leaving them there ready to drag to their homes when the snow comes and transport is easier.

We came to Omoutninsk in late August. At first things were not so bad. There was still a weekly market and it was possible to buy some commodities. But as winter approached, food disappeared from the markets. The peasants, who resented the presence of the evacuees, needed food for themselves and certainly would not part with anything for money that would be useless to them for feeding their families. They had prepared for the winter, and we evacuees who were unprepared became very resourceful. Our lives revolved around the acquisition of food: where we could get it, what we could get, and how we could keep it.

Marousia, whose mother's house we had previously rented, was friendly. She had gone with me to the library in an unsuccessful search for any books in English; she had taken me to the river to show me where to do the washing, and had promised to let me have some potatoes. I went to see her and after a couple of hours of talk and bargaining, she opened the trap-door of the cellar and came up with a sack of potatoes. They were too heavy for me to carry, but I daren't risk leaving any. She might change her mind. So I dragged the sack as far as possible, and waited till someone I knew came to help me. The potatoes were stored on wooden slats in the basement of our house, and once a week it was necessary to turn them over and take out any that were rotting.

Marousia told me that a cousin of hers had grown carrots in the summer, and might have some to sell. It was rather far away, but her cousin did let me have some, at a price, and these were buried in a deep box in the cellar.

I had bought cabbage in the autumn market. We threaded string around the stalks and hung the heads of cabbage from rafters in the cellar.

Before the winter set in I had picked wild raspberries in the forest which we had dried on the Russian stove. Then I had gathered the wild rose hips which were also dried and used for tea.

Onions were the most difficult to find, and they were essential to prevent scurvy. I tracked my onions down in a distant part of Omoutninsk. It was a poor hut and it was the first time I had seen animals living in one room with people. The hens and goats had been taken in for the winter, and the place stank. But I got my onions. They were too precious to put in the cellar, so they stayed in the little room with us, adding to the smells of the unventilated house.

Now we were ready for the winter.

Panic in Moscow

The Moscow panic – the day of the 'great skedaddle' as it was later called – began on October 16 when it was decided to evacuate government and party organisations and foreign embassies to Kuibyshev and other cities in the east. A rumour spread through the city that the Germans had already occupied Khimki, one of Moscow's northern suburbs. When the State and party officials began to leave, often in large cars with their families and everything they could cram in with them, or were seen crowding the railway stations, the people felt they were being abandoned. Panic was fed by hysterical rumours – that German parachutists had landed in Red Square, that Germans were among them dressed in Red Army uniforms, that government had broken down and that millions of Muscovites had been abandoned to their fate without food or weapons.

Technically no one could leave Moscow without a pass, but now all order and discipline broke down – in any case, the officials who should have checked all passes were themselves fighting to get out of the city. There was a deep fear of German occupation and a mass flight from the city began. For three or four days Moscow was in the grip of mass panic as tens of thousands crowded the roads, flooded the stations, and fought to get onto trains.

A graphic picture of the situation at the headquarters of the Soviet government is described in the reminiscences of Alexei Kosygin, who was at that time Deputy-Chairman of Sovnarkom, the executive committee of the government.

'The Sovnarkom building was empty – the doors of offices swung open, papers blew around and rustled underfoot, everywhere telephones rang. Kosygin ran from room to room, answering the phone. No-one spoke at the other end. Silence. He understood they were checking whether there was anyone in the Kremlin… One of those who rang identified himself. It was a well-known person. In a business-like way he enquired 'Well then, are we going to surrender Moscow?'[20]

The flight from the city and the evacuation continued throughout October and the first half of November. About half of the population and a large part of its industry left the city. But there were those who could not leave. There were civilian and military installations that had to be sustained. The hospitals were crammed with thousands of wounded and thousands more were arriving every day. And there were those who could leave, but would not; for though it seemed the whole city was demoralised, many hung on in grim determination to stay at all costs, never to leave Moscow.

Now the Soviet people were fighting for their very survival; by the end of October the first German offensive against Moscow had been halted and the German advance had exhausted itself.

News of the progress of the war filtered through to the Urals in a thin trickle. In Omoutninsk they did not hear of the chaos and incoherence that had overcome the great city, nor did they get news of defeats. To those so far away the news of the war became, as in Matthew Arnold's words, as though from the 'darkling plain, Swept with confused alarms of struggle and flight, Where ignorant armies clash by night'.

The Winter Forest

The autumn rains turned colder and suddenly it was winter. We woke up one morning to find a new landscape. Everything was covered in snow. But we still couldn't go to the Uchastok – the site. 'It's too treacherous, till the heavy frosts come and the earth freezes hard,' I was told.

Each day the snow fell steadily. The little wooden houses seemed to sink down into it. Narrow paths were cleared along the streets and small tracks up to the doors of the houses. On these paths the snow packed hard and was firm underfoot, but off the well-trodden paths it was loose and shifting, and a false step could send you up to your knees or deeper in soft snow.

At last Nickolai said, 'We're going to the site tomorrow. You can come, but you'll have to spend the day on your own.'

We left for the railway tracks in the early morning darkness. It was misty and cold, and we buried our faces in our scarves and concentrated on keeping to the track. The step from sleeper to sleeper was too big a stride for me, almost a jump, but going to the station by road would have added a mile and a half to our walk.

We reached the station in good time. The other engineers were there, but there were no crowds as there had been before, going north towards the labour camps, and we waited on the unusually quiet platform where the snow was hard and grey.

The train came round the bend in a sudden rush of lights and noise, and we were on our way for the two-hour journey. Inside, the lights were dim and there was a haze of cigarette smoke. The windows were so completely frosted over that it was impossible to see outside. Even breathing hard on one spot of the pane and then scraping the softened ice with a coin made no impression. In any case it was still dark outside.

The train whistled and slowed down for the halt. No station here – just a snow-covered platform in the midst of the forest. It was a big jump down from the high platform, then a wait for the train to get up speed again; and in the cold light of the northern winter's day, we saw the forest around us.

The site was at a forest halt, and the forest was magnificently beautiful. It stretched, it seemed to me, forever, but I was never afraid there. Thoughts of wild animals, wolves and bears, did not disturb me. I only avoided the sentry, who stood on the railway-bridge with his rifle ready. I would creep into the forest, make a detour and come up again near the railway line well past the bridge. I kept my bearings by the railway and tried not to wander far off.

I had been here several times in late summer and picked rose hips and wild raspberries to dry for the bleak winter. Everything then had been a symphony of greens; light coloured birch leaves, dark pines and firs. Once, too, I had come in the early autumn before the rains, and seen the brilliant reds and orange-yellow of the birch trees between the dark blue-green firs.

Now the forest was transformed; everything was glistening white. The branches of the trees were heavily laden with fresh-fallen snow. Their shapes were grotesque, but even more grotesque were the shadows they cast as the wintry sun came up. The snow, which at first had been pure white, now took on many colours; deep blue and purple in the shadows, bright yellow where the direct sun fell. The forest, which had been so still, seemed to find its voice. There were soft plumps as snow fell from over-laden branches. Every now and then there would be a sharp crack like a rifle shot, as a bough broke under its heavy burden and came crashing down.

We walked along the railway track to the clearing where the two log cabins stood. The men went in to prepare for their day's work, and I was alone in the forest. I really had to keep the railway in sight, as all footpaths had been obliterated by the snow.

I walked as always to the bridge where the sentry stood guard. He was stamping his feet to keep warm, and I made my usual detour, keeping out of his view, floundering in the snow, but not losing sight altogether of the railway line.

Beyond the bridge was the spot where the wild roses had grown and where I had picked hips that gave us our life-saving vitamin tea. And here it was that I saw the pin-points of bright scarlet peeping out of the snow.

Surely not raspberries! As I brushed the fluffy snow off I could see brilliant little shining red berries – winter cranberries – sparkling in the snow, the blanket that had enabled them to ripen slowly. They were firm and fragrant, and I filled my pockets, feeling I had been amply rewarded for my journey to the winter forest. All we would need now for our Christmas dinner was the turkey!

The Market at Yar

Now the real winter had set in the problem of washing clothes became acute. Local inhabitants mostly did a big bi-annual wash – spring and autumn. They washed their clothes in the bath house, then went down to the river to rinse them in the clearer water of the river where it flowed into the lake.

In the winter the men cut holes in the thick ice covering the lake so that they could fish. And the women then rinsed their washing in the open holes.

After seeing the raw hands and arms of her landlady – the result of plunging them into icy waters – Olga decided to wash her clothes in the bath house and hang them to dry on strings that had been stretched across to dry the clothes in summer. The wet washing froze solid, as stiff as boards. It took two weeks to thaw out before it could begin to dry.

For two months it was below forty degrees centigrade all the time. 'You froze absolutely. You had to be very well clothed, and you covered everything, leaving just a little aperture to see and to breathe.'

In this bleak midwinter Olga and three of her evacuee friends – Katia, Ella and Ella's niece Rosa, decided to take the overnight train to a larger town, Yar, where a weekly market was still held.

Yar market square is not far from the wooden station buildings, but most of the peasants bring their goods to market by road. They come on horse-drawn sleighs, the man walking beside the horse, and his wife sitting on top of the bags of potatoes or the frozen carcass they are trying to sell. Some walk down the bare winding road from the forest hauling small sledges, or carrying their bundles on their shoulders.

Most of the buyers, on the other hand, have come on the only train, arriving at five o'clock in the morning and waiting near the dark, deserted station or in the unlit village street till the market opens. They peer impatiently up the hill and at last, as the day begins to break, out of the misty darkness appear small clouds of steam – the breath and sweat of the first horses and peasants who are approaching Yar down the snow-covered road.

Only the eyes of the people are exposed, their faces covered by scarves, and their heads and ears protected from the frost by shawls or fur hats. Voluminous coats, often patched and shabby, envelop their bodies completely, and on their shuffling feet they wear valenki – clumsy felt boots made in the village during the long winter when the fields are covered with snow and farming is at a standstill. Their breath freezes and forms icicles on their eyelashes and brows, and on the horses' forelocks, giving them a frosted appearance.

The market square comes to life with daylight and the official opening time. In the grey light of early morning the village itself appears grey, the wooden houses are small and dilapidated, and the snow in the streets and on the square has been churned into a grey mass. Market officials, with bands on the arms to show authority, try to hustle the peasants to the stands, but there are not enough trestle tables, and many people prefer to sell their goods direct from the sleighs. Some hopeful buyers have walked up the road to meet the sledges, trying to obtain short-supply goods before the farmers reach the village and set too high a price for their produce.

Milk comes frozen in plates, and is sold in blocks looking like thick, pale pancakes, to be stored at home and melted when needed. Potatoes, which are sold by the bucket, are kept well-covered under sacking so that they *shall not freeze and turn sickly sweet and black. The carcasses of lamb and beef and horse-meat are frozen solid and are chopped and sawn through.*

Crowds of drably dressed country folk surround the sleighs where the meat is sold, bidding for parts of the carcass, and hoping to get enough to stock up for the long, hungry winter ahead. Eggs have been snatched up by the eager purchasers before they even reach the stalls. It is definitely a sellers' market; food is scarce, and the peasants do not want money that can be devalued, but to exchange goods for goods; so there is a lot of hard bargaining. A bottle of vodka will buy you the moon; a bouhanka – a large loaf of black bread – will get you enough beef for a week; a city trinket will purchase some solid pork fat.

The only vegetables grown in these northern parts are potatoes and cabbages, but it is possible to find dried forest raspberries and strings of dried mushrooms (used for soup) and there are plenty of cranberries shining brightly in little mounds on the dark stalls. The berries have been gathered in the late autumn by children who stand with their mothers eyeing prospective purchasers.

A young soldier exchanges a tin of army rations for some makhorka, cheap, foul-smelling tobacco, and then tries to find some newspaper to roll for a smoke. His companion, who carries an accordion slung over his shoulder, starts to play a popular tune, and at the sound children leave their stalls and gather round to watch and be entertained.

By mid-day all the goods have gone and the peasants start on their way home, past the wooden village houses and up the road towards the forest.

*

They had travelled all night by train to get to the market, and now they had to queue at the crowded station for tickets to take them and their expensive bargains on the night journey back to Omoutninsk. If they failed there would be a wait of twenty-four hours for the next train, and they were desperately anxious to get back to their families with their precious purchases.

The waiting-room at the station was packed with people and a long queue had already formed in front of the ticket office. Ella and Katia were assigned to stand in the queue and Olga, as the foreigner whose Russian was not so fluent, and Rosa, who was only fifteen, were left to safeguard their purchases.

The room was dense with cigarette smoke and stale with the stench of so many winter-wrapped bodies. Unable to stand the noise and smell any longer, Olga left Rosa in charge of the purchases and went outside to get a breath of fresh air.

Outside it was dark and still. The snow had stopped falling and it was freezing hard, the stars bright in the pitch black sky. There were no lamps on the platform, only a hazy light from the frosted windows of the waiting room. Beyond that the station was deserted, in complete darkness, a world totally encompassed by the blackness and intense cold, as though there was nowhere on this continent – on the whole planet – that was not in the metallic grasp of the icy night.

But as her eyes became accustomed to the dark Olga could see the outlines of a train standing on the siding. They had not heard it arrive; it looked dark and empty.

She heard the crunch of heavy footsteps behind her, and a little alarmed turned back to the waiting room. Three men who had left the train were coming towards her. As she reached the area of light she heard her name called, and one of the men came up to her. It was Nikolai, head of the organisation that had brought them out of Moscow. He was warmly dressed with the collar of his coat turned up and the flaps of his hat turned down, but it was unmistakably Nikolai.

He was amazed to see her and said: 'What on earth are you doing here?'

'We came to the Yar market yesterday to try and buy some food for the winter, but we can't get tickets for the way back. There's a fight going on in the waiting room.'

'We're returning to Omoutninsk from Glazov,' he told her. 'We just got off the train for a breath of fresh air and a smoke. You can come back with us.'

'But I haven't got a ticket.'

'We'll arrange that. Get your things. It's leaving very soon.'

Olga explained that she was not alone. 'There are four of us.'

'I can take you and your things,' he said, 'but no-one else.'

She tried to persuade him, and after much pleading he agreed to take Rosa, but not the others. 'It will be easier for two of them – they'll only need two tickets,' he said.

Inside, Olga pushed her way through the people and bundles. Rosa, standing over their purchases, was looking apprehensive at the thought of not getting back to her mother. Katia came towards her, picking her way gingerly through the crowded floor. Her luxurious grey fur coat looked out of place in the midst of the crowd of peasants, as she herself did with her fresh appearance and delicate colouring. She, too, was anxious at the thought of not seeing her small son for another twenty-four hours.

Ella beckoned to Olga urgently. 'They haven't started selling tickets yet, and the train is due. They must be letting their friends get tickets first.' Her dark eyes flashed angrily and there were red patches on her cheeks. 'The train is in already,' Olga told her. 'I've just seen Nikolai.' She explained that he had agreed to take her and Rosa and their bundles, but not the other two.

Ella looked furious. 'Typical!' she spat out through clenched teeth. 'I could have told you he wouldn't take me.'

'He says it will help you if you only have to get two tickets. But I don't like going back without you.'

But Ella and Katia said she must go. If they could not get on that train, she would be able to explain to their husbands why they were not back.

Inside the train it was warm and comfortable. The men had been on a business trip, travelling 'soft', with sleeping compartments. Olga and Rosa shared a berth, and when the train started the men brought warm blankets for them.

CHAPTER 3

Typhoon

Iɴ November 1941 the second stage of Operation Typhoon was launched. But the offensive petered out. For the first time the *Blitzkrieg* stalled, lost its momentum.

In the beginning Barbarossa was a brilliant success for Germany. In the first few days the German onslaught wiped out the Russian air force in the west and smashed or captured the Red Army units confronting it. Within five days the German forces had already taken Minsk, capital of Belorussia, and were advancing through the Ukraine. They had swept aside all resistance and were on the way to achieving their objectives.

In October the Germans launched what was to be their knock-out blow against the city. This assault lasted for a month; by mid-October Moscow's situation was critical. Even the bravest and most determined people doubted that the city could be held.

From a conquered Russia they planned to obtain all the raw materials for their future attack on Britain. They were in sight of the big prize – the capital city of the whole of the Union of Soviet Socialist Republics. It seemed that resistance to total German occupation could only degenerate into scattered Red Army remnants and partisan groups; these, the German generals believed, would be dealt with easily.

Hitler had not reckoned on a winter offensive. The troops outside Moscow had no experience of the intense cold of this city in winter and were not equipped for the freezing temperatures further north than they had ever been. As the mud turned to frost, weapons and men began to freeze into immobility. The offensive lasted barely three weeks. Winter was in full force, with temperatures below minus twenty degrees. Tank engines froze solid, and the ground was as hard as cement. The German soldiers were without proper clothing for such extreme cold, and many suffered from frost-bite. Typhoon came to a standstill; and now the Germans faced a long and bloody war under conditions they had not anticipated and for which they were not prepared.

On December 6 the Red Army launched a counter-offensive outside Moscow. It was a most significant, critical moment. For the first time since they had started the war, the first time in all the countries they had invaded, the Germans had lost their strategic initiative. Although the national survival of the Soviet Union still hung in the balance in effect it signalled the beginning of loss of strategic initiative in the war as a whole.

Germany had invaded a country unprepared for war. Yet now, paradoxically, it was that very factor that helped bring the military advance to a halt. Their superior arms and experienced fighting power had taken them too far and too fast to a front 600 kilometres deep and 1,500 kilometres wide. Their supply lines had become too long and their problems of recouping food and fuel shortages had been compounded by the scorched earth policy of the Soviets.

Their transport was clogged. They had to cope with the huge number of prisoners they had taken; they needed to bring up necessary supplies to the front and in addition equip their armies for even harsher weather. As the mud turned to ice men and arms froze into immobility.

And a change had taken place in the attitude of the Russian people. Ten years before the country had been at war, but it was a war with itself as the peasants fought a policy of forced collectivisation which was robbing them of their rights over their land and way of life. They had been destroying their own livestock rather than hand them over to the collectives; and they and the whole population had been stricken by the famine that resulted from this disastrous conflict.

Now the people were again immersed in a life-and-death struggle, and once more they were destroying their own livestock and cattle, everything they could not take with them as they fled before the German advance, destroying their own homes, buildings – anything to deny the invaders the supplies they needed. But this time it was against an invader from outside, an intruder, and all that same deep and stubborn resistance which had been so fatally divisive was now aroused in a way that unified the whole population.

Stalin finally was alive to the need to unite the country. He had to rally the people to a struggle now based not on class, not town against country, but on a unifying patriotism. On the night of November 6 Stalin spoke in the central hall of Mayakovskaya Metro station, and the following day in celebration of the 24th anniversary of the revolution he spoke again in Red Square to troops that listened in the grey, bitter cold as fighter planes patrolled overhead and the distant boom of Russian and German guns punctuated his speech. His appeal was not political, he did not speak of the socialist Soviet Union; he called up deep Russian feelings of nationalism, invoking Russian heroes of the past, those who fought Napoleon; and the great men of Russian civilisation: Nevsky, Pushkin, Tolstoy. He appealed for a revival of the deepest instincts that his years of terror almost destroyed – love of country and a specifically national Russian pride.

'The mystique of a great national war, of a life and death struggle took deep roots in the Russians' consciousness within a very short time.' Pasternak wrote: 'Everyone took a deep breath and flung themselves into the furnace of this deadly, liberating struggle with real joy, real rapture.'[21]

*

The Russian counter-offensive pushed the Germans 200 kilometres back from Moscow.

And now the consequences of Nazi occupation were laid bare to the Soviet troops as they entered the villages. They were devoid of all living men; a few women and children had returned to the charred remains of their homes; the corpses hung from telegraph poles; and there they saw the first mass graves.

German soldiers were instructed to live off conquered lands even if the local populations would suffer famine. The planning for the subjugation of a conquered Russia was as detailed as it was for military triumph.

The invasion of the Soviet Union was predicated on the fascist belief in the superiority of the Aryan race and the inferiority of all others, and on the Nazi view of Bolshevism as a Jewish-Slavic conspiracy against Germany. Thus the Russians and other nationalities in the Soviet Union were *Untermenschen* – subhuman, barbarians. who could be treated as you would treat disgusting or dangerous animals. There would be no adherence to the laws of war.

This was a war terrible beyond belief, a war of hideous brutalisation. After Kiev was captured in June more than 33,000 Jews were shot and thrown into a ravine at Babi Yar. German troops were exhorted and encouraged to act with maximum cruelty against both the Red Army and against civilians. All war conventions applying to civilians and to

HILDA BERNSTEIN

prisoners of war were abandoned. Russian soldiers taken prisoner faced an agonising fate by exposure and starvation, by inhuman treatment and sometimes by execution. Of five million, more than three million would never return.

German cruelty and criminality, of indiscriminate murders of civilians, of the twisted piles of corpses in mass graves that were exposed when the Soviet soldiers re-took occupied areas, led to a deep hate and desire for revenge that would bring cruelty and brutalisation in return.

That December Japan bombed the United States naval base at Pearl Harbour bringing America into the war on the side of the allies. The following day America and Britain declared war on Japan. By Christmas that year the Soviet Union had two powerful allies.

In the four years of war that were to follow, the battle front at its widest would stretch two thousand kilometres across Europe, from the Baltic Sea to the Caucasus mountains.

The Order of the Bath

There were two types of bath houses in Omoutninsk: the one in which you had a bath 'the black way', and the other 'the white way'. The 'black way' bath house had no chimney and no flue. The fire was lit under a cauldron of water and smoke filled the place. Soot settled on the walls and ceiling, and you came out – clean perhaps – but smudged. The 'white way' was the way the wealthier peasants had their bath. This bath house had a chimney and a proper stove in which great logs were burned. When only the embers were left the flue was closed. Uncovered iron cauldrons stood on top of the stove and as the water temperature rose steam filled the bath house.

There were wide wooden shelves at different levels. The higher you sat the warmer it was, and the greater the steam. There was no light in the bath house; only a small oil-wick, if any paraffin was available.

After weeks of fruitless waiting for my landlady to feel that she was in need of a bath, I was persuaded by some friends to go to the public bath house with them. Most of the women there were evacuees. Many of them from Latvia and Estonia had escaped when their country was occupied by the Germans. They had travelled for weeks, some had been separated from their families, and now they were here in Omoutninsk waiting for the war to end. Near me an emaciated Latvian woman was rubbing ash over her little daughter's skin and then washing it off. She had no soap.

I did not go to the public bath house again, but waited for the promised day when my landlady would prepare her bath house. Finally, she decided to clean up her family for the New Year holiday.

We all got up early on bath day, which happened to be 25 December, and fetched endless pails of water from the well. The bath houses were never built close to the house for fear of fire, but always stood beyond the well. We stamped a path in the deep snow and tried not to spill any water, as it turned to ice immediately. If we touched the metal bucket or the well handle with bare hands our skin would be burnt by the icy metal, so we wore gloves inside our mittens. The freezing water splashed onto my mittens which stiffened at once, making it hard to carry the pails.

At last the old grandmother declared there was enough water. The fire was lit in the stove, and I waited to be called to take my bath. I waited a very long time.

This was the order of the bath:

First came Marie Ivanovna, as head of the household while her husband was away. Then the eldest son, who was fourteen and had done a great deal of the water carrying. After Vanya came the eleven-year-old daughter. Then the grandmother took the two little boys and bathed first them and then herself. After that, the pig was taken and given his New Year bath. And lastly, after the pig, came the impermanent and unacceptable evacuee. That was me.

Christmas in the Urals

In mid-winter it was no longer possible for Olga to go to the site; the days were too short and it was dark most of the day. It was dangerous for her to be wandering by herself in the forest after dark.

The village hibernated, snowbound. Sometimes she would meet with the wives of other engineers. Often alone for long hours, she read poetry, played Patience, and as her Russian became more fluent, began to get books in Russian from the library. With no electricity she cherished their tiny oil lamp with its wick in a saucer. She was told that the fat for the lamps came from bears that were hunted in the forest.

The windows of the house were sealed and in the room all the smells accumulated. When someone came in from outside they brought the freshness with them. Into the room, filling it with his presence, snow sparkling on his hat and dripping as it melted, came Alyosha.

His eyes were shining. 'I've something for you,' he said.

He put his hand in his pocket and carefully drew out a fish wrapped in his handkerchief; a fresh river trout, its scales blue and glistening.

'I was crossing a little wooden bridge over a stream,' he explained, 'and I noticed a string tied to the handrail. When I looked down I saw a hole in the ice; I pulled it, and there was a net, with this fish in it!'

'It was my Christmas present,' Olga said later, and wrote a little poem about Alyosha and the fish, in which she said, 'We travelled so far and then returned, But you will return no more.' For Alyosha was one of the millions killed in the war.

So for my sister Christmas in the Urals was marked by having a bath and by Alyosha's fish. But, as always, January 1 was a holiday, and a party was held on New Year's Eve. Olga and Henry took along their portable gramophone and records for the celebration. 'We played the records and danced a little, but although we had chosen the records carefully, taking those we thought would last, we were tired of them already.

'There wasn't really any food. We had black bread spread with butter that had been reclaimed from cooking and sprinkled with a little sugar; we called them "pastries". Surprisingly they tasted quite nice.'

There was real cause for celebration: the news that the Germans had been driven back from the gates of Moscow; and that with the Japanese attack on Pearl Harbour America had declared war on Japan and Germany. The Soviet Union now had powerful allies, and material aid from Britain and American would soon arrive.

The American Girl

My Russian had improved rapidly since we had come to Omoutninsk, as nobody, apart from Henry, who was away most of the time, spoke English. But I was longing for the sounds of the English language. So I was excited when Nina Stepanovna told me that there was an American girl living on the other side of the lake and that she would find out her address and take me to her.

On the morning of our expedition I woke early and tried to guess what the day was like. I could hear the children's voices and the sound of heavy logs being brought in to light the big Russian stove which was the heart of the home. It was placed centrally so that it heated the whole of the house. We did all our cooking in it; anyone who felt cold climbed onto it to warm up, and my landlady slept on it at night.

It was dark in my room, for the thickly snow-frosted window hid the outside world, and there was no need for curtains. I hoped desperately that it was fine, for we couldn't go if it was snowing, and I had been looking forward to our expedition for a long time.

When I went out to fetch water from the well the sun had risen, a brilliant ball of fire hanging over the distant forest. The sky was an icy blue, and clear. The desolate expanse of the lake stretched ahead. On the outskirts were a few minute houses, and beyond them the deep forest, reaching away to the far horizon. Everything was white, with blue shadows in the distance. Near the banks of the lake were some small boats frozen in and snowed up for the winter. Round the holes made in the ice and kept open all winter a few people were fishing, their breath rising in puffs of steam.

The water in the well was frozen and I had to drop the bucket several times to break the ice; but still, it was a good day for our outing.

Inside the house the stove was well alight. There was a smell of charcoal mixed with the earthy smell of unwashed jacket potatoes boiling in a cauldron. That was the children's breakfast, and two little boys were watching and waiting for it to be ready. All day long the cauldron of potatoes would stand by the side of the stove, and whenever they were hungry the children would take a potato, peel it, and eat it.

I prepared for our evening meal: vegetables and meat that I had obtained at the Yar market; put them in a cast-iron pot, and with a long-handled fork pushed it to the far corner inside the hot stove to simmer slowly all day. It would be ready, deliciously cooked, when I returned.

Nina Stepanovna, with her dog, was waiting for me near her house. We had discussed many times how to get to the other side of the lake, and in the end had decided to walk across. Spare skis were hard to find; anyway, I had had very little practice in skiing, and it was essential that we should be back on our side before the early northern night with its severe frosts set in. The lake was wide, the further shore only just visible; to walk round would take too long – the quickest way was to take, as the Russians say, 'the bird's eye route'.

So we set out on foot to go across the vast expanse of snow-covered ice to the doll's houses on the opposite shore. Our feet crunched on the rough surface and we tried to keep to the tracks across the frozen lake which were so snowed over that we might have been walking across fields. Once well away from the banks and the protection of the trees and houses there, the wind was biting, and we covered our faces so that only our eyes were exposed.

The going was hard, and I banished the thought that each step we took now would have to be taken again on the way back. Instead, I thought of the reason for our visit. I was filled with joy at the prospect of talking in English to a real American after all these weeks of hearing only Russian spoken. I wondered what had brought her to this God-forsaken place. I had been looking forward to meeting 'the other foreigner' ever since Nina Stepanovna had told me about an American girl living somewhere in Omoutninsk, and that she would take me with her when she visited her 'on business'.

I didn't ask what the business was, though the thought had crossed my mind that perhaps I was being used as an excuse for it. I remembered how I had met Nina Stepanovna. She had been sitting outside my room in the house where we first stayed when I came in one afternoon. A large Alsatian was lying in front of my door. I hesitated before it, and she spoke to me, asking if I was the evacuee, and how I was getting on. Her excuse for visiting me was that she had heard an animal had died, and that there was dog meat for sale. No animal had died in our house, nor in the street for that matter, but it was a fair excuse for checking up on the 'foreigner'.

That was how we had met, accidentally, it seemed. I had concluded that she was my watchdog but even so she had taken me under her wing, invited me to her home, given me papers to read, scoured the library for English books (there were none) and now she was taking me to find the American girl so that I could speak to her in English. It would help her too, for perhaps the American spoke no Russian!

At last we reached the further bank, scrambled up the slope and, after some searching and questioning, found the house where the foreigner was living. It was really no more than a log cabin, with icicles hanging from *the eaves and drifts of snow piled at the sides; but it was warm inside, and our faces tingled as life came back.*

We asked for the American, and Nina Stepanovna introduced herself and then triumphantly me – the 'Englishwoman – the American'.

Delighted, I burst into English. But what was the matter? The American girl didn't seem to understand what I was saying. She spoke first in a strange language I didn't know, and then in French. Bewildered, I spoke to her in my halting Russian. Oh yes, she was from America, but not from the United States. She had come from Portuguese-speaking Brazil.

To Nina Stepanovna America was America. 'North, South – what's the difference?'

The Pink Nightgown

The first news I had was from Ella, who whispered to me excitedly: 'The train has come, but it's not going East. It's taking a short list back to Moscow.'

The train came from Moscow every two days on a branch line and the next station after ours was where the prison camps of the North began.

Ever since our arrival the previous August our one hope was that we would be able, in time, to return to Moscow. At that time the possibility seemed a long way away – if ever. So when we had been told that some of us were to be shifted East, to the Chinese borders, there were many volunteers, hoping to end up somewhere more amenable than this little dot in the frozen North.

But now we heard that the train was not going East, but that a select few would be taken back to Moscow.

There was a scramble for places. Perhaps the Metro engineers were particularly valued, for we were among the fortunate ones.

We had left for Omoutninsk in the heat of summer. Now it was March, and the world was still frozen. We would be returning the way we had come – in cattle trucks – and we now knew that the journey that should have taken two days would take two or three weeks. We needed food; the only issue on rations was black bread, and salt once a month. Food would not be obtainable en route and to get it we needed something to barter.

What was left? All our clothes were now very worn; besides, we needed them. We all walked around in that severe cold wearing several layers of clothing. I looked through our trunk again. Crockery could be bartered in the hope that it could be replaced in the city.

We had inherited some cotton blanket covers from American friends who had left Moscow. They were simply lengths of cotton print sewn to-gether to make a bag for the blankets. They had a pretty design of blue flowers. I carefully unpicked and washed and ironed them to see if they, too, could be bartered for food to take back to hungry Moscow.

Another friend leaving Russia had left me a pink silk night-dress trimmed with coffee-coloured lace. It was fine and soft. I did not bring it to the north to wear; it had been used to wrap the crockery. It was still wrapped round the dishes when I took them to the market.

As I was unwrapping the plates, one of the women asked about the pink 'dress'. I explained that it was a night-dress, but there was some confusion between the words 'evening' and 'night'. The woman was convinced that the pink crepe-de-chine garment with its deep lace trim was a fine evening gown.

The people of Omoutninsk were poor peasants. They had brown, weather-beaten faces. Their hands were rough, their nails broken. There was no such thing as make-up, hair-dos or manicures. They wore long skirts, thick cotton stockings, and heavy overshoes.

I could not visualise the occasion on which the purchaser would wear this delicate piece of underwear as a dress. My hesitation in selling it as such seemed to make it more desirable to the purchaser, and the result was that we got butter – real butter, quite beyond our dreams – for the night-dress. The cotton material was exchanged for flour.

Nina Stepanovna, who had taken me across the lake to meet 'the American girl' must have been the kindest 'watchdog' I ever had. She de-hydrated the frozen meat that I had by drying it for days in her slow oven. She came to see me off triumphantly producing a box of carrots she had dried for me as a parting gift.

With a few onions, the dried carrots, some bread and dehydrated meat, we were ready for the journey to Moscow.

Return to Moscow

They went back on the first train, among the chosen few with the Metrostroy engineers, some people who were in the army and technical experts, together with their wives and children.

The journey back was very, very hard, much harder than going. Deep snow covered the whole countryside; the cold was intense. In the middle of each wagon there was a stove in which they burned logs. The logs of wood occupied precious space in the over-crowded truck, but while the stove burned they kept warm. When it went out they froze.

For nearly three weeks they journeyed through the silent white wastes, the rhythm of the clack of the wheels only broken by unpredictable pauses, sometimes at stations, sometimes where there was nothing to be seen but the dazzling white expanse under an iron sky. The doors of the trucks were tightly closed to keep in the warmth. Only when the train stopped could they open them briefly and they saw that they were in a landscape so obliterated by the shroud of snow that they could have been anywhere in the world – or nowhere.

Somewhere there were great armies at war; but for them the war was reduced to a train isolated in this vast, anonymous, frozen, snow-shrouded world.

They were all underfed and had little resistance to cold. Life filtered down to a slow and low ebb, a hibernation that conserved what energy remained from their inadequate diet. As on the way out, the train, after stopping for unspecified periods, would start again just as unpredictably without warning. At one stage when they ran out of water, the men in their truck got off to collect snow; and they were all left behind.

Then Olga and another young woman – Tamara – were really the only able-bodied ones left in their wagon. There was an old engineer, Aleksandrov, who had a broken arm and was accompanied by his sister and his grandson. The wife of another of the lost engineers had four children, and needed assistance as she had a burned hand.

Olga and Tamara attended to the stove, prepared the food, and helped the women with children as best they could. The men left behind managed to get another train, and they caught up with them before they reached Moscow.

Volya, a boy of fourteen, also disappeared. They were not quite sure what had happened to him. He must have jumped out some time when the train stopped, either to relieve himself or to go to another truck, but he did not return. His mother was very upset but Olga said, 'We were not so worried as we would have been on the outward journey. Then we hadn't known our exact destination, and families completely lost track of each other. Now we knew we were returning to Moscow, and a resourceful fourteen-year-old can usually find his way home.'

When they were approaching Moscow they began worrying about the time of arrival. There was a curfew operating in the city, and if they arrived after curfew they would have to spend another night on the train.

They arrived at midnight. And there, sitting on a bench on the station, looking tired and disconsolate, was Volya. He had managed to get on a train that had arrived three days before, but he had been unable to leave the station. Moscow was a sealed city, no one was allowed in or out without a permit, and his mother had the necessary papers.

'Volya, why did you leave us?'

'I couldn't stand it any more. The pace was so slow.'

By a happy chance the curfew had been lifted for that one night, in celebration of Easter. This was a concession to religious observance through which Stalin sought to cement the unity of the Russian people during this intensely critical period; and to make a gesture of friendship to the Allies.

CHAPTER 4

Wartime City

THEY returned to a city damaged and darkened by war, silent and austere. There were no lights – the black-out was complete – no traffic, no children, no dogs. The schools were closed; the children with their immaculate white blouses and red scarves, the girls with big bows in their hair, would not return for another two years. It was a city shut in on itself in a season of darkness, cold, strange, empty, completely quiet. The only sound from the streets was the squeaking of valenki on the hard-packed snow.

The bombs had not fallen on the block where Olga and Henry lived, and they were fortunate to find their home more or less intact. Most of the flats in their building were empty.

The panic of the past October was a shameful memory, but hundreds of thousands who had left then had not returned. The embassies and many government offices and huge industrial plants with all their workers were still in the east, in Kuibyshev and other parts of Kazakhstan. But Stalin had remained in Moscow, which had been essential for morale, and with him the generals and most of the Politbureau. The Moscow Town Council and the Commissariat of Defence also had not budged. But half the population was still away; only those who were recalled for work were beginning to return.

The sky was dotted with barrage balloons. Those who had stayed in the 'danger months' – October to December – had lived through weeks with barricades and anti-tank obstacles in the main streets. There was a considerable amount of bomb damage. And everyone was short of food.

The Metropol was no longer the hotel of faded splendour of its former days. With little lighting and minimum warmth the large rooms with heavy furniture were shadowed and gloomy, the chilly corridors dark by 3 p.m., and the crystal chandeliers unlit, dusty, shrouded with cobwebs. It was now the base for foreign correspondents from Europe and America who had flown in to report on the war.

'Moscow had a lean and hungry look' wrote Alexander Werth. 'It had lived through a hard, and for many people, terrible winter.'[22] The American correspondent, Harrison Salisbury, describing how he first saw Moscow in the fading light of a wartime winter's day, wrote of the city as beleaguered, the people thin, gaunt and wolfish under their padded cotton jackets and sheepskins, moving with shoulders bowed and heads bent under the burden of war. He wrote of the inevitable queues, the cold, the hunger, the heartbreak and tragedy; the markets where men and women sold, bit by bit, the heritage of a lifetime for bread or a scrap of meat.[23]

There were many homeless people, some who had been bombed out of their own homes, others who had fled from villages as the Germans advanced on Moscow. Because so many people had not yet returned there were many empty apartments; the homeless found their way into some; others were stripped by thieves.

All able-bodied men between the ages of sixteen and fifty-five and women aged sixteen to fifty who were not already working in state enterprises were mobilised for work in industry or construction. Only sixteen - eighteen year olds who were receiving vocational training, students in higher or secondary education, and mothers with several children were exempted. Olga was welcomed back to the Foreign Languages Institute.

They had finished all the food they had brought with them from the North, and there was no food in the shops. In the shopping streets like Kuznetsky Most or Gorki Street, shop windows were mostly sandbagged, or displayed cardboard hams and cheeses, covered with dust. Once again it was a case of exchanging clothes for food, sometimes by going into the country and bartering with the peasants; and in Moscow itself to the *kolkhoz* markets where peasants were permitted to sell produce grown on their own plots of land.

Everything was hard to get. Rations were too small for survival, except for the minority who were in special categories; often ration coupons were not honoured, and many basic foods were not supplied on the ration, while a large part of the population – the peasants – did not get any rations and had to survive on what they could grow themselves.

Because the supply of food and goods in the shops was so erratic and arbitrary people found methods of distribution that by-passed the formal system. In her book about the 1930s, Sheila Fitzpatrick describes this as a second economy which operated alongside the official one. Goods leaked out of factories at every stage of production, and industry itself relied on more or less illegal practices to get necessary raw materials.[24]

This second economy was also used by speculators and other criminal operators. The *kolkhoz* markets became a channel for black market goods. They traded in everything, legal and illegal. It was in the markets that people traded their personal possessions and family treasures for food. They were the most important unofficial source of food for the urban population. Prices were unregulated and as demand far exceeded supply, they were far higher than official prices. But for many they became essential for survival.

Olga had learned how to barter, but she grew very thin. 'It taught me to love food,' she said, 'so I never achieved that slimness again.'

The Hardest Winter

When she returned to the Institute, there was Larissa. 'No, we hadn't left Moscow.' She and Nickolai, she told Olga in confidence, had decided they had nothing to lose and would simply wait for the Germans to come. 'We're not communists or Jews, and we thought it couldn't be any worse with the Germans.' There were so few teachers left that Larissa's position at the Institute had in fact grown better.

Every available male was absent on war service; the only male students in the Institute were those who were totally unfit for any war duties. The students were almost all female, mostly girls straight from school.

The year was divided into two terms, with examinations in June, at the end of the school year. The Institute owned a small farm at Istra, a well-known beauty spot not far from Moscow. The farm supplied vegetables for the students' canteen and the students went there in summer to help with the weeding, hay-making and harvesting. They would come back after their life in the open-air fresh and sunburned and more eager for study.

It was a very beautiful place, surrounded by extensive forests and situated on the clear, swift-flowing river Istra. There had been a famous ancient monastery there, the New Jerusalem renowned for its beauty. When the Germans were finally driven out of Istra everything had been destroyed. All but three houses had been burned to the ground, and the New Jerusalem monastery had been blown up.

In normal times there would have been plenty of social and sports activities. But now in the summer vacation the students were mobilised for construction jobs. They went to the forests, cutting wood for

Moscow's winter. They worked hard; but they were young women, physically weakened by insufficient food, and they could not provide a city the size of Moscow with enough wood for heating.

Winter came, and the classrooms were unheated and freezing. Students and teachers wore all their outdoor clothes – hats, gloves, boots. They would get up every half hour and jump and run around the rooms. Even so it was often impossible to write, to hold a pen or pencil.

These spartan conditions produced a camaraderie between teachers and students. Olga formed lasting relationships with her students who loved her for her for her clear, 'proper' English pronunciation, her attractiveness and her cheerful good nature.

The gas supply flickered lower and lower, and sometimes went off altogether. Electricity was limited to a single bulb for each room. Not a house in Moscow was heated by coal; the wood cut from the forests was thinly spread and soon exhausted. People used tin stoves, fuelled with chopped up furniture and torn up books. All down the streets you could see the smoke from the chimneys of these little stoves sticking out of the windows and the smudges left on the outside walls.

Hunger would prove to be the most pervasive of all wartime hardships. 'While many people experienced violence, injury, bereavement and homelessness, all but a small minority were hungry for much of the time.'[25] They lost weight, became weaker and more tired; and at its most extreme, malnutrition culminated in starvation. The largest number of deaths by starvation was in blockaded Leningrad, but in Moscow, also, people fell dead of starvation in the streets.

For Olga and Henry, although they were on very stringent rations, the food situation was not as critical as for some Muscovites. Now that the Germans had been driven back from Moscow the engineers were back at work on the Metro where work continued underground twenty-four hours a day during the rest of the war. Henry was on a higher ration which they supplemented by bartering whatever they could in the markets.

Often Henry was on night-shift, and she would be alone in their room at night, with insufficient light to read by, in a building ghost-like in its emptiness.

Rowena

As soon as we returned to Moscow from evacuation the Dean of the English Faculty was delighted to see me. Would I start teaching again? Tomorrow, please! There were two advanced groups who had been struggling with Russian teachers. The only native English-speaking lecturer they had at the college who had not left Moscow was Rowena.

She was an American and her subject was maths. Still, she spoke English – and could teach it, although they did not much like her American accent.

Nobody liked Rowena. She was extremely short, but by no means petite, and very self-centred. Her one aim in life seemed to be to amass enough roubles to buy herself an expensive fur coat so that she could return to America in style. That was why she had stayed in Moscow just before the war when the majority of other Americans had left for home.

In October when the Germans were only fifteen kilometres away and there was general panic, even part of the college was to be evacuated. Rowena came along with her bag but was unable to get on any of the transport. She saw books, equipment and other peoples' luggage being loaded onto trucks, and witnessed one eminent professor throw another, equally eminent, off the truck so that he could take his belongings away with him. After that Rowena, together with some of the less important members of the staff and many students decided to make their own way out of the city.

They walked all day until they were well away from the town and getting deep into the forests surrounding Moscow. By this time they had split into groups and scattered in different directions. It was getting dark. Rowena, with her short legs and plump figure, had difficulty in keeping up. She had been brought up in Brooklyn and was a real New Yorker who had never walked in a forest at all, certainly never after dark and alone. The terrors of the wild wood were greater to her than human ones. So Rowena turned round and walked back again, still carrying her suitcase.

She went to live in the nearly empty students' hostel to wait for the Germans. But the Germans never reached Moscow, and gradually other teachers and students drifted back, the College reopened, and classes began again.

Those were hungry days.

During the time Rowena had been on her own in the students' hostel bread supplies had been fairly good, and she had dried crusts of bread daily on the slightly warm radiators. She had in this way collected a large quantity of dried bread. Once an old peasant woman from the country outside Moscow had come looking for bread, and Rowena exchanged her sack of dried crusts for a stringy, but whole, chicken. She told me that she had cooked the chicken behind locked doors so that no one should know about it. She hadn't tasted chicken for a long time. She could hardly wait for it to cook. When it was about ready she sat down and ate the whole chicken straight off. But poor Rowena had become unaccustomed to such a feast, and immediately brought it all up.

After my flat was organised with illicit supplies of gas and power, Rowena used to come round on her way to College. In winter it gets dark very early in Moscow and I had to do the cooking whenever I could as there were usually power cuts all evening. Rowena would stand over the electric toaster to keep warm and watch me prepare the evening meal: cereal made from grain (oats that I had once considered only fit for horses) frozen cabbage and frozen black potatoes. She invariably said: 'It smells delicious,' and I always thought she must be much hungrier than I was.

One day Rowena was buying her bread rations in Gorki Street when a bomb was dropped on the shop next door. She came out to see the street looking, as she said, like a butcher's shop with meat strewn all over the place. It was an unnerving sight.

By this time America had entered the war, and Rowena's brother was a Major in the American army. He wanted his little sister to come home, and Rowena felt she had had enough and began to make preparations to leave.

Most Americans donated useful little articles of clothing to their friends when they went back to the States, but not Rowena. She sold everything she could, still aiming for her fur coat. She didn't want just an ordinary astrakhan or karakul. What she wanted was the rarest of all, broadtail, made from lambs that were taken from the sheep before birth when their coats had a silky quality.

She haunted the government commission shops where people sold their clothes for money, and finally found the coat she wanted. She wore it when she left to fly to Iran, and from there to America. It was spring, and the coat was heavy. But no matter; winters are cold in New York too.

I last heard from her from Teheran. The American Airforce had been very gallant and given her a marvellous time there.

She advised me to leave by the same route.

Masha

The three sisters in Chekhov's play, one of whom was named Masha, were always longing to go to Moscow, but never went. My Masha did go to Moscow from the village where she had lived all her life.

Olga's Masha was a domestic worker who once a week came to do the washing. She would hang the sheets in the yard and sit watching them billowing in the wind. It was not safe to leave them unguarded.

Masha's husband was in exile, in a labour camp. He had killed a man in a drunken brawl and was serving five years for manslaughter. With three young boys to keep she had found things hard in the village and had sent the middle son to her husband's parents in Moscow. The parents lived in poverty in a shack. The boy contracted tuberculosis. The letter telling of his illness had lain unread; Masha couldn't read. By the time she understood he was really ill, he had died.

So she came to Moscow to find work. Six days a week she worked as a cleaner in the Lenin library, and on the seventh day, her free day, she went to Olga. This was before the German invasion.

She had not told her husband of the son's death. He was the bright one, his father's favourite.

Masha's husband was released in 1941, and they returned to their village, but war was imminent and he was called up only days after their return.

So Masha came back to Moscow to work bringing her eldest son, who was now fifteen, with her. She sent her youngest son to a cousin in Leningrad, believing that there he would be safe. And once more she dusted the books in the Lenin library. When Olga returned to Moscow from the Urals, Masha was there again to do her washing once a week.

When her eldest son turned sixteen he was mobilised for construction work. Masha had a bed in a hostel, and was trying to learn to read and write at evening classes.

The Russians had managed to evacuate some of the women and children from Leningrad before the end of the siege, but Masha's youngest boy was not among them, and there was no news of him.

Perhaps he had died of starvation. Perhaps he had been killed by bombs or shells that rained on the city.

Masha, in Moscow, had no more news of him.

Blat

The key word used, and the most important word in the language, was blat. It was impossible, without the necessary blat, to get a railway ticket from Kiev to Kharkov, to find accommodation in Moscow or Leningrad, to purchase a new valve for a wireless set, to find a man to mend a hole in the roof, to obtain an interview with a government official… For many years blat was the only way to get what was needed.

Edward Crankshaw, *Kruschev's Russia* (Harmondsworth, 1959)

Blat was Soviet jargon for a system that was not exactly bribery; it was more a reciprocal relationship involving goods and favours, sometimes involving money, but more often of friendship and informal exchanges; a system of networking. You needed to know people in different occupations and positions. The Russian proverb was 'one hand washes the other'. This is how *blat* worked for my sister.

The Telephone

My friend Zyama was an actor in the Moscow Arts Theatre. For Russians it is a great honour to work in this theatre, and Zyama had been an actor with them since his youth, even going to Paris with them as a member of the company before the war.

In Moscow the Bolshoi Theatre produces opera and ballet, and the Mali Theatre is the national theatre of the classics; but the Arts is the theatre that was idolised by all. It is Chekhov's Theatre, the one that first produced his plays. The emblem over its entrance, embroidered on the heavy curtains, and printed on all the programmes is the flying seagull taken from his play of that name. His wife, Knipper-Chekhova, acted for the Arts Theatre all her life, and the play 'The Cherry Orchard' was written for her.

The actors in the main characters produced by the Arts Theatre are always famous, usually venerable; the frustrated younger ones rarely get a chance to perform the big parts. But they do get practice by understudying. The only part that never had an understudy was 'The Cherry Orchard' – Knipper-Checkova said that the part would be played by someone else only over her dead body. If she was ever indisposed, then another play had to be substituted.

The first performance I ever saw at the Arts Theatre was Maurice Maeterlinck's 'Bluebird' at a children's matinee, the one play for which tickets were more readily available. When my friend Zyama told me that his favourite part was the cat in 'The Bluebird', I was very impressed. 'But of course,' he hastened to add, 'I'm only the understudy. It's one of our greatest actor's (Moskvin) favourite roles too.'

The Arts has an affiliated theatre and a large permanent company. In the summer months the theatre buildings are used by visiting provincial companies, and the Arts Theatre itself forms groups that travel to various places. When the Germans attacked Russia in 1941, Zyama was with a group performing in Minsk. Minsk was bombed on the first night of the war, and this section of the Arts Theatre, stranded there, abandoned everything – personal possessions and all their stage props – and set out at night on foot, leaving Minsk in flames behind them. Actors old and young walked until they managed to get some transport and eventually made their way back to Moscow. From there they were evacuated in October with other theatres and the Government and Diplomatic Corps to Kuibyshev.

A year later part of their company returned to perform at their smaller theatre, the Filial. All the costumes and sets for their latest production – Sheridan's 'School for Scandal' – had been lost in Minsk, and at that stage in the war it was not possible to have new ones made. Undaunted they decided to open in Moscow without period costumes, and with sets borrowed from another play.

Zyama got me tickets for the opening nights.

In the interval he came round to see how we were liking their production of the English play. I thought it was enchanting, and explained the meaning of the names. But why, I asked, did the actors pronounce them so strangely? 'Snike' for 'snake', for instance. Oh, they thought they had the correct English sounds, but all would be put right in the second act.

He made a note of the correct pronunciations, and at that performance of 'The School for Scandal', the names changed suddenly, half way through the play.

After that Zyama decided it would be useful to learn English. My students were preparing to put on a play for the end of the term. They had chosen Bernard Shaw's 'You Never Can Tell'. Rehearsals dragged; it was cold at college, there was no heat. I couldn't help my students with their acting. All I could do was to correct their pronunciation and their speech.

Then Zyama said, 'Could I coach them? It would help my English.' I rose enormously in my students' estimation; not only did I speak English with a real English accent, but I knew an actor at the Arts Theatre – and a young and good looking one at that. It was like knowing Clark Gable. Zyama coached them magnificently. He gave us an insight into how meticulously the Arts Theatre actor goes into every detail to reach perfection. The students began to act really well, and Zyama's English improved immensely.

In Moscow, that winter of 1942-43 was the hardest winter of the war. There was no fuel for heat. There were constant electricity cuts. Each flat had only sufficient for essential lighting. The gas pressure was so low it couldn't pass the meter. There were no telephones. The previous year, when the Germans were approaching Moscow, all the instruments had been removed and taken from the city. In my flat the wires were still sticking out from the wall where the telephone had been. I had found out that *our number had not been reallocated to anyone else, and I had actually managed to acquire an instrument, but only official organisations were allowed to have their telephones re-connected.*

One day Zyama said, 'How can I contact you when I can't manage a rehearsal? What, no phone? We'll have to do something about that.' He went to the local telephone exchange, made some enquiries, and came back elated. He had met someone there who would help, but it would take a little time – and some theatre tickets.

Only a few theatres had re-opened in entertainment-starved Moscow, and tickets were unobtainable unless one had 'influence' or 'connections'. Actors in the theatre were allowed to buy two tickets for each of their own performances. Zyama went to the telephone exchange a number of times with precious tickets for the lady in charge of connecting telephones. Finally he said 'She wants to see you. You will have to take these two tickets yourself. Give them to her when no one else is around, and ask her what play she wants to see next. That should do it.'

By this time our flat had become a little more comfortable. We had been shown how to by-pass the electric meter, which enabled us to use the electric toaster and iron for heat. It had been too cold in the flat, and the gas pressure too low to allow a kettle of water to boil. But a friendly engineer had constructed a pipe that by-passed the gas meter. Now we would have a telephone as well, and at last it was installed.

That evening Zyama came in for a brief rehearsal on his way to the theatre. My students were already there. I carefully put the chain back on the front door after I had let him in. The room was pleasant, although there was a faint smell of gas.

Zyama said, 'It's warm in here! What comfort!' He took the glass of tea I handed him. No tea leaves floating on the top.

'Tea made with boiling water! What luxury!' A dramatic pause, and a significant look towards my students… 'And I see you even have a telephone!'

CHAPTER 5

Stalingrad

THE terrible winter of 1942-43 was also felt by the German army. In January 1942 the Russians had launched a general counter-offensive with the aim of lifting the siege of Leningrad and clearing German forces out of the Donbass and Crimea. But the Soviet Army failed in its objective; although they had pushed back the German lines by up to 350 kilometres, by April the offensive had petered out.

The German divisions, however, had lost more 400,000 men and a considerable part of their armaments. It was becoming clear that Hitler's lightning war against the Soviet Union had failed. The Germans now faced a different kind of war, a long, grinding, devastating war, entailing enormous losses and sacrifices.

Stalled outside Moscow the Germans now launched an attack in the Crimea. In the Caucasus they continued their relentless advance. An attempt by the Soviets to retake Kharkov ended in failure, with the loss of 200,000 men. Kerch and Kharkov fell to the Wehrmacht. In May they pushed towards Sevastopol, which endured a two-month siege and bombing by hundreds of planes before what was left of this vital port on the Black Sea was occupied. The Germans took 90,000 prisoners; then they turned east towards Stalingrad.

The order from Stalin and his supreme command to the Soviet forces was 'not one step back'. The city was to be defended to the very end. The German leader, General Paulus was also under instructions to take the city at any cost.

In August the Germans reached the Volga, and at the end of the month they broke into Stalingrad north and south; six thousand planes carpet-bombed the city and 40,000 civilians were killed. The city was reduced to a wilderness of ruins, a burned out wasteland. By September the Russians had been driven back into three small bridgeheads. October was the most terrible month. The German offensive was being pursued in a battle unequalled in cruelty and ferocity.

But at the same time its forces were slowly being sucked into the vortex of a small area within the city where the grinding attrition of urban infantry fighting suited the Russians. With the Germans in control of large areas of the city, the Russians were fighting 'for every brick and stone, for every yard of the Stalingrad earth', as the Commander of the 62nd army, Marshal Chuikov, later wrote.* The losses on both sides were appalling.

Yet after five months of battle 10,000 civilians, including 1,000 children who had been unable to leave, still survived in the cellars and sewers. The soldiers had rations, but the civilians trapped in the city had nothing. In his powerful book, *Stalingrad*, Antony Beevor describes how each time there was a lull in the bombardment women and children appeared out of holes in the ground to cut slabs of meat off dead horses before dogs and could strip the carcasses. The chief foragers were children. Younger, small and more agile they presented less of a target.[26]

The worst of the weather arrived in November when the temperature dropped to minus eighteen degrees centigrade and the German's last major attack petered out. Then, in the middle of November Soviet forces launched their counter-attack: Operation Uranus, a pincer movement around Stalingrad which closed a ring around the German troops, trapping 330,000 men.

Eleven weeks of purgatory now followed for the German Sixth Army and its Axis allies, Italians, Hungarians, Rumanians, and others. Beevor describes the terrible conditions of all soldiers, not just the wounded. Starving, suffering from frost-bite, with no chance to wash or change clothes, their bodies crawled with lice. They limped on frost-bitten feet, their lips were cracked right open from the frost, their faces had a waxen quality. Exhausted men slumped in the snow and never rose again. The corpses were stripped of clothing as soon as possible after death to be used by those still living. Once a body froze, it was impossible to undress.

In the middle of December a hard bitter wind blew up and the ice floes on the Volga froze into a solid ice highway over which the Russians could advance with thousands of vehicles with men and arms. Over 200,000 of the trapped Germans died from fighting, from hunger, from wounds and disease and from the ferocious cold that in January reached forty degrees below zero. Hitler signalled that surrender was out of the question.

But at the end of January, in defiance of Hitler's orders, the recently promoted Field Marshal von Paulus surrendered. When the last German survivors crawled out of the dark ruins of the city they had destroyed, in addition to the Field Marshal the Russians had captured twenty-four generals together with the remains of the Sixth Army, gaunt, frost-bitten and wrapped in rags. The Wehrmacht had lost 800,000 troops, as well as vast quantities of guns, tanks and aircraft.

It was the turning point in World War Two.

Christmas 1942

The only place where bartering could be done more or less legally was an out-of-town open market at Serpukhov. I went there with an American friend who had recently received a package from the States and wanted to exchange the shoes she had been sent – if possible for a festive chicken. It was the time of the New Year Festival.

As I stood waiting for my friend to clinch her bargain, a pretty young girl approached. My clothes always marked me unmistakably as a foreigner. But I had nothing to sell.

'Perhaps you have an evening gown at home to sell me?' the stranger asked; and I remembered the green velvet dress at the bottom of my trunk.

When I came to live in Russia I had taken only those things I knew I would need, mainly utilitarian clothes, leaving luxuries behind. At the last moment, however, I had pushed into the trunk my favourite evening dress and cape. It had been the first evening dress I had actually bought, and not made myself. Perhaps I took it as a remembrance of past good times.

When inflation and shortages meant money had no value, many clothes had been bartered, but no one had any use for an elegant velvet evening gown. It did not go with me to the Urals; I knew that wherever we were going there would be no use for it.

But now I thought this young Moscow girl looked as though she could use it. I gave her my address; and when she came to see me we made a deal: a bottle of vodka and the know-how to by-pass the electric meter for the dress and cape.

The girl's husband was some kind of wartime profiteering engineer who understood electricity and meters. With only one electric light bulb for our room, and no electricity for heating or cooking, this was a valuable – though obviously illegal – deal. Vodka was the most prized commodity. Only army officers and important officials could buy it legally in their closed shops. After vodka came flour, because it could be kept, and bread was the basic food. Potatoes were bulky, froze in winter, started to sprout in spring and went bad. Fats were luxuries that were completely unobtainable. We took the bottle of vodka to a village some kilometres away and exchanged it for a pood (36 lbs.) of flour. It sounds easy, but the complications were immense. One had to have a permit to go out of town, and another one to travel on a train, even a local one. Flour was quite unobtainable in town.

But back in the flat there was no gas, and no way to bake anything, so after another out of town expedition the flour was exchanged for a sack of potatoes to keep for winter. And some of the potatoes were traded as part-payment to a little old Russian dressmaker for making, out of two old dresses, a nice new dress for my Christmas.

An Offer Refused

Captain Fielding said: 'We could arrange to send you home now, if you wish, on a convoy sailing from the north.'

The possibility of such a route back to England arose because of the Soviet alliance with Britain and the United States. On the night of the German invasion into Russia Churchill had made an historic broadcast promising that Britain would support Russia and would never make a deal with Hitler. Three weeks later the two countries signed a mutual assistance pact. By the end of the month Roosevelt had sent an envoy to Moscow to discuss the supply of military and economic aid.

At first Allied aid had been largely symbolic, but it grew in importance as 1942 progressed. The first joint action between Britain and the USSR had enabled a military force to open up a land route through Iran for vital supplies to the Soviet Union. It was a slow and hazardous journey, but lorries and planes were getting through to the Red Army.

Sea convoys had started in 1941. British convoys were bringing arms and ammunition to the Soviet Union by sea to Murmansk and Archangel. The journey was a harsh and difficult one in Arctic conditions. But by the beginning of 1942 the Germans had moved a considerable force of U-boats and submarines to the convoy route, and British losses began to mount catastrophically.

So when Captain Fielding suggested that she could return to England on one of the convoys, Olga looked at him and said: 'Isn't it rather dangerous?'

'He hesitated, and then he said: "Mmm… yes, it is rather."'

Then she thought: And I would be the only woman on an all-male ship, and perhaps it would be dangerous from every point of view. So she said, 'No, I don't think I would like to go back on a convoy.'

Part of her strength had always been her ability to accept a situation and to adapt to the present. So she had put the thought of returning to England into some recess of memory – filed it away, as it were, for the duration.

The war was here, in the Soviet Union which had become her home. But the war was there, too, in the country she still thought of as home. The German defeat at Stalingrad made it possible to imagine a time when the war would end. But it was not possible for her to return yet except by such a hazardous route. She did not wish to contemplate it.

Deep War

With the surrender of the German armies in Stalingrad in February 1943, there was a wave of hope and of real joy. At last people permitted themselves a cautious optimism.

But the state of war was the reality, peace a distant memory of the past, a distant hope for the future. In the words of the writer, Ilya Ehrenburg, a 'deep war' had set in; a time of ferocious fighting, hardship and sacrifice and death still lay ahead.[27]

And in the frozen north the gulags were still there.

When news of the war first reached prisoners in the camps in Siberia, it re-awoke in them a deep patriotism that had not been destroyed by the injustices and hardships inflicted on them. Most of the prisoners hoped for the defeat of the German invaders and wished that they, too, could participate in defending their country, Russia.

'We tried our best to discern what lay ahead. Not just for ourselves but for everyone. We, the outcasts, racked by four years of suffering, suddenly felt ourselves citizens of this country of ours. We, its rejected children, now trembled for our fatherland. Some of us managed to lay hands on scraps of paper and to trace a message with a stubby pencil: "I ask to be sent to the most dangerous section of the front. I have been a member of the Communist Party since the age of sixteen…"

Just as if the thirteen thousand kilometres of hatred, calumny, and suffering which separated our Kolyma huts from the land of human beings had ceased to exist.'[28]

But they were still 'enemies of the people'. Their appeals were ignored and they remained outcasts.

Irina and Leonid

My sister was head of the fourth year – the advanced students – at the Institute. She had become confident in her work and more fluent in her Russian.

In 1944 Irina Volosova entered the Institute.

Irina had been eight years old when Olga first arrived in Moscow and when she and Henry had become friendly with Irina's parents, Kseniya and Grigorii.

When Irina's parents were arrested Olga and Henry kept in touch with the two children. Olga felt a special closeness to the little girl, and when Irina decided she wanted to study English at the Foreign Languages Institute Olga had coached her.

Olga was immediately recognisable as a foreigner even before she spoke. Although they would have been unremarkable in England, in Moscow the fabrics and style of her clothes stood out among the very drab, dark and shapeless clothes of the Muscovites, all that was available at that time.

She would pin a brooch to her jersey, or wear a colourful scarf, and the girls – there were very few boys at the Institute during the war – would go to the teachers' room to see what she was wearing and to listen to her speaking.

'Everybody at the Institute adored her,' Irina said. 'She was very popular. Thanks to her I became a first-year student. She visited me regularly, coached me thoroughly, and helped me pass my exams.'

There is a postscript to be added to the story of Irina and her family. After the war Stalin's persecution of his own people began all over again. Now among the targets of the new paranoia were the children of former victims. In 1949 Irina's beloved brother, Leonid – Lenya – who had cared for her when both their parents disappeared, was arrested. He was accused of saying in public that his father had been an honest man and a true communist. Lenya was then twenty-eight, and his wife had just given birth to a son.

He was kept in prison for some time, where he was accused of plotting something illegal with a group of his friends – a false allegation. He was sentenced to eight years in a camp, and was sent to Krasnoyarsk in Siberia.

In the camp he worked as an engineer. He was told that if he worked well, each day would be counted as two, and his term of imprisonment would be reduced to four years.

In 1953 Stalin died and the following year Lenya was released. But when he returned to Moscow he was prohibited by the KGB from living in the city. So he went to Rostov-on-the-Don where Irina was teaching at the University, and their mother, released from the camps but also debarred from returning to Moscow, worked as a nurse at the hospital.

But the KGB refused to allow Lenya to be registered in Rostov, and he had to go to a small town 100 kilometres away, where he got a job at a chemical plant.

In 1958, when he and his parents were 'rehabilitated' he returned to Moscow.

When I met her Irina told me the story of her brother. This was sixty years after Olga first became friends of Irina's parents.

I also met Irina's husband, Vladimir and learned that Vladimir's father, like my own, had also left his home in Russia and emigrated to America; but that he had returned to Russia in 1924.

I think of the parallels with my own family, of the constant shift of peoples from country to country, and how our lives interweave in such strange and unpredictable ways. Of how oppression, racial and religious prejudice, injustice and cruelty, and most of all wars between nations and civil wars drive people to leave their own countries in search of peace and safety. And that although we put down new roots and merge into the customs, the culture, the politics of our adopted lands, something of that other world which we or our parents long left behind permeates our lives. We belong to more than a single nation, we have tasted more than one culture; and this brings its own riches and rewards – but at the same time it troubles us. For all that has been gained, something has been taken away; something has been lost.

And then I think how right Simeon – Papa – had been at that time not to want to bring us to the Soviet Union, despite all his beliefs, his hopes, his dreams of a better, more just future for us all.

In one of the letters that he sent to his family by hand he had written:

'Our lives are so short that at times it seems senseless to strive for things that cannot be expected to mature in our lifetime. The desire to live *personally* and live *well* takes very often the upper hand. It requires the world of strength to withstand all temptations.'

And I now know that what had seemed the senseless tragedy of his death, the chance drinking of a glass of infected milk, which had brought us so much sorrow, such an acute sense of loss so long ago, was in a way fortunate. He was spared from a greater tragedy: the knowledge that he had exercised that 'world of strength', left the family he loved so deeply, sacrificed himself for that greater good in which he believed, only to see the betrayal of his life's purpose and to become a victim.

For he, surely, after his years in the West, would have been caught up in that time of terror, and shot as an enemy of the people.

Strangers at the Door

When the Russians occupied eastern Poland in 1939 they had taken 200,000 prisoners of war, and most of the officers and thousands of the soldiers were sent to the camps. Hundreds of thousands of Polish civilians were also arrested and deported to remote places. Thousands were murdered in captivity.

Two years later when the Soviet Union had itself been invaded by Germany it signed an agreement with the Polish government in exile. An amnesty was granted to all Poles imprisoned on Russian territory. Surviving soldiers and civilians alike were free to leave Russia.

They were free, but most of them were located in distant places, far to the north and east. It was a freedom constrained by where they were and by the volcanic disruption of the war.

Some found work and stayed in the area where they were released. Some embarked on the long and hazardous journey towards their own country. They had no money, no food, no transport. Hundreds of miles separated them from the frontiers of Poland.

Many of those who had been in the camps beyond Omoutninsk followed the line of the railway, and this was the first town that they came to.

Perhaps because Olga and Henry's room was in a house on the edge of the town, a traveller passing through might choose to knock on the door where they lived and ask for food.

To Olga such strangers would be instantly recognisable as one who had come from the vast, empty, dark obscurity that lay beyond the forests to the north-east. She would remember how the peasants on the stations during their journey from Moscow had crossed themselves and called it a 'God-forsaken place', the last stop on the branch line beyond which lay the camps.

She would recognise such strangers at the door; not only by their ragged and insufficient clothing, not only by their gaunt, half-starved faces, not only because they would ask for an onion; but also by a look in their eyes, by their remote and haunted expression that marked them indelibly as having come from the camps.

Now that they were back in Moscow another stranger with the same look on his face knocked on her door.

There had not been any graduates for two years. During the early days of the war, in order to prepare translators and interpreters quickly, the authorities had decided to cut the course of English language studies by a year, making it three instead of four years, plus the introductory Course for Beginners.

By now, in 1944, conditions were a little easier; the course for students had been extended to four years again, and the previous summer there had been no graduating students, which made this State Examination more nerve-wracking than usual.

I was sitting in my room typing the examination tickets. It was always a last-minute job, so that there could be no leak. My thoughts went back to my school-leaving, not so many years before, when I had been asked what I wanted to do. My answer had been that I did not know what I wanted to do – I only knew what I didn't want to do: teach or type. Here I was doing both.

There was a knock on the door. I answered it, impatient at the interruption. A stranger stood there saying: 'I've come from Ray.' But one look at him told me where he had come from, and I took him quickly into my room, hoping no one had caught sight of him on the way up. Ragged, wretched, though still young behind the aged, tired look, he spoke hesitantly.

'I'm only passing through Moscow. I was trying to get a train tonight. Ray said you would put me up if I didn't manage it in one day.'

I told him: 'You know I'm a foreigner. It would be awfully bad for you if you were caught here.'

He was clearly used to taking risks.

'I have no where else to go. Is your neighbour all right?'

'Just don't let her see you.'

He was on his way to the Ukraine. Was that his home?

'No.' He had married a fellow prisoner in the labour camp, but although he had served his full term of imprisonment and was now ostensibly free, his wife was still serving her sentence, and was not allowed to leave the North. She had come from the Ukraine where she had a seven-year-old son whom she had not seen since he was a baby. The boy was being looked after by a relative, and my visitor was going to fetch him and take him to Verkuta in the far North. They would settle there, and the boy would live with them.

I said, 'Of course you must stay,' and offered him food. He ate sparingly, carefully, not to appear greedy, although it must have been the first good food he had eaten for years. Then he said, 'No more.' I made up a bed for him, and despite my typing he went to sleep with the ease of sleeping in any surroundings that only prisoners acquire.

But I could not sleep. I cried all night. I cried for Ray, who was not yet free; for the stranger sharing my room, for the mother and child, for all the cruelly separated families. And I cried, selfishly, for myself, having to share my home with a stranger, and for fear of the two o'clock knock on the door.

No one came in the night, and in the morning he asked, 'May I come and stay with you again when I come back with Vanya?' He showed me a tattered snapshot of a little boy with tousled hair and big round eyes, and I said, 'Naturally, you will stay here.'

He went off for his ticket, and I left for the Institute.

CHAPTER 6

A World at War

I have been writing about the war only in relevance to my sister's life; as though during those years the whole war was contained within Russia. But of course this was a *world* war; it began in Europe, and everything that happened in Europe, in Africa and in the Far East had tremendous bearing on the war in Russia.

But I have not attempted to write a summary of the history of the Second World War, only to give shape to a certain time in the life of one woman. So I have narrowed the perspective of those cataclysmic world events to focus only on her, the milieu that surrounded her, the events that shaped her life.

When Germany invaded Poland Olga had had no expectation of returning to England for a time that no one could foretell. A sign that she had accepted this – she was always a realist – was the fact that she and Henry made a second attempt to get married legally. Again they confronted bureaucratic difficulties and delays. It seems clear that the authorities were pressurising her to become a Soviet citizen. But though she had resigned herself to an indeterminate – perhaps even permanent – life in Russia, she was not prepared to be anything but British.

While my sister was wandering through snow-filled forests

somewhere in the far North, the Allied Armies were fighting the Germans in the Western Desert, and war was also raging at sea as German submarines sank British ships.

While she was still in Omoutninsk Hong Kong, Singapore and Rangoon surrendered to the Japanese. And by the time she had returned to wartime Moscow, Rommel was on his offensive in the Western Desert, taking Tobruk and El Alamein.

As the tide of battle turned at El Alamein and Rommel was in retreat the final German assault on Stalingrad was failing. When the Russian counter-offensive was launched, the Allies were landing in French North Africa. The Germans were withdrawing from the Caucasus as the Eighth Army swept across North Africa to reach Tripoli.

It was one war, spread across countries and continents, conducted by alliances that breached political systems. For as long as the war lasted the alliance among the nations held.

It was the catastrophic defeat that the Germans suffered at Stalingrad that now changed the whole course of the war. And as it gave hope everywhere that the Allies would finally defeat Nazism, it also kept alive my sister's hope that one day she would be able to leave the Soviet Union.

Moscow Celebrates

At midnight on August 5 in 1943 the Moscow sky was lit by great bursts of falling stars, while the whole of the blacked-out and silent city reverberated to twelve artillery salvoes from one hundred and twenty guns.

It was the first of the era of victory salutes, Russia's celebration of major victories. More than three hundred such salvoes and fireworks displays would take place in the next two years.

The victory salvoes would register every major town recaptured, mark every significant advance, as though only by so doing could the Russians confirm their reality to themselves. There was still a long way to go.

After the massive and humiliating defeat that the Germans had suffered in the Caucasus, Hitler needed a resounding victory. In July he had launched his offensive, Operation Citadel, in the Kursk salient – the heart of Russia, hoping to trap the considerable Russian forces there, and at the same time open up the way to a new attack on Moscow.

Operation Citadel failed. Once again the Germans suffered catastrophic losses. The battle was described by one reporter as concentrated carnage more terrible than any that had yet been seen. The opinion of a post-war German historian, Walter Goerlitz, was that Stalingrad had been the politico-psychological turning-point of the whole war in the east, but the German defeat at Kursk was its military turning point.

Final victory was still far ahead, and would cost another million lives or more. But the Russian celebration of the victory at Kursk with those first salvoes and fireworks was testimony to the Russian belief that in winning the Battle of Kursk, Russia had, in effect won the war.

Now at last Moscow was completely out of danger; for though the Germans had been driven back from the outskirts of the city, throughout the dark summer of the previous year they had clung to a position still close enough to the city to be a threat and to act as a springboard for bombing raids. With their withdrawal from the Caucasus, the Germans had also been forced to abandon their position outside Moscow.

The Soviet command now felt secure in the advances they had made. The whole of the diplomatic service was brought back to Moscow from Kuibyshev.

Stalinism

There was a drive at the Institute for 'raising one's qualifications'. Even the staff with foreign diplomas were called in. Nobody would be allowed to teach without the necessary Russian diploma, which included a political subject. This was a 'short' course of Political Economy, Dialectical Materialism, Marxism-Leninism and the History of the Communist Party of the Soviet Union.

We took all the exams required leaving the most difficult – the political one – to the last; and that's where I stopped. Most of the political material could be read in English translations, but Stalin's works had not all been translated into English. He had written many volumes, and his Russian was awkward and hard to read.

My students didn't want me to leave the Institute. I was the only 'real' English teacher there. They kept reminding me: 'You haven't taken your political exam yet.' Finally they said: 'Next week's the last date for the political exam.'

'I know. But I'm not taking it.'

They were aghast, and I explained.

'I can't manage Stalin. He's written too much. It hasn't been translated, and I couldn't possibly read it all in time.'

They looked at each other.

'We'll coach you,' they volunteered.

'There's too much to read. It's too difficult for me, and there's no time,' I repeated.

They looked at each other again. We'll come to your flat and coach you. We'll show you what we do. You'll see, it's not as difficult as it seems.'

They took no notice of my protests, and six of them turned up that afternoon. 'This is what we do,' they said, carefully unwrapping some tattered old notebooks. 'You don't think we read Stalin, do you? We wouldn't have time. No one would, and he's so difficult for us too. We have all the questions and answers here. We'll teach you them.'

'Where did you get those from?'

'Oh, they're passed down from year to year. As soon as you've taken the exam they'll be handed down to the next year's graduates. Nobody reads Stalin.'

They took it in turns to come and coach me. On the day before the exam three of them came home with me for the final coaching – Galina, who was the leader of the class, Grisha, who was the best student, and Suzanne. Suzanne was Polish, and she had studied English in Paris and Warsaw, and spoke more fluently than the others.

That morning at the Institute she had triumphantly presented her book review. She had chosen Hemingway's 'Farewell to Arms'. It was a memorable occasion, and she had read the passage 'If she should die – she can't die – she won't die – but if she should die...' so emotionally that half the class had been in tears. Death, of course, was close to us all. Her father, a doctor, had been taken into the army in Poland and was killed. She and her mother had travelled westwards and worked on a collective farm. Her mother had died there, and Suzanne had come to Moscow to live with an uncle, and had entered the Institute as a fourth year student.

She wore a beautiful fur-lined coat, obviously foreign and expensive. She told me it was her mother's. Gradually it became shabby as she wore it all the time. That was not remarkable. We all wore our coats all the time. That winter the ink froze in the inkpots and we had to keep marching around the desks to stop ourselves from freezing.

In the Moscow Metro, on the way to my flat, we saw two men from the Royal Navy in obvious difficulties. They were standing gazing helplessly at the milling mobs of people pushing and squeezing themselves into the trains.

I said to them, in English: 'It's no use being gentlemanly and polite; you just have to push hard. Get in front of us and shove.' We squeezed into the *train and stood packed tight. They told us they had been on a northern convoy. Over half the ships had been lost, and they were being treated to two days in Moscow before they returned to Murmansk for the voyage back to England.*

Suzanne was the only one of the students who understood their rapidly-spoken English, and I can still see the expression on her face when one of the sailor's said to me: 'You know, you do speak awfully good English.' I didn't bother to explain to them.

I did take the political exam, and even passed it. But out of the blue I was asked a new question relating to after-war conditions in the world, a question which was not in my students' tattered notebooks. So although I have 'First Class' for everything else on my Russian diploma, my Stalinism is only second class.

Vava

With the Allies' military and economic aid came military personnel.

The British seamen whom Olga and her students had encountered in the Metro were only chance visitors on leave before returning to Murmansk. But gradually there were big, well-fed Americans and smart British army men in the streets of Moscow, their foreignness made more glamorous by their uniforms. And for young Russian women their attractiveness made more tempting by gifts they brought with them from the Western world.

They met in all sorts of places. In the streets, the parks, the canteens, the offices where the Allies employed Russian women in clerical and other capacities. Many were drawn into fleeting affairs, a romantic fling. Some became serious.

*

Vava was a student learning English at the Mopinia – the Moscow Institute of Foreign Languages. She was not one of my students, but I knew her because she was a star performer in the choir I had organised for the English faculty at the last end-of-term concert.

All of us working in a State institution had to do some voluntary work to keep a 'social face'. As a foreigner I was allowed to do 'light social duties' – I organised the light entertainment, ran the college English language choir and produced plays and student concerts.

During her second year of studies Vava went for a walk in Gorki Central Park, by the river, and met her American. All the students dreamed of meeting and marrying Americans or Englishmen and going to live abroad; but only a few actually met any.

Vava's American had been drafted into the army, but his service was being carried out in the American Embassy in Moscow. In civilian life he worked in the film industry – a young producer. That was convenient for Vava as she was extraordinarily lovely to look at and had a beautiful voice. Her aunt, Novikova, was the best-known star of the Theatre of Operatta, renowned and very popular. Vava had studied music, singing and the piano, and sang arias in Italian and German, as well as popular Russian and English songs. But you are much more likely to meet a foreigner if you learn a foreign language; and, after all, during the war, weren't the British and Americans allies of the Russians? What harm could there be in meeting and talking to an American?

In Vava's case they really fell in love, and her American married her. He had to get permission from the army first, and they were reluctant to let him get involved; she could always be a plant. But they gave way, and Vava and Ed got married.

However, Americans married to local Russian girls were considered a security risk; so he was promptly sent home. They had a week together, and she applied for permission to leave the country and join her husband in America. But Russians were not allowed to leave the country, and Vava became one of the notorious Russian wives, who had married a member of the British or American armed forces, but were not permitted to leave the country to join their husbands.

'It'll take a few weeks,' Ed reassured her, 'and you'll be in my next film.'

The weeks lengthened into months. All the papers were signed, the war was nearly over, but poor Vava was still in Moscow. She tried to pull strings. Her aunt was reputedly the mistress of Kalinin, the President of the Soviet Union. But the strings were most probably a disadvantage. The outside world shouldn't know that Russian leaders had mistresses.

Vava was now in her third year at the Institute, and due to take exams. She came to see me to ask if I would give her some private lessons.

'Why? You don't need them,' I said.

'I'm afraid of failing my exams.'

'But you can't. Your English is too good.'

'They'll find an excuse. You'll see.'

I told her to go to her own teacher – an American.

'They'll say I have an American accent. They like you. It will give me some protection if they know I'm having extra lessons with you.'

So we had some lessons; conversations, really, and I did not want to take money from her. Anyway, in wartime Russia money had no value. As an American wife, Vava received rations from the American Embassy. Most of it she sold on the open market. But she would come along to my flat bringing something different each time from her food allowance.

Once it was a tin of pineapple and grapefruit juice, unknown in Russia.

'Do you like it?'

'It's delicious.'

'We don't like grapefruit. It tastes bitter, so we don't like it. I'll bring you more next time.'

The next time Vava came it was just before Christmas. Though the lift was working I could hear her running up the stairs. Shoes were just about unobtainable in wartime Russia, but she was wearing shoes her husband *had sent to her from the States. They had little bells on them that tinkled as she walked. Pretty, but quite unsuitable for the Russian winter.*

I opened the door. There she was, smiling broadly, no make-up on her face except for mascara on her long eyelashes. Her cheeks were flushed from the frost. She wore no hat, and her chestnut curls fell on her shoulders. She was wearing a new winter coat, obviously not made in the USSR. Russians wore winter coats with fur collars, and Vava's silver fox furs were the sleeves of her coat – very smart; and of course she was wearing the shoes with the silver bells.

We had our lesson. She said she had been interviewed by an important official who did not give her much hope of leaving. She cried a little. Then she laughed.

'He told me, the big chief, that I'd only done one thing right.'

'What was that?'

'I could have married an Englishman. That would have been much worse.'

She worried about her exams. If she failed she would have no 'social face' and no permission to stay in Moscow. She would have to go to a village somewhere and lose all contact with Americans, the Embassy – her husband.

'What shall I do, Olga Semenovna? Give me some advice.'

I said, 'Perhaps if you were less different in your clothes, people wouldn't notice you so much.'

'What do you mean? These are ordinary things I'm wearing.'

'Well. your shoes, for instance. Everyone hears you coming. In the street everyone looks at you.'

She stretched her legs in her beautiful imported nylons. The bells tinkled. 'They're lovely shoes. They make me happy. Don't you like them?'

'Of course I do. But they're for special occasions. Don't you have others you can wear for ordinary times?'

'*Oh yes. My husband has sent me a case of shoes. That will help me a lot.*'

Fashion shoes, if you could get them, cost a thousand roubles a pair. I could not calculate what a whole case of shoes was worth on the black market. No wonder she was prepared to pay for private coaching.

She cheered up, and followed me into the kitchen.

'*I went to the Ambassador's Christmas party yesterday, and sang the latest song; they taught me it, just before. It's a big hit in the States, and they made me stand on the table and sing it again. I'll sing it for you.*'

And she sat on the little wooden stool in the communal kitchen I shared with both my neighbours, and sang 'I'm dreaming of a white Christmas...'

That was our last lesson. I had no time for any more, and anyway, I was preparing to leave the Soviet Union.

That, really, is the end. But would you like to know what happened to Vava Novikova?

She didn't fail her exams – her English was too good. But after I left, and she had no one to speak up for her, she was expelled for being unsuitably dressed for classes. No, she didn't wear the fox furs and the shoes with bells to classes. She was expelled for wearing trousers.

Some years later I read a book by a woman, Nora Murray, a Russian who with great difficulty had left early in the war with her English husband. She mentioned the 'Russian wives', as the girls who had married Englishmen and Americans were called, and she mentioned that Vava Novikova was sentenced to two years imprisonment for 'not conforming to the registration normalities'.

As the wife of a foreigner she was now subject to a new law – passed after the war – that made it illegal for Soviet citizens to marry foreigners. But in addition, as she was no longer a student, and had no work permit, she must have been living illegally in Moscow.

1944...The Year of Victories

The people of Moscow had never seen anything like it.

It was a glorious sunny day in Moscow; the women in their floral cotton frocks, the men in linen suits or embroidered tunics came pouring out of homes, offices, work-places at the sight of 57,000 German prisoners, walking twenty abreast down the centre streets of the city. At their head, twenty German generals, their iron crosses tinkling on their chests; and dozens of other officers. Mounted Russian soldiers with drawn sabres guarded them, and Russian infantrymen, with bayonets thrust forward, marched behind each contingent.

A crowd of about a million people lined the streets. At first youngsters booed and whistled at the Germans, but when they started to throw things at them they were restrained by the older people. From the radio loudspeakers came a message: 'Citizens must keep order and must not permit themselves any demonstration in regard to the prisoners.'

Then a grim silence settled on the crowds as the endless procession continued. For these wretched, ragged, unshaven columns of men were those who had set themselves up to be the rulers of the world. They had come with their polished boots, their Panzer divisions, their swastikas and their blonde arrogance to bomb and shell cities, to burn villages, to hang partisans from trees to take men and women as slave labourers, to fill mass graves with murdered Jews, Slavs, gypsies, communists. They were the master-race, Aryans. Now their uniforms were torn and ragged, their shoulders hunched, their eyes vacant. Now they carried with them the stench of their incomprehensible defeat, while the silent crowds in their summer clothes watched them shuffling past; and vendors sold ice cream at the street corners.

They were the remnants of 100,000 men who had been caught in a huge encirclement by the Red Army in Belorussia. More than 40,000 were killed or wounded. The rest surrendered.

The Russian offensive in Belorussia was the gravest defeat that had ever been inflicted on the Wehrmacht on the Eastern Front. Twenty-five German divisions were destroyed. It was July1944, the year the Russians were to call 'the year of ten victories'.

The first great victory was at the end of January when Leningrad was completely relieved. The 900 days of the siege were over.

In February and March Russian troops encircled several German divisions and crashed through into Rumania. Odessa was liberated in April and in May the Crimea was completely cleared.

In the Ukraine American shuttle-bombing bases were established, and Flying Fortresses started coming in from Italy dropping bombs on Hungarian and Rumanian targets on the way.

'It was strange to see,' wrote the BBC war correspondent, Alexander Werth, 'there, at Poltava and Mirgorod, in the heart of the Gogol country, those hundreds of GI's eating vast quantities of American canned food – spam, and baked beans, and apple-sauce – drinking gallons of good coffee, making passes at the giggly Ukraine canteen waitresses.'[29]

In June the Russians broke through German lines in six places, encircling large German forces and taking tens of thousands of prisoners. In June, also, the American Fifth Army entered Rome; and the long-awaited second front was opened with an Allied invasion of Normandy.

But as the Red Army advanced the terrible cost of the war was becoming apparent to the people of the Soviet Union. Millions of civilians and war prisoners died as a result of mass slaughter, starvation, or the deportation of nearly three million prisoners to Germany as slave labour. Villages were burned down and entire populations, men, women and children, exterminated. Partisans, hostages, commissars and Jews were shot.

Then, as Russian forces advanced into Poland they discovered the industrial slaughter of human beings at Maidenek, the death factory outside Lublin. Alexander Werth who was among the first to visit Maidenek, wrote of the industrial quality of the unbelievable Death Factory.

'Unbelievable it was; when I sent the BBC a detailed report on Maidenek in August 1944 they refused to use it; they thought it was a Russian propaganda stunt, and it was not till the discovery in the West of Buchenwald, Dachau and Belsen that they were convinced that Maidenek and Auschwitz were also genuine.'

In two years an estimated 1,500,000 people had been put to death there.

A Visit to Captain Fielding

Captain Fielding said, 'Now we can fly you. We've got a route, and you can fly back.'

Olga had gone to the British Embassy to renew her passport.

In the outer office was a Russian clerk – 'a little bloke', she said. Olga felt a strong resentment towards him, with his assumed air of importance. According to her the British should never have employed Russians in their embassies, because all of them were spies. 'The Russians in Britain would never employ British in their embassies and consulates,' she said.

She told him she wanted to see the Consul.

This little bloke was smoking, and when he lit a cigarette he threw the empty matchbox into the waste-paper basket; then he went out of the office.

I got up. I mean, we occasionally had matches but we never got boxes for them, and there was no way of lighting them. I was going to take the matchbox. And then I thought, I just can't bring myself to scrabble around in his waste-paper basket. We didn't have anything. Can you imagine? But I didn't take it.

Now she was sitting in front of Captain Fielding.

This was the moment she had waited for, the opportunity so long deferred to go to England. And how beautiful! No long wait to get out, no bureaucracy and red tape, no tiresome journey by train and by boat – a swift and safeguarded departure. What could be better? Except that, as she realised the import of his words, she knew that she could not go; at least, not now, not until the war had finally ended.

For, without her wish, and certainly without her intention, this tremendous and terrible period of Soviet history had, for her, become personalised in so many different ways.

She had wanted to go when those brave and beautiful refugees from Nazism – whose history and fate remained unwritten – had begun to disappear; when her friend Probst had turned his face towards the wall. It simply reinforced her wish to depart, to leave behind the increasing and inexplicable atmosphere of secrecy and fear. She had not intended and had not wanted to live in this society, to have any part in it.

It was as though she had not really been part of either of the two Russian dramas – neither the one of living ordinary lives, nor the other one with its shrouded, dark players. She had been observing that other play, that drama at the back of the stage, a member of the audience, and, as any member of the audience, with the right to leave the auditorium. She had only postponed her departure because of Henry and his need of her assistance, her care and attention during his period of disablement.

But then, with the arrest of Ray, she had been drawn inexorably into the show, the pageant of injustice, of terror and insanity of the Stalin era. By her decision to stay at that time – at least until she knew what was happening to Ray – she had become an active participant in devious conspiracies to maintain contact with her sister-in-law. The elaborately devised secret messages, the long and fruitless wrestles with bureaucracy, the queues outside prisons, the hours of waiting in cold corridors, the exhausting stratagems to get parcels accepted and sent – these were the acts that had impelled her into the drama of that era of Soviet life.

Then came the war; and forced by the war to remain, she became part of the millions in that vast country seeking ways to keep alive. In later life it might become possible to reflect on all that had been endured as a distant memory, but at this time it was still all with her, the present. The struggles to board packed trains, the weeks-long journeys in cattle trucks in summer heat and in bitter winter cold; the harsh winter in Omoutninsk; the stratagems to obtain and store food; the bartering at distant markets; the adjustments to living in a tiny room, lacking any modern conveniences, in a peasant's home in a poor village.

And the hard days in Moscow when they returned to a city stripped bare of power – no heat, no light, little food; and always the bombing, the tensions of Panzer divisions menacing the city. The nights when Henry was working on the Metro when, without adequate light and warmth, she would sit in the cold and lonely darkness of her room until Henry came home.

Maintaining her classes when students and teacher alike were wrapped in every item of clothing they possessed, covered with coats, hats, gloves; and had to stop studying to jump and run around the room to keep some circulation going; yet still determined to continue their studies and pass their exams. Organising and taking part in the choir and plays, the cultural activities that were never abandoned even during the most dangerous and difficult times.

These were all still part of the present. It was all too close. She was no longer a spectator; she was at one with them. It was not that she had become reconciled to living in Soviet Russia, nor would she ever feel that it was her home. But she had become part of the people who had been forced into this enormous life and death struggle, she had lived through the time of semi-starvation, she had jumped around with her students to keep themselves from freezing, kept the classes going, shared their struggles and their laughter with them.

The great armies fought out the war on the battlefields, on the seas and in the air. But the non-combatants, the mass of the people, had to live out the war in their own way, each in their own countries; their homes bombed from the air or razed to the ground by the Nazis, their cities devastated, their lives totally constrained, accepting privation, enduring loss and death; their sacrifices an essential part of the ultimate defeat of fascism. She was part of those millions whose lives had been formed in this way.

She had lived through a time when survival and sanity had depended on a web of love and co-operation between friends and strangers. She could not desert them now, not until the war had come to an end. And here, in Moscow which had for nine years been her home, the final chapter had not yet been written.

She looked at Captain Fielding and said, 'No. I'd feel guilty. Now I think I'll wait and see it through.'

He said, 'Just imagine. Tomorrow you could be in London.'

She found herself weeping.

When she left he gave her a bar of chocolate. It was quite a small bar, divided into four sections. She had not seen chocolate – oh! for so many years. She walked home thinking, now, who will I share these four little sections with?

'Of course, by the time I got home, the four little sections had gone.'

CHAPTER 7

The Final Push

THE final Russian offensive began on January 12, 1945. Even at this stage there was fierce and prolonged resistance, the Red Army suffering more than 300,000 casualties in the last two-week battle of Berlin before Germany finally capitulated four months later. They surrendered to the Anglo-American command on May 7 and to the Soviet command on May 8. The war in Europe was over.

In terms of destruction of industry and agriculture, of towns and villages, of countries laid waste, but most of all in terms of human lives. it had been the most costly war in history, and the wounds of war were everywhere. The Soviet Union paid a high price for victory. Nearly twenty million people died, among whom were nine million soldiers, about three million of whom died in German captivity; two million Jews were massacred; one million people died in the siege of Leningrad; and 60,000 civilians were killed in the battle of Stalingrad. The burden of the seriously wounded, those who were blinded and lost limbs, would last for decades.

The paradox is that the Russian victory was achieved not only in the face of such monstrous slaughter, but under the leadership of a despot who, before the war began, had been responsible for the deaths of almost every one of the old guard of the Bolshevik party, had beheaded

his armed forces of their most experienced officers and had condemned millions to suffering and death in concentration camps.

From the first the Soviet forces were fighting against fearful odds,
confronting a military might that had conquered Europe. Initially they
suffered enormous losses of armaments, fighting forces, land and factories. Hitler's belief that he would conquer the Soviet Union within a
matter of months was shared by political and military observers in the
West. It had, after all, taken the Germans less than three months to
reach the outskirts of Moscow. They saw a country whose people had
become appeared to become passive and silent during the years of terror and mass arrests.

But to the Soviet people the German invasion posed a threat that
over-rode the disruption and fear that Stalin had brought into their
lives. Despite the barbarous acts and mounting injustices of the 1930s
the people of the Soviet Union were proud of their achievements and
of the many ways in which their society had advanced. Stalin recognised this and in his speeches invoking heroes of the past, he played on
and stimulated Russian pride.

It was the pride of patriotism that united and aroused ordinary people to anger and to resistance. They were fighting for their country, for
their lives. They called it the Great Patriotic War, and it was indeed this
powerful and positive patriotism that inspired the self-sacrifice, devotion and heroism and ultimately brought them victory.

And then there was the nature of the Soviet Union itself that had
contributed to the German defeat, not only the vastness, its sheer geographical immensity; but of a continent of many nations, diverse in
every way, its armies fighting under a unified command. The German
panzer divisions that had sliced through the continent of Europe with
such speed, almost as though there were no frontiers, now entered a
land without frontiers. Beyond every region they conquered, every
river they crossed, every town they laid to waste, every division they

captured, lay more lands and more towns, more rivers and more peoples. The further they advanced, the longer became the road back.

The Soviet Union was an empire that stretched from the Gulf of Finland to the Bering Sea, from the Arctic Ocean to the Caspian Sea. Far, too far. Every step forward increased the distance between them and their victory. When they reached the town of their ultimate advance, Mozdok in the Caucasus, the German armies were two thousand kilometres from Berlin. This was the measure of their retreat.

May 1945 – Victory Day

The end of the war was not publicly proclaimed until the early hours of May 9. Fifty years later Irina Volosova recalled that day in Moscow, Victory Day.

'Early in the morning everyone went out into the streets. The streets were full of people, crying, singing, playing guitars.

'We made our way to Red Square. I turned my head and I saw a huge sea of people coming down Gorki Street. It's a broad street, and it was filled side to side. I thought there would be a disaster, as they had to pass through narrow entrances. But somehow they found their way through.'

It was an unforgettable day. In the evening two to three million people thronged Red Square, the Moscow River embankments and Gorki Street, all the way up to Byelorussian Station. Searchlights were making patterns in the sky. At night the sky was lit up by a spectacular fireworks display.

It was a mass release of emotions, a joy that obliterated for a while the suffering and loss. Reserve was thrown to the winds as the people danced, as they sang in the streets, as they kissed and hugged every man and woman in uniform. They were intoxicated by victory.

And now, people believed, everything would change, everything would be different. There were the slogans of the great freedoms declared by the leaders of the Allied nations. In all the countries whose peoples had suffered and sacrificed in this world war a new idealism flourished, the belief that the defeat of the Nazi armies meant the defeat of the idea of dictatorship, that the democratic rights they had fought for would now be extended, entrenched, safeguarded; that greater power would evolve to the people everywhere; that the world was entering a new era of peace between nations; that the defeat of fascism meant the defeat of the theories of *Untermensch*, of racism.

A Time of Mourning

Love of country and an intense national pride had sustained the people of the Soviet Union during those four years of war and had impelled them to victory.

But at such appalling cost.

It was not only the millions killed and wounded, the burden of destruction, the loss of homes, ruined industries, the countryside devastated and impoverished. It was the destructive effect on society and social relations. The cost to Soviet society as a whole was incalculable. Scarcely any family remained untouched.

Nearly every family had suffered prolonged separation from loved ones; many families had been ripped to pieces never to be restored. In the chaos of the German advance countless families were split up. For weeks, months, even years millions of parents lost contact with their children. Decades later people would still be searching for relatives lost in the war.

Most suffered long separations as families were scattered, as the war drove millions first eastward, then westward; as the majority of adults became soldiers, war workers or farmers. The loss of a generation of young men meant that millions of women would never have husbands or children – there were thirteen million more women than men at the end of the war.

The war irreparably damaged personal relations throughout the Soviet Union. Millions of men and women had been drafted into work which took them far from their homes. Millions of youths still in their teens had been mobilised into the State Labour Reserves, taken from their families and sent to live in factory barracks under strict discipline.

There would be a long period of struggle and sacrifice to rebuild devastated industries, build homes in villages and cities and to try to eliminate some of the worst scars of war.

The tears of joy at victory had passed. Now it was a time for sorrow, for mourning the millions killed, for the destruction of homes and villages, even of cities, for a whole generation of young men who would never return, for the returned soldiers with missing limbs; for the lost children.

And for the gradual realisation that far from initiating political change the end of the war had entrenched the power of Stalin. While he lived the power of dictatorship would not be broken; and while he lived his paranoia would continue to destroy peoples' lives.

Primorskaya

A few months after the war ended Olga and Henry went on holiday to the Caucasus. Their destination was a little village, Primorskaya.

Primorskaya was in a small Soviet republic, Abkhazia, which stretched along the north-east shores of the Black Sea. Here the Caucasus Mountain range reached to the edge of the curving coast, and there were many small bays and inlets where the clear mountain streams flowed down to the sea.

The soft Southern climate and the mountain waters created a bounty of fruit and flowers. Pomegranates and wild figs grew by the roadside. Tall cypresses and lombardy poplars shaded the dusty roads, and eucalyptus and bay trees made the air fragrant. On the lower slopes were olive groves and orchards, and higher there were wooded hills with the snow-capped peaks of the high mountains beyond.

The coast road meandered along, following the line of the sea. According to the Abkhazians the road was constructed in the late nineteenth century by an Englishman who had a contract that paid him by the mile. And – as Englishmen have good heads for business, the local population maintained – it was not to his advantage to make the road run straight; so he simply followed the curves of the coastline.

Fifty years after the coastal road was constructed, the railway was extended from the popular resort of Baku to the administrative centre of Abkhazia-Sukhumi. Because the mountains were so close to the sea, the railway ran along the coast, and because the railway could not meander, it cut across the coast road in many places.

Of the various holidays that they spent together the best of all was in that small village high in the mountains, overlooking the Black Sea. It was rather inaccessible, the journeys there always difficult and tiring; but, Olga said, 'it was indescribably beautiful, and we always had such a welcome from our village friends that it felt as though we were coming home.'

This journey, so soon after the war, was chaotic. They had reserved a sleeping compartment on the train, but when they arrived at the station they found that it had already been occupied, crammed with packages and bundles and with their owners – speculators who had come to Moscow to acquire goods unobtainable elsewhere, and were returning to sell them in the provinces.

Friends had come to see them off, and the argument with obdurate illegal occupiers of their compartment degenerated into a fight, 'a real free for all,' Olga said, before they were able to evict the intruders.

The train, as usual, was overcrowded. People climbed into the luggage racks which they would use as beds. The journey, which in the past had taken two days, now took three.

They arrived at their destination at night. The train stopped barely long enough for them to scramble off; and with a whistle it was off. The lights that illuminated the halt – hardly a station – went off as the train departed. They were left standing in the dark with their holiday luggage.

How Paul Became Mark

Primorskaya is a tiny hamlet in one of the small bays all along the coast. The name means simply 'By-the-sea'. Originally it was called Petropavlovskaya – Peter and Paul – but that name had religious connotations, so after the revolution it was changed, and officially it is now By-the-sea.

In Primorskaya the railway goes along almost on the beach, with the sea to the south; and to the north the scattered houses of the village, climbing up the wooded mountain. There are no shops, not even a post office; but at the foot of the mountain, in the cleft of the bay, there is a small clearing that serves as a market-place. Here there is a trestle table where the peasants display their fruit and vegetables for sale: mounds of bright red tomatoes, yellow sweet corn, peaches, melons and grapes. There are always eggs, and live quail (usually caught by illegal methods) and, on a red-letter day, pork. The peasants do not kill their animals in the summer. The pork is supplied by workers who live in local barracks.

We arrived after dark, and did not know the way to the cottage that had been booked for us. But our friend who had arranged the booking had said: 'Go to the barracks and ask for Rima. She will show you the way up the mountain.'

When the railway was being built along the coast a standard two-storey hostel was erected not far from the market place to house the railway workers. It is the only two-storey building in Primorskaya, and stands square and solid between the railway line and the beach. The villagers have plots of land round their houses, where they grow their fruit and vegetables and keep their poultry and pigs. But the barrack-dwellers have no gardens, and their pigs and poultry roam about freely. There is hardly any traffic on the road, and the train passes only two or three times a week. So when the whistle of the train is heard, people dash out of the barracks to collect their children, poultry and pigs off the line.

Sometimes the train was early, or a pig is obstinate and not rescued in time; and after that a disconsolate woman stands in the market place selling pork.

The barracks were not hard to find, and Rima was there. But it was too dark to climb up the mountain, and Rima said we could stay with her for the night. She shared the room with her two sisters, but both of them were away, and we could have their beds for the night. In the morning someone would show us the way up the mountain.

The room in the barracks was large and bare, and in one corner there was a cot. As we came in a little boy of about two called, 'Mama, Mama.' Rima picked him up and introduce him as 'Marik' – little Mark. We sat and talked over glasses of Russian tea, and Rima said she had come to Primorskaya from her home town of Kiev after the death of her husband, who had been killed at the front in the early days of the war.

I must have glanced involuntarily at Mark, for Rima laughed and said: 'Oh, he's not mine really. He calls us all Mama.'

They were three sisters living together in Primorskaya, the remains of what, before the war, had been a large family. The eldest, Manya, was a civil engineer who had worked on the construction of the railway. She had sent for her second sister, Rima, after both their husbands had been killed. Mark's mother, Bronnia, had joined them before she had the baby. She was a doctor, working in the nearest town, coming back whenever she could. Rima, herself a teacher, was the housekeeper. And to the baby they were all his mothers. There was no difference.

Rima told us that they had lost all their relatives in the massacre at

Babi Yar. For a long time they had no definite news of their parents and hoped desperately that perhaps they had survived, and would be found later. When the baby was born they had wanted to call him after their father, but as Jews, their tradition was not to name a child after a living relative. They had waited until the last permissible date before registering the baby's birth, but no news came, and they finally registered him as Paul, after the name of the village where he was born.

But later confirmation of their father's death arrived, and they longed to name the baby after him. They managed to acquire a bottle of vodka – almost unobtainable in those days – invited the local militiaman to supper with them, and got him so drunk that he agreed to alter the records.

And that is how little Paul became Mark, to perpetuate the memory of his dead grandfather.

The Phone Call

In ten years together, particularly years of such hardship, people form powerful emotional bonds. Even more so when their whole time is spent in the closest possible intimacy imposed by the limited living space. Olga and Henry had maintained their harmony and love through their life together in one room.

The end of the war confronted her with a bitter choice. She still longed to go back to England to visit her family, to re-connect with them again, and to assuage her home-sickness for London and the English countryside. But it was clear that Henry would not be able to leave. They had seen the attitude of the authorities to the Soviet women who had married British or American men; the men left, and their wives were not permitted to join them. With Henry working on a project that was of such importance to the authorities there could be no possibility of his being allowed to leave.

She would go to England. She had her British nationality and her British passport. The bureaucrats might seek to delay her departure, but ultimately they would have to release her. Yes, she would go. But would she return to live in Russia – to Henry?

During the war it had been hard for Olga to write home. All letters were censored. She could not have written about the course of the war itself even had she known the truth of it; the terrible defeats, the massive numbers killed, were hidden from the whole population. She could not have written about the journey to the North; that would have been revealing secrets. Even if she had written about the classes at the Institute she would not have been able to describe the conditions. None of that would have passed the censors. But then, how could you write that everything was all right? It wasn't. So she did not bother to write at all.

From London the family had tried to get in touch with her through the Red Cross. They sent packages, but these never arrived; probably stolen on the way.

She heard through the Moscow grapevine that it was now possible to receive telephone calls from overseas. The rumour was that their friend Selma had spoken to her brother in New York.

She went to see Selma. 'My brother put the phone call through,' Selma said, 'but I was too choked to speak, and we didn't know what to say to each other. But it was heavenly just to hear his voice.'

It seemed that there had been some sort of international agreement and that it was possible to phone one's relatives abroad, and to pay in roubles. There was, of course, no direct dialling in those days. She decided to go to the Central Telegraph Office to find out about it.

The main Post Office was a large, modern building in Gorki Street. She was directed to a room around the corner where calls to foreign countries were made. On one side of the room were benches where you could sit and wait for your call; on the other side curtains that concealed a number of phone booths. From time to time a voice came from one corner of the room announcing the next call, and directing you to the booth where you could take it.

She enquired about making a call to London, and gave them Vera's phone number. She had expected to wait for a long time, or even to be told to come back later, but almost immediately her name was called.

'I heard this faint, rather squeaky-sounding voice,' Vera said. 'It said: Vera, is that you? This is Olga.'

'Olga! Is that really you?'

'Yes, it's me. How are you?'

'I said: How are you?

'We kept saying this to each other: "How are you? Are you all right?" That's all I can remember of the conversation. It was so unexpected. After all those years. Perhaps if I had been expecting it I would have prepared something intelligent to say.'

What could Olga have said – that I was hungry all the time? That in the frozen North I bartered a silk night-dress for some butter? That I went on teaching English in sub-zero temperatures?

What could Vera have said – that they evacuated children from London and I went with them to Wales, and they cried all night for their parents? And some of the country families took the older ones in to use as cheap labour on their farms? That sometimes, when the bombers came over London, the whole building shook, and I would still be shaking long after they had gone?

For them both it was the ties of childhood, the ties of blood. For Olga it was also the intensity of hearing a voice from what would always be home. She had applied for an exit visa. Her stated intention was to visit her family in England, then go to America to visit Ray and Henry's relatives. She was living in expectation of receiving it.

She continued teaching at the Institute. The building of the fourth line of the Moscow Metro had started in 1945, and Henry was still working there.

Ray had served her sentence in the camps and been released, but had not been not allowed to return to live in Moscow. She had gone to live in Kursk, not far from Moscow, and was lucky to get a job in as a teacher at the Foreign Languages Institute there.

A year went by; still the exit visa did not arrive. In September Olga and Henry went to Primorskaya once again, to be welcomed back as old friends.

The houses were strung up the hill and raised on stilts, with front terraces on which corn was husked and then strung up to dry. Hens lived under the terrace. Their house was painted white, and they had two rooms opening on to the terrace where they sat in the evenings.

The climb up to the house from the beach was steep, especially when they returned in the heat of the day. Then they would pause to get their breath and to see how the curve of the bay opened widely. The view expanded as they climbed, the sea becoming even more intensely blue, and the houses and people down below diminishing to the size of toys.

What a Pity!

September in the Caucasus is called the golden month, but local people talk more descriptively of 'the velvet season'. The great heat of summer is over, but the sun is still warm and shines each day from a clear sky. At night the dew falls, and a light breeze blows cool air from the sea. The stars are bright in the dark sky, and the atmosphere is truly 'velvet'. This is the month when the figs ripen and the grapes are picked for wine.

All month our little old landlady had been saying, 'What a pity you won't be here when we make the wine!'

Then she would reflect and brighten.

'But the black grapes will be just right for picking when you leave. You'll take some back to Moscow with you.'

One day she would say, 'What a pity you weren't here when the strawberries were ready.' And the next, 'What a pity you won't be here for the tangerines.'

The day before our departure I asked, 'Shall we pick the grapes?'

'Oh no! Grapes must be picked in the morning with the dew on them. Vova will climb up the trees tomorrow and pick them at their best.'

In the night I woke and heard the rain, light at first, just pattering on the corrugated iron roof of the little hut; but then falling more heavily and noisily. By morning it was teeming down, and Kseniya Philipovna was almost in tears.

'The grapes! You can't pick the grapes in the rain! They will split, and they won't keep.'

'Then we won't take grapes back with us.'

'But you must take grapes back! How can you go without any? What a pity you can't stay a little longer.'

Her thirteen-year-old grandson, Vova, came in barefoot, his usually unruly hair plastered to his head, his clothes dripping, a basket hidden under his jacket.

'I tried to pick the driest ones. I've covered them with vine leaves. The figs weren't worth picking.'

Poor Xseniya Philipovna was still worried. 'What a pity we didn't pick them yesterday.'

Then she cheered up a little. 'Next year come early and leave before the rains start.' Then she said sadly, 'Even the sky is crying because you are leaving us.'

Return

They had to go to Sochi to get a train back to Moscow. Sochi lay to the West of Primorskaya. But as a foreigner Olga had to register her arrival and departure in the district with the local militia, and that meant first going to Sukhumi, the capital of Abkhazia, which lay to the east.

The skies were indeed crying as they left 'By-the-sea'. The only transport to Sukhumi, apart from the train which did not run every day, was to get a lift in a two-wheeled peasant cart pulled by bullocks or mules, or if they were lucky, on an occasional passing truck.

There was a huge old oak tree at the market place, and they sat there on its roots with their pile of luggage for a long time before they managed to get a lift in an open truck.

By the time they arrived in Sukhumi, in the late afternoon, the office of the militia was closed. They went to an address given to them by a friend; the occupier said they could stay the night, and that there was a plane flying to Moscow in the morning. They went at once to the Aeroflot office.

As they expected, they were told that the plane was full; their only hope was to come to the office at 6 a.m. to see if there was a cancellation.

It was still raining in the early morning; there had been a cancellation, but the plane was leaving right away. If they took it Olga would leave without the necessary stamp on her identification card, which might lead to difficulties when they arrived in Moscow. If they stayed to register they might not get transport for days, even weeks.

They decided to take a chance. In a sub-tropical downpour they got a lift on a truck to the airport. The small plane was standing in the middle of a field, its wheels half-submerged in pools of water. The rain stopped, the sun came out, and as they waited, they and their luggage dried in the warmth.

It was an informal flight. There were no safety belts, and everyone smoked the whole way, regardless of any safety regulations.

They flew back along the coastline, and they strained to see if they could identify Primorskaya. As the plane turned inland to go between the mountains they looked down, and surely that was Vova, waving a white towel to them from the top of the garden. It was a last glimpse of a small paradise; there would be no return.

Waiting

Now there were no pressing reasons for her to stay, she had to endure the seemingly endless frustrations and misery of battling with Soviet bureaucracy. They did not refuse her an exit visa – presumably as a British subject they could not, ultimately, do that. They just found endless ways of impeding its issue. She believed they wanted to hold her to use as a bargaining weapon to get one of their own people back from the British.

I do not know if this is so. It may have been. But by this time it was obvious that it was pointless to search for a reason.

She became very depressed. She felt her life was purposeless, she had lost all sense of belonging, either to her work at the Institute or to her partner in their home. It was as though she had detached herself from Moscow, from the Soviet society in which she lived, but was unable to break free.

She had been drawn inexorably into one of the most extraordinary and significant periods of Russian history, almost, it seemed, by a series of accidents, of external factors which had seemingly controlled this long episode in her life.

Yet the decisions about how to react to these accidents were her own. She could have dealt with them differently; how she did react to them revealed the fabric of her own complex personality: a strong sense of self-survival into which was woven her ability to relate to and to love others that kept her conscience alive and made her capable of self-sacrifice.

It was not only a question of cultural differences. She adapted easily to the warmth and open acceptance of the Russian people. Although she was aware of the straitjacket that confined the arts, she appreciated their love of poetry, of intellectual argument and of literature, the theatre and ballet. Yet despite the courage and sacrifices she had witnessed, despite her close and loving relationship with her students, despite the many Russian friends that had enriched her life, she had never become Russianised. Her roots remained deep in the country where she was born and brought up.

Her homesickness was physical, a longing for geography and climate: the informality of London parks; the green fields and open spaces; the random way the countryside joined the towns; the places where we had always walked when we were young, and sisters together – Stanmore, Burnham Beeches, Hampstead Heath and Kenwood; the gentler, softer, seasons; hearing the language you had grown up speaking, your own language, around you in the streets, on the underground. Even the way townspeople lived, not in sealed-in apartment blocks but in semi-detached houses in the suburbs with their trim lawns rimmed with ordered rows of flowers.

Nothing could reconcile her to staying longer, not her familiarity with and acceptance into Moscow society, not her love for the man she had come to marry, nor his adoration of her; not the intense daily physical closeness of all those years together. She was being torn apart by her own decision to reject all this and by the extended period of marking time that had become so meaningless.

An Amputation

The special circumstances that had enabled ordinary people to behave with extraordinary heroism and sacrifice were no longer there. A powerful purpose had disappeared.

So it was, on an individual and purely personal scale, with my sister. There was no more objective reason for staying, only the subjective one – Henry. Her desire not to remain in the Soviet Union for the rest of her life had to be stronger than all the years of their close relationship. But to make such a break, to take such a decision, was hard. She could not bring herself to tell him the truth. She was going to visit her family, she said, and she left the rest open. He believed she would return. In her heart she knew she would not.

Will you come back? Was this the 'only awkward question' that she once said that Ray had ever asked her? I believe it was; perhaps Ray sensed her conflict and her sorrow.

I look through all the pieces she wrote, incorporated now in this record, as well as the jottings on scraps of paper, names of people she meant to write about, episodes begun but not completed; and Henry is never there. In all her later reminiscences he is never mentioned.

The one person with whom she had so closely and constantly lived through those extraordinary times, those eleven and a half years, virtually disappears, or appears only as a shadow cast on a screen.

She was not simply leaving one country for another, one kind of life for a different one, choosing one social and economic system against another. She was amputating a portion of herself, cutting away something that was not as physical as a limb, but nevertheless was real. To leave meant she had to sever those powerful invisible connections and the continuity of both their lives. When you have shared times of such extreme difficulty and danger there is no way of breaking free without inflicting a kind of destruction on yourself and the other.

The long wait was like a provocation, almost a challenge, to make her change her mind. Thus the last year of frustrated waiting became unbearable. It was not enough to reject her lover, her friends, her students, a major portion of her youthful years.

W.H. Auden has written, 'We must love each other or die'. The war had taught so many to love each other so that they could survive. To end all those associations was something of a death.

What was left was her overwhelming sense of sadness and despair.

She had a friend Isa who, like her, had been born in England and whom she had known when they were children. Isa was also desperately miserable, but she was married to a Russian and had no hope of leaving.

We used to walk around together and discuss ways in which to commit suicide. I suppose we never would have done it, even if we could think of a painless way. I used to say to Isa: 'But you couldn't possibly, because you have a son to care for.

But I mean, it was hard, very hard, and we didn't want to go on living like that.

On October 25, 1947, she was finally given her visa, and a week later, at the beginning of November, she left Moscow for Leningrad from where she would travel by boat to Southampton, retreating the way she had come nearly twelve years ago.

Leningrad

The city was deeply scarred by the war. Its outskirts were a vast ruin, and the famous historical palaces around the city – Pavlovsk, Tsarskoie-Selo, Peterhof – were vandalised and destroyed.

When the German army had been threatening Moscow in August of 1941 and Olga and Henry were leaving for Omoutninsk, the irresistible tide of the Nazi Panzer divisions at the same time swept closer and closer to the gates of Leningrad. By the beginning of September the Germans had reached the Luga line, 125 miles south of the city, captured all the surrounding towns and cut railways and roads. Within three weeks an iron ring closed around the city, with only a slender lifeline – Lake Ladoga – linking it with the Russian mainland.

The population of more than three million were trapped in a blockade that would last for over two years.

Shelling and bombing was intense, but an all-out attack on the city failed. Hitler thought that the city would be mined – as Kiev was when the Germans entered it – and there was no question of it being declared an open city, as Paris had been, which saved it from destruction. The war in Russia was different from anywhere else in Europe – it was a war of extermination. Hitler had an intense desire to destroy Leningrad; Russia, the Russians, had no right to a sophisticated, cultured city that rivalled many in the West; nor could he accept that Russia had any place as part of the Western world. He wanted to destroy this cultured city and all its fine monuments totally and completely. He stated that he would accept no capitulation, and that Leningrad would be wiped off the face of the earth.

Now the people of Leningrad were condemned to death by starvation.

In the besieged city there were no food markets. The chief food warehouse was an old wooden building covering several acres. The Germans bombed the warehouse and it burned to the ground. The smell of burning meat, wrote a war correspondent, the acrid stench of carbonised sugar, of burning oil and flour filled the air. The whole city was covered in clouds of blood-red and black smoke, casting the fateful shadow of famine over Leningrad.[30]

In November the lake was half frozen and no longer navigable. Until the ice was frozen to sufficient depth to support the weight of vehicles, it could not be used. Food was only obtainable on ration, and the ration could no longer support life. At its lowest point the ration of bread for workers was 350 grams daily; dependants, non-workers and children were entitled to 200 grams, but often only got 125. By December people were already dying of starvation. In January up to 4,000 were dying every day.

Starvation was compounded by the bitter cold. Furniture was chopped up to fuel stoves, and when there was no more furniture, millions of books were burned as fuel. Death overtook people in the streets, in the offices and factories, in the courtyards and cellars of the great apartment houses. In the streets the corpses lay where they fell, frozen and covered by the snow. Some concealed the frozen corpses of their relatives so that they could claim their rations. There were some who stole or murdered to get another's rations, and there were some who ate the flesh of the dead.

Death modified the problems; with a smaller population there was a little food more to go round.

All winter the corpses lay in the streets, blanketed by snow. When people collapsed others walked by – there was nothing they could do. Soon there would be just a vague human form covered with snow.

In February, when the ice was two metres thick, a motor road was es-tablished across Lake Ladoga for lorries to bring in supplies. It was a hazardous journey. The transports were bombed by the Germans. Some trucks fell through the ice as it weakened but many got through, although they brought in only a fraction of what was needed. In 1942 nearly a million people were evacuated from the city across the lake, by the ice road in winter, and when the ice melted, by ships in summer.

Only when spring came, when the ice over the Lake began to break up, when the snow-shroud melted to reveal the thousands who had died in the streets and in their homes, could those who still had the strength collect the corpses. Silently, without ceremonies and without coffins, the dead were buried.

Yet it was at the height of the sufferings, in August of 1942, that the Leningrad Symphony Orchestra played Shostakovich's Leningrad Symphony for the first time. Shostakovich had been ordered by the government to leave the city before it was entirely cut off. The score of his new composition was sent to Leningrad. To assemble an orchestra of people still alive and able to play was a difficult task. Some members of the orchestra had already died of starvation. A call went to soldiers in the front-line of the defence of the city for any who were musicians, and those who responded were taken to augment the orchestra. Although it was summer, all suffered from the cold of semi-starvation and played their instruments wearing gloves with the fingers cut off. And despite the fact that some of the audience were so weak they could hardly stand, there was a great queue seeking admission. The Russians had placed loudspeakers in their front lines and the concert was broadcast loudly towards the German troops – a gesture of pride and defiance.

The Ladoga lifeline continued to assert the existence, the defiance, the endurance of the people of Leningrad until January 1944, when the blockade was broken, 900 days after it began.

One million citizens of Peter's City had died during, what Salisbury had described as 'the greatest and longest siege ever endured by a modern city, a time of trial, suffering and heroism that reached peaks of tragedy and bravery almost beyond the power to comprehend'.[31]

Closing the Circle

Olga arrived in Leningrad in the evening, and booked in at a hotel for the night.

She saw a city sullen, shabby, strained, still suffering from war weariness, and now also from neglect. Grandiose plans for restoring and recreating a magnificent new Leningrad had been put on one side. The needs of its people were once again subordinated to the building of heavy industry.

When she had arrived there in 1935 it was just after the murder of Kirov, the signal for the savage purges that spread throughout the USSR. Now the war, the blockade, the siege, the 900 days – all these had become a backdrop to renewed paranoia.

A new series of purges began. Leningrad's intellectuals were targeted. Writers and artists were the first victims of the savage political warfare. Anna Akhmatova, the classic purist of Russian poetry, and others were expelled from the Leningrad Union of Writers, which meant that they were unable to get their work published.

Stalin wanted to purge from the history of Leningrad the heroic sufferings of the people of the blockaded city. The Museum of Leningrad's
Defence was closed, its archives seized, its director sent to Siberia. A
chronicle of the blockade which had been prepared was never published. Public records, speeches, memoirs were destroyed. Thousands
who had survived the most terrible days of the blockade were shot or
sent to the camps.

Now, at the end of 1947, my sister was leaving just as the people of
Leningrad were subject to this new assault; as though all those years of
suffering and sacrifice had been simply part of a monstrous cycle that
had never ended.

Walking the streets of the night-time city, it was as though her own
depression was part of the collective pain of Leningrad. But it was a
personal pain that could not be shared and lived within her.

She knew what Henry did not. That she was leaving her partner, her
companion, her lover, and would not return.

Goodbye to Leningrad

*When I hear travellers' tales of what a magnificent city Leningrad is, I do
believe them. But for me Leningrad will always remain a city of utter despair – grey, gloomy and forbidding. I can imagine the sun shining on the
beautiful buildings painted in pastel colours, as I am told they are now.
But in my mind's eye I see only a city of mist, fog, rain and slush, with un-
painted buildings, broken pavements and ill-fed, ill-clothed people.*

*I left it on a bleak December day in 1947, and in the taxi taking me to
the docks I wondered how I would be treated there. Would I be searched?
Would some excuse be found to detain me again? I had been waiting so
long to leave, and now I was gripped by fear. How could I have been so
foolish as to agree to take other peoples' gifts and letters out of the country
for them?*

On the ship I was conducted to my cabin and told not to unpack, but to wait for the Customs Officer who would come to me there. I felt numb with foreboding as two security men entered the cabin and began to unpack my things. I had taken very little of the accumulated possessions of eleven and a half years, just two small suitcases and a few packages.

But the inspection seemed endless. Every item was lifted out separately, and documents and papers carefully scrutinised. Hours seemed to be spent on the examination of each snapshot. A thick finger would point to a now unremembered person in a group picture taken years ago on a holiday. 'Who is this? What is he? Where does he work? How don't you know? You must know. You must remember.'

They asked for my Russian money. I had hoped to take a few coins back as souvenirs, but was not allowed to do so.

At last the search of my possessions was over, and I watched as they put away in their little cases the photographs and papers they had abstracted for themselves. Would they now search me? And what about those wretched letters I had on me that I had recklessly promised to deliver to friends' relatives abroad?

Finally, after a long, agonising pause, they handed me my passport and walked out of the cabin. I waited, still apprehensive, for what seemed an age, until I heard the engines of the boat throb, and the creaking and strain of wood. Relief swept over me.

I left my cabin and went on deck; and stood with three other passengers as we passed the fortifications of the Kronstadt, and approached the Gulf of Finland. Relief swept over me.

I was on my way home at last.

EPILOGUE

THEY tell us that the past is another country. Yet think how the past shapes the lives that come after. My father, my mother, had made England their home. We three were British-born; the furthest we had ever travelled from our London-suburban homes were when we went on holiday to the Isle of Wight. Within the framework of our social status, our class, our lives had a logical normality.

Then came the Russian Revolution. Our father, who had discarded the religion and social customs of his childhood, who believed that émigrés should assimilate in their new country, who brought up his family to live as the English lived, found himself pulled back to the country from which he had sprung.

His letters from abroad were kept by my mother and after she died they were left with my sister Vera. I think for her, even more than for me, they were too painful, and were put away, out of sight, out of our minds. It was my own daughter who resurrected them and began recovering facts about my parents – her grandparents – that I had not known. She put those letters into chronological order, had them transcribed, and interviewed people (now no longer alive) who had known her grandparents. She was intrigued by the story they revealed, and thought of writing a book about her grandparents and the distance – both physical and in understanding – that opened up between them. But she was busy with other work, and put them to one side.

When in her later life in England Olga showed me the essays that she had written for her writers' class I urged her to write more and connect them together, as I believed they were interesting – unique in a way – and could be published. But her life was a busy one, and she died leaving only these episodic pieces.

It seemed to me so strange, and strangely fascinating. Father and daughter had both lived for years in a country they wanted to leave, but could not, and both had left disjointed and limited records of their experiences. There was not only a generation gap between them but also a deep division between their attitudes. He was totally committed to the aims of the new society, and sympathetic to and understanding of its faults. She felt no personal connection with it and was hostile to the way it operated. And both were, in their own ways, trapped in it.

I wanted to put their experiences together, and to do that I had to enter that other country, the past, their past, that I had shut out of my own life.

Yes, it is true that what we lived through is a far-away distant place to those who follow after. To them it is the present that is reality, and the future that occupies their imagination. Just one generation, and the door on the past begins to close. Perhaps there are glimpses to be had through the lives of their parents and the memories of their friends when they revisit the once-shared territory of their past. But for the younger ones these events seem so far away, so long ago – *But that was before I was born!*

Yet their lives, too, will become that other country. There are not many years between them and the next ones to separate them totally from their own history. Then it is they who will be told that things have changed since then; that's old stuff. It's not like that any more. And they will want their young to understand that there is so much to be learned from the past; that the lives of this new generation have been profoundly shaped by their lives, their times, what they lived through.

What I have written is only an episode in the private lives of two people, insignificant, of no historical importance. I have taken some small spots from a vast panorama and enlarged them to make visible those influences at which we can only guess. The panorama is part of Russia's horrific period of Stalinism, the aftermath of the First World War, together with the epic history of the Second.

No one grows out of a vacuum. The history of our lives is your history, as your lives will be the ground from which your children will grow. The days of our years, the years of our lives, so terrible and so beautiful, so base and so heroic may seem strange and hard to comprehend, but they are irrevocably part of yours.

What right have we to forget?

AFTERWORD

I had not intended to write an Afterword to Olga's story, but have yielded to my readers' wish to know what happened after Olga returned to England.

When she arrived in London she found that all the members of our small family were in Johannesburg with me – our mother, Vera, and Vera's husband Morgan. So she joined us in Johannesburg.

After a while Vera, Morgan and our mother went back to England, but at my special request to her, Olga stayed on until my second child, Patrick, was born. We loved each other, and we were happy together, but it was not until many years later, after I, too, was living in England, that we talked about her life in the Soviet Union.

Why? Vera and I were both members of the Communist Party at the time Olga joined us. She understood our reluctance to accept what she would have to say, and we, in turn, refrained from asking questions because – I believe now – instinctively we did not want to accept the truth. And when I did find out the reality of life in the Soviet Union it was not through her revelations that I changed. I came to recognise the truth of the Stalin era in my own way.

Olga, in turn, did not speak to us about her true experiences. Later, when Toni became interested in her family's past life, she asked Olga, 'Did you tell them what it was like?'

Olga replied, 'No. Because I like to keep on good terms with people. It would not have changed them, they wouldn't have believed me, people believe what they want to believe. And they didn't ask. And they must have had an inkling at the back of their heads that things weren't perfect, because otherwise they would have questioned me more. Nobody really questioned me. And then I was asked to talk at peoples' houses, and I used to go around and talk. And it was dishonest, I suppose, but I talked about the good aspects of Russian life – things like education, like the treatment of children, which was very good, and about the country itself; to evade other things.'

Clara Friedman – the American woman I mentioned earlier who wanted her application for Soviet citizenship to be returned to her, but was told it was too late – told me that Henry was very charming, very good-looking. 'I wondered,' she commented, 'I often thought, did she do the right thing? I thought they were so much in love with each other. Well, it was a hard choice to make. I suppose she knew what she was doing.' Irina also told me that he was handsome – very active, tall and slim.

Olga never returned to Henry.

After the war, when Olga left the Soviet Union, the storm-clouds were gathering as Stalin's new era of oppression was just beginning. Underlying it was a paranoia about anything connected with the West or with 'cosmopolitanism'. Jews and foreigners were among those targeted. Henry was taken off his job, and had to go to work in a laundry factory.

Henry died of a heart attack when he was still quite young; I do not know the date.

Olga married in England, had a daughter, and lived in a bungalow in Harrow. She did translation work for foreign embassies and spoke a few times on the BBC. After her husband died of cancer, she took over his small business, made a success of it, moved to a house where she built a beautiful garden full of the flowers she loved. She enjoyed a full social life, joined various clubs, went to opera, played bridge, ran her business; and – ultimately – attended a writers' class, the results of which formed the basis for this book.

She began going on visits to Moscow to see her old friends and former pupils. By that time Henry was dead, but his sister Ray was still alive.

On December 31, 1976 – New Year's Eve – I joined Olga, her daughter Linda and son-in-law Stuart on a short trip to Moscow. Linda and Stuart stayed only four days, but Olga and I stayed for a week. The days were crammed with visits to museums, galleries, and theatres, including superb ballet; and visits to Olga's former pupils and friends, all of whom were delighted to see her and loaded us with food, and Olga with gifts to take back to England.

*

Olga had returned to England in 1948 after her stay with us in Johannesburg. She left us some months after an election that brought the Nationalist Party to power. So she left to begin a new, happier phase in her life as we were entering a darker, harder time in ours. For this was the inauguration of more than forty years of apartheid, of the time when we, too, in South Africa would be forced to confront a system based on the belief in the *Untermensch* – of security police, detention without trial, imprisonment, torture, murder, under a regime determined to maintain minority control over a majority of the population.

We were being drawn onto the stage with two plays; and inevitably would have our lives changed by the moral choices we were forced to make, as the strident voices from the back of the stage came to the front, and we, too, came to know the men in dark suits and hats.

ENDNOTES

1. E.H. Carr, *The Russian Revolution from Lenin to Stalin (1917 1929)*. MacMillan Press, 1970.

2. Ibid.

3. Robert Service, *A History of Twentieth-Century Russia*. Allen Lane, 1997.

4. Walter Duranty, *'I Write as I Please'*. Hamish Hamilton, 1935.

5. Sheila Fitzpatrick, *Everyday Stalinism. Ordinary Life in Extraordinary Times. Soviet Russia in the 1930s*. OUP, 1999.

6. Margaret Wettlin, *Fifty Russian Winters: An American Woman's Life in the Soviet Union*. Pharos Books, 1992.

7. Victor Serge, *Memoirs of a Revolutionary, 1901-1941*. OUP, 1967.

8. Ernst Fischer, *An Opposing Man. The Autobiography of a Romantic Revolutionary*. Livewright, 1974.

9. Robert Conquest, *The Great Terror: A Re-Assessment*. Hutchinson, 1990.

10. J. Arch Getty, 'Palaces on Monday', in *The London Review of Books*, 2 March 2000.

11. Margaret Wettlin, *Fifty Russian Winters: An American Woman's Life in the Soviet Union*. Pharos Books, 1992.

12. Ernst Fischer, *An Opposing Man. The Autobiography of a Romantic Revolutionary*. Livewright, 1974.

13. Eugenia Ginzburg, *Journey Into The Whirlwind*. Harcourt, Brace & World, 1967.

14. Cited in Robert Conquest, *The Great Terror: A Re-Assessment*. Hutchinson, 1990.

15. Lidiya Ginzburg, *Blockade Diary*. The Harvill Press, 1995.

16. Cited in Robert Conquest, *The Great Terror: A Re-Assessment*. Hutchinson, 1990.

17. Robert Service, *A History of Twentieth-Century Russia.* Allen Lane, 1997.

18. Ibid.

19. Alexander Werth, *Russia at War, 1941-1945.* Barrie and Rockliff, 1964.

20. Cited in John Barber and Mark Harrison, *The Soviet Home Front 1941 to 1945: a Social and Economic History of the USSR in World War II.* Longman, 1991.

21. Boris Pasternak, *Doctor Zhivago.* Collins and Harvill Press, 1958.

22. Alexander Werth, *Russia at War, 1941-1945.* Barrie and Rockliff, 1964.

23. Harrison E. Salisbury, *The 900 Days: The Siege of Leningrad.* Pan Books, 2000.

24. Sheila Fitzpatrick, *Everyday Stalinism. Ordinary Life in Extraordinary Times. Soviet Russia in the 1930s.* OUP, 1999.

25. John Barber & Mark Harrison, *The Soviet Home Front 1941 to 1945: a Social and Economic History of the USSR in World War II.* Longman, 1991.

26. Antony Beevor, *Stalingrad.* Viking, 1998.

27. Ilya Ehrenburg, *Men, Years, Life.* MacGibbon and Kee, 1964.

28. Eugenia Ginzburg, *Within The Whirlwind.* Collins and Harvill Press, 1981

29. Alexander Werth, *Russia at War, 1941-1945.* Barrie and Rockliff, 1964.

30. Harrison E. Salisbury, *The 900 Days: The Siege of Leningrad.* Pan Books, 2000.

31. Ibid.

HILDA BERNSTEIN
SEPARATION

Moscow, 20-IX-26

My dear Vera,

Many Happy Returns.
Sorry can-not be with
you on your birthday, but hope to be with you
on Christmas.

Love Papa